Idyllic Splendour

Idyllic Splendour

A pictorial journey through Germany's stately homes, parks and castles

Castles and Gardens
of Germany Association (eds.)

SCHNELL + STEINER

Contents

- 7 Introduction
- 8 **Meissen Albrechtsburg Castle**
  A trendsetter since 1471
- 11 **Altenstein Palace and Park**
  Summer residence of the "Theatre Duke"
- 14 **Wasserburg Anholt**
  Noble gem with museum and hotel
- 17 **Arolsen Palace**
  A residence steeped in family history
- 20 **Bad Homburg Castle and Park**
  Seat of the landgraves of Hesse-Homburg and summer residence of the German emperors
- 23 **Belvedere Castle and Park**
  A floral paradise at the gates of Weimar
- 26 **Benrath Palace**
  Most beautiful palace on the Rhine
- 29 **Bentheim Castle**
  A journey into history
- 32 **Bothmer House**
  A piece of England in Mecklenburg
- 35 **Branitz Palace and Park**
  Prince Pückler's masterpiece and refuge
- 38 **Bückeburg Palace**
  Living tradition
- 41 **Celle Castle**
  A noble residence with a living history
- 44 **Cochem Imperial Castle**
  A fairytale castle on the Moselle – a dream come true
- 47 **Dennenlohe Castle – House and Park**
  An English garden paradise in the centre of Franconia
- 50 **Detmold Castle**
  Seat of the counts and princes zur Lippe
- 53 **Dornburg Castles – a Triad of Stately Homes**
  Gardens with views
- 56 **Dresden Zwinger**
  Home of world-famous artworks
- 60 **Dyck Castle**
  Architectural, garden and landscape culture through the centuries
- 63 **Eberbach Monastery**
  From medieval economic powerhouse to modern secular institution
- 66 **Ehrenbreitstein Fortress**
  From military stronghold to cultural forefront
- 69 **Eltz Castle**
  Nine centuries of German family history
- 72 **St. Emmeram's Palace, Regensburg**
  From Benedictine abbey to stately home of the Princes of Thurn and Taxis
- 75 **Schloss Fasanerie (The Pheasantry)**
  The most beautiful Baroque palace in the State of Hesse
- 78 **Friedenstein Castle**
  The Baroque Universe of Gotha
- 81 **"Fürstenlager" State Park, Bensheim-Auerbach**
  Idyllic village on the Bergstrasse
- 84 **Glücksburg Castle**
  Home to "Europe's father-in-law"
- 87 **Granitz Hunting Lodge**
  Rügen's crown
- 90 **Greiz – Summer Palace and Princely Park**
  Art and nature in harmony
- 93 **Hambach Castle**
  Cradle of German democracy
- 96 **Hämelschenburg Castle**
  An authentic fairytale castle
- 99 **State Park Hanau-Wilhelmsbad**
  From quarry to fashionable spa
- 102 **Hartenfels Castle, Torgau**
  Renaissance masterpiece and political centre of the Reformation
- 105 **Heidecksburg Palace, Rudolstadt**
  Rococo *en gros* and *en miniature*
- 108 **Heidelberg Castle**
  Truly romantic – the world-famous ruins
- 111 **Royal Gardens of Herrenhausen, Hanover**
  The Splendour of Garden Art
- 114 **Hohenzollern Castle**
  History with majestic views
- 117 **Hundisburg Palace and Baroque Garden, Althaldensleben Landscape Park**
  Baroque splendour in the Magdeburg Börde
- 120 **Langenburg Castle**
  A castle through changing centuries

123 **Lichtenstein Castle**
Württemberg's fairytale castle

126 **Lorsch Abbey**
From medieval spiritual centre to site of knowledge and learning

129 **Ludwigsburg Palace**
One of the largest Baroque palaces in Germany

132 **Ludwigshöhe Castle**
"A villa in the Italian style"

135 **Ludwigslust Palace**
Sandstone, gold and papier mâché

138 **Mainau Island**
Baroque splendour, botanical treasures

141 **Marienburg Castle**
Seat of the Royal House of Guelph

144 **Marksburg**
Home of the German Castles Association

147 **Maulbronn Monastery**
UNESCO World Heritage Site with a vibrant atmosphere

150 **A Cultural Landscape of Manorial Estates and Houses**
Mecklenburg-Western Pomerania

153 **Mirow Palace**
A Baroque and Rococo jewel

156 **Moritzburg Castle**
A fairy-tale castle and its treasures

159 **Oettingen Castle**
A noble residence in an enchanting town

162 **Pappenheim Castle**
Gateway to the Altmühl Valley

165 **Pillnitz Palace & Park**
A *maison de plaisance* with botanical rarities

168 **Rochlitz Castle**
Fat, one-eyed revolutionary!

171 **Salem Monastery and Palace**
One of the most majestic Cistercian monasteries in Southern Germany

174 **The Europa-Rosarium, Sangerhausen**
The world's biggest collection of roses

177 **Sayn – Castle and Schloss**
"A veritable fairytale castle"

180 **Sayn Palace Gardens**
Delight of princes and butterflies

183 **Schwerin Palace**
Fairytale castle at the pulse of the state

186 **Schwetzingen Palace and Gardens**
Gardens of extraordinary European renown

189 **Three Saxon Highlights**
Triad from the Ore Mountains and Central Saxony

193 **Sigmaringen Palace**
A millennium of political, cultural and family history

196 **Stolzenfels Castle**
Monument of Prussian Rhine-romanticism

199 **Tiefurt Mansion and Park**
Garden landscape of the Muses

202 **Trier**
Roman city

205 **Trifels Imperial Castle**
Mighty fortress of kings and safe stronghold

208 **Ulrichshusen Castle Estate**
Cultural centre and jewel of Mecklenburg's lakeland

211 **Wartburg World Heritage Site**
Living history in ancient walls

214 **Weilburg on the Lahn – Castle and Gardens**
From medieval castle to Renaissance residence and Baroque palace

217 **Weimar City Castle and Park on the Ilm**
An ensemble of castle, park and artworks

220 **Weissenstein Palace**
Baroque splendour in the Steigerwald

223 **Wernigerode Castle®**
Centre for the History of 19th Century Art and Culture

226 **Wilhelmsburg Castle in Schmalkalden**
A Hessian castle in Thüringia

229 **Schloss Wilhelmshöhe**
Palace with international flair

232 **Schloss Wilhelmsthal**
A Rococo pearl

235 **Wittumspalais in Weimar**
Dowager seat of Duchess Anna Amalia

238 **Schloss and Park Wörlitz**
Iconic classicism

242 **Annex**

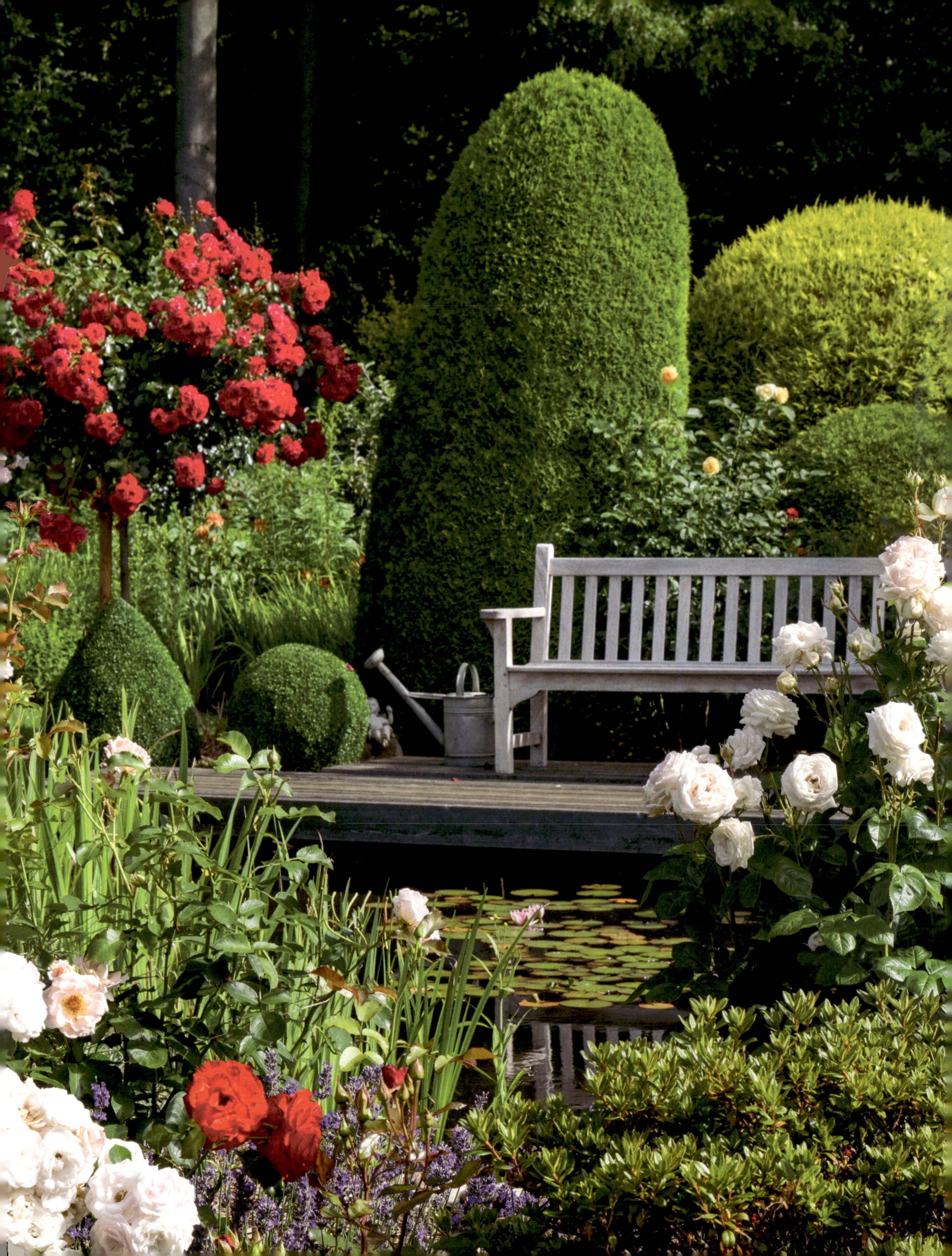

Introduction

Germany is a country of palaces and castles, of abbeys, parks and gardens. They define our regions, give our cultural landscapes their unmistakable character, and create a sense of home and belonging, of regional rootedness and touristic flair. They offer leisure and regeneration; they are centres of culture and communication; and for the cultural historian they are an indispensable, tangible archive.

Their origins lie in the centuries-long juxtaposition of innumerable dynasties, estates and rulers, secular and sacred, in the multifarious patchwork of the Holy Roman Empire of the German Nation. Inspired to imitate one another or consciously compete, they built their increasingly conspicuous seats of government, capital cities and residential landscapes. To us they left an incomparable legacy signposted by its many and varied architectural and horticultural monuments. We today are called upon to preserve this heritage, to enable people from near and far to share in its enjoyment, and to pass it on unscathed to posterity.

Founded in 2012, the "Castles and Gardens of Germany Association" brought private, municipal and state owners and administrators together for the first time in a common endeavour to meet the demands of the monuments – institutions of national importance – entrusted to them. Irrespective of ownership structures, they seek, in mutual cooperation and support, to represent the interests of the historical estates and buildings and their visitors, and at the same time to highlight the importance of this heritage to society. This involves a regular exchange of knowledge and perspectives on issues of conservation, economics and tourism, as well as in the areas of research, communication and cultural education. Of prime importance is effective public information: Only on this basis can the acceptance of these sites of regional identity and historical remembrance be sustainably secured. As specialists in the politics and economics of tourism, we are an informed and reliable partner at all levels.

With its wealth of photographs, this volume is an invitation to dip into the endless variety of stately homes and parks between Lake Constance and the Baltic Sea. With more than 15,000 castles, mansions and palaces to choose from, the selection presented here is necessarily incomplete. But each example is an ambassador for the many other jewels numbered among Germany's great houses and estates.

From celestially inspired Gothic to proud Renaissance, from exultant Baroque to gardens of earthly paradise, the book presents a journey of discovery through epochs, styles, and thematic worlds. We invite you to enjoy it and find in it an inspiration to personally explore one or other of these worlds – the choice is overwhelming.

Michael Hörrmann
Chairman

Alexander Prince zu Sayn-Wittgenstein
Deputy Chairman

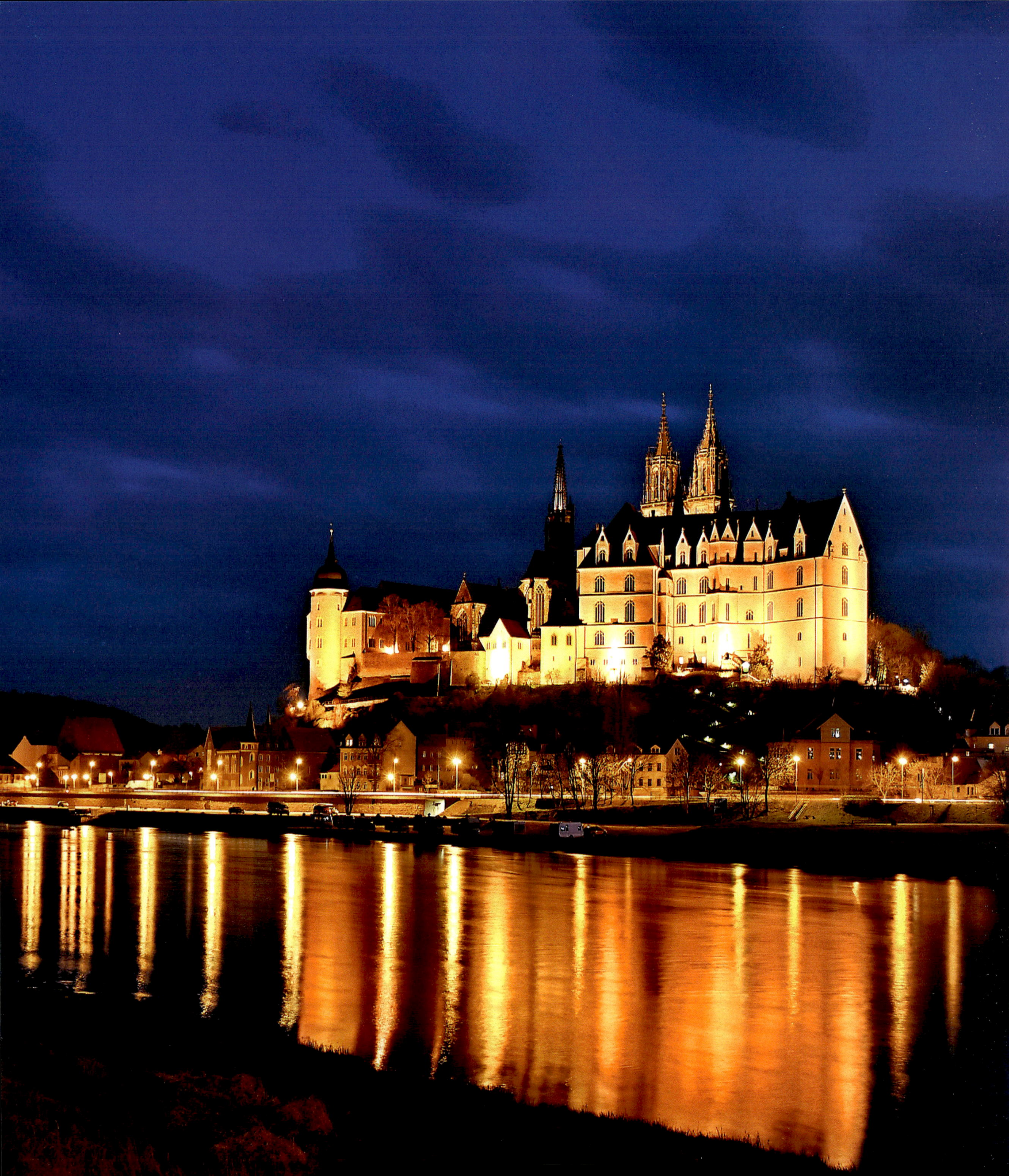

Meissen Albrechtsburg Castle
A trendsetter since 1471

Majestically enthroned above the picturesque valley of the Elbe, Meissen's Albrechtsburg Castle – built in 15th century Late Gothic style – ranks as Germany's oldest residential castle.

In 929 King Henry I erected a wooden fortress on a cliff above the Elbe at Meissen, making the city the centre of the "march" (or borderland) facing the still Slavic territories to the east. The margrave ruled over the entire March of Meissen and resided in what would later become the Albrechtsburg, which has consequently come down in history as the "cradle of Saxony".

Commissioned by the brothers Ernest and Albert of Wettin, who then ruled in Saxony, Meissen's Late Gothic castle was built between 1471 and 1524 as both a residence appropriate to their rank and an awe-inspiring administrative centre of their lands. As such it was less a defensive stronghold than a schloss in the true sense of the word – the first in German history.

But Albrechtsburg Castle was destined never to be used in its appointed function. Before it was finished the brothers had already divided the Wettin territories between them, and Albrechtsburg Castle was not used actively until, two centuries later, Elector Augustus the Strong transformed it in 1710 into Europe's first porcelain manufactory – a role it fulfilled for the following 153 years.

Production of porcelain in the castle halls ceased in 1863. Prolonged industrial use had, however, caused massive damage; repairs were necessary, and thorough restoration of the interior and exterior Gothic forms was planned. Extra funding soon became available in the form of French reparations in the

Meissen Albrechtsburg Castle with the landmark twin towers of Meissen Cathedral

The "cradle of Saxony" on the River Elbe ranks as Germany's oldest castle residence.

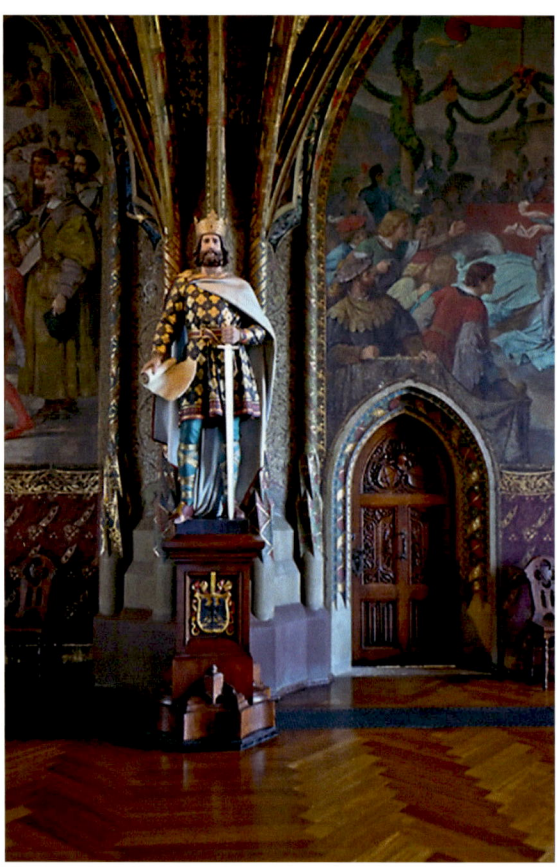

wake of the Franco-Prussian War, and this enabled the inauguration of a new artistic programme for the castle. Starting in 1873, wall paintings were commissioned, mostly depicting historical events around the Meissen Albrechtsburg Castle, the march of Meissen, the House of Wettin, and the origins of "white gold" – as porcelain was familiarly called. As well as these intentionally modern works, decorative artwork along Gothic lines was also executed, and the apartments were fitted out with historical reproductions extending from furniture, floors and doors, through flags and weapons, to lighting, stoves and fireplaces.

The focus now was on stylish living. Meissen Albrechtsburg Castle was already a trendsetter when it was built, causing wonder and astonishment at the grandeur of its Late Gothic architecture. Today, with every floor of the castle accessible to the visitor, a state-of-the-art interactive presentation maintains this reputation, providing in five sub-sections fascinating insights into the castle architecture, the House of Wettin as rulers and residents in Meissen, and Meissen Albrechtsburg Castle in its passage from noble residence to china factory. Finally a book of paintings illustrates the dynastic and political history of the state.

The Great Court Chamber features large coloured statues of the former margraves of the March of Meissen.

Looking into the Great Court Chamber. A wealth of 19th century wall paintings gives the castle's biggest room a festal atmosphere.

Altenstein Palace and Park
Summer residence of the "Theatre Duke"

Altenstein Palace, with its 160 hectare (c. 400 acre) landscaped park, lies north of Bad Liebenstein, Thuringia's oldest spa town. It is not often in Germany today that horticulture, landscaping and nature meld into so perfect a park landscape – the work of three garden designers, Prince Hermann von Pückler-Muskau, Eduard Petzold and Peter Joseph Lenné. At the heart of this idyll Duke Georg II of Saxe-Meiningen built his summer residence.

The park was laid down in 1798 and later extended several times. Today it reveals three distinct phases of development: the Early Sentimental landscaped garden complete with architectural elements, the broad, defined spaces of the first half of the 19th century, and the trend towards decorative flower beds and sculptures marking the turn of the 20th century. At Altenstein these three modes blend into an artistic synthesis.

In the late 19th century Duke Georg II of Saxe-Meiningen, aka the "Theatre Duke", replaced an earlier Baroque residence with a house in the style of an English stately home. With its stepped and curving gables, bow windows and arcaded portico annex the house has a particularly striking silhouette. Immediately surrounding it, the pergolas, statues and fountains are set off by two elaborate flower beds: The great "Altenstein tapestry bed", already much admired in descriptions from the turn of the century, fills the centre of the trapezium-shaped lawn between palace and Idolino fountain, while the intricately woven "bed of knots" has graced the middle terrace since the second half of the 19th century.

As well as the gardens around the house, Altenstein Palace has an extensive landscaped outer park with a dense network of paths and numerous lookouts, like the Boniface and Morgentor cliffs, offering wide views of the Werra Valley and across to the Rhön Hills. Wide meadows punctuated by single or clustered trees open between

Altenstein Palace in Bad Liebenstein

generously wooded parkland. A tour of the park takes one through different landscapes – the Morgentor meadow, the Luisental etc. – passing features like the Blumenkorbfelsen with its stone basket of planted flowers, a delight since 1800.

Architectural elements from this period enhance the charm of the tour – the Neo-Gothic Knights' Chapel, for example, perched on a needle of rock, or the alarmingly undulating Devil's Bridge, or the Chinese Cabin reflecting the fashion of the late 18th century. An entire valley with an artificial waterfall and Alpine herdsman's hut was incorporated into this picturesque landscape – a classic example of the discovery of natural beauty as a design principle of horticultural art.

"Tapestry flower bed" with view across the Werra Valley

Chinese Cabin

Knights' Chapel

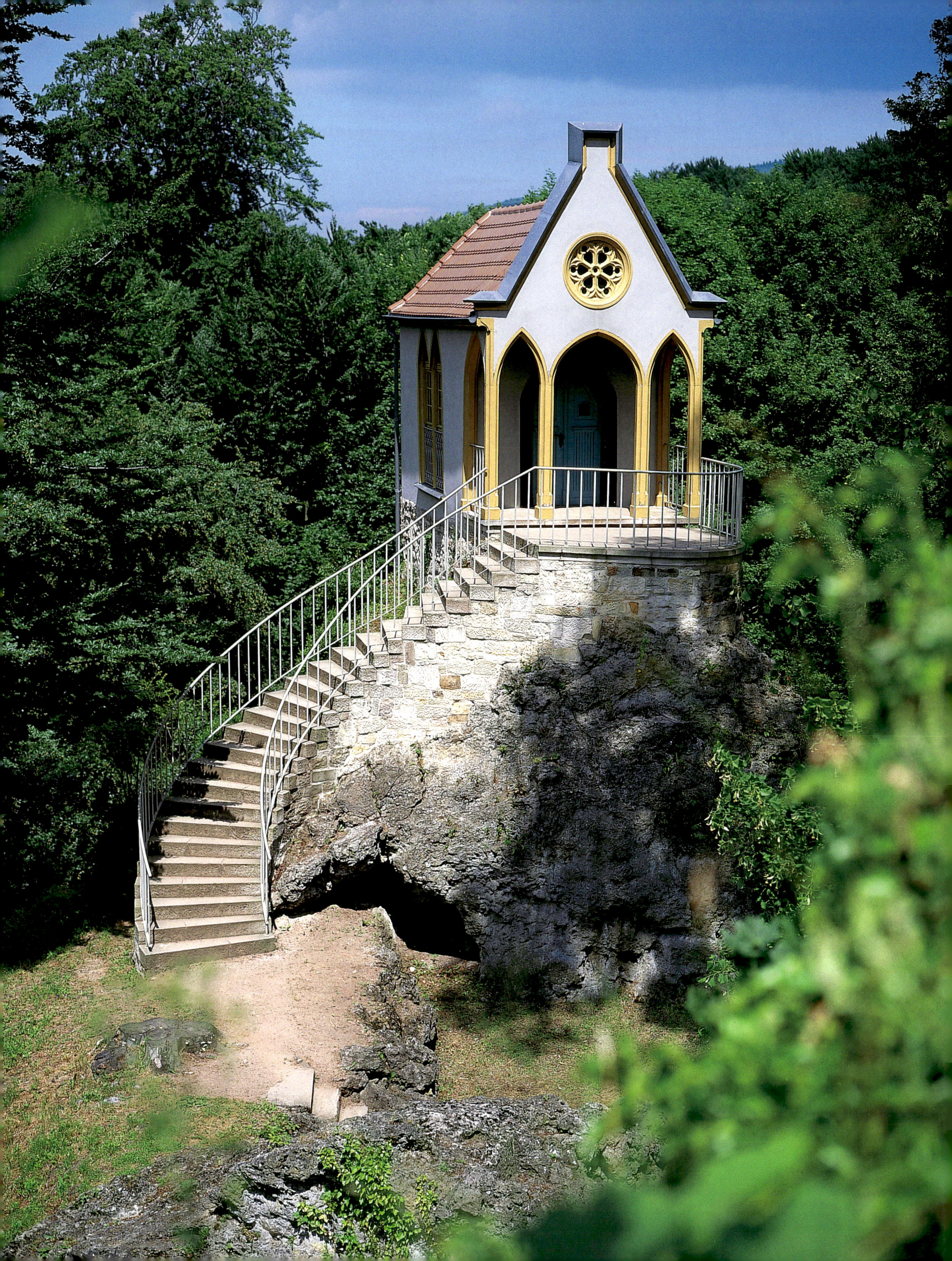

Wasserburg Anholt

Noble gem with museum and hotel

Between Isselburg and the Dutch border, the imposing moated castle of Anholt stands guard, one of the Western Münsterland's most impressive stately homes.

With its circular keep, corner turrets, and helmet-roofed Baroque gate tower, Wasserburg Anholt owes its origin to Godfried van Rhenen, bishop of Utrecht (†1178), who around 1165 had a fortress built in the south-west corner of his territories to control the Rhine delta. In 1402 the castle and its lands passed to the House of Bronkhorst-Batenburg, who guided its fortunes for the following 250 years. Despite their involvement in armed conflict and their rank of bannerets (leading knights), the family sent their sons to university and left a considerable cultural legacy, including an extensive library with medieval manuscripts and a gallery of paintings. Both collections are still extant and open to the public.

Under the rule of the princely House of Salm, who came into possession of Anholt through marriage in 1641, a period of peaceful development began for castle, town and lands. Prince Carl Theodor Otto zu Salm (1645–1710) transformed the medieval fortress into a Baroque residence, notable measures being the conversion of the late medieval front castle a three-winged lodge, and the replacement of the defensive gatehouse with a Baroque entrance portal. The interior of the castle was at the same time lavishly renovated in the Baroque style, with furniture and artworks purchased in the European centres of Vienna and Paris. After his father's death, Prince Ludwig Otto zu Salm (1674–1738) continued the work, laying down the unrivalled Baroque gardens.

The French Revolution brought less tranquil times, culminating in the incorporation of the principality in the Kingdom of Prussia in 1815. However, the House of Salm-Salm retained the moated castle of Anholt as their sole seat and the administrative centre of their lands. In the course of the 19th century, economic consolidation brought renewed prosperity; the already impres-

Wasserburg Anholt with water gardens

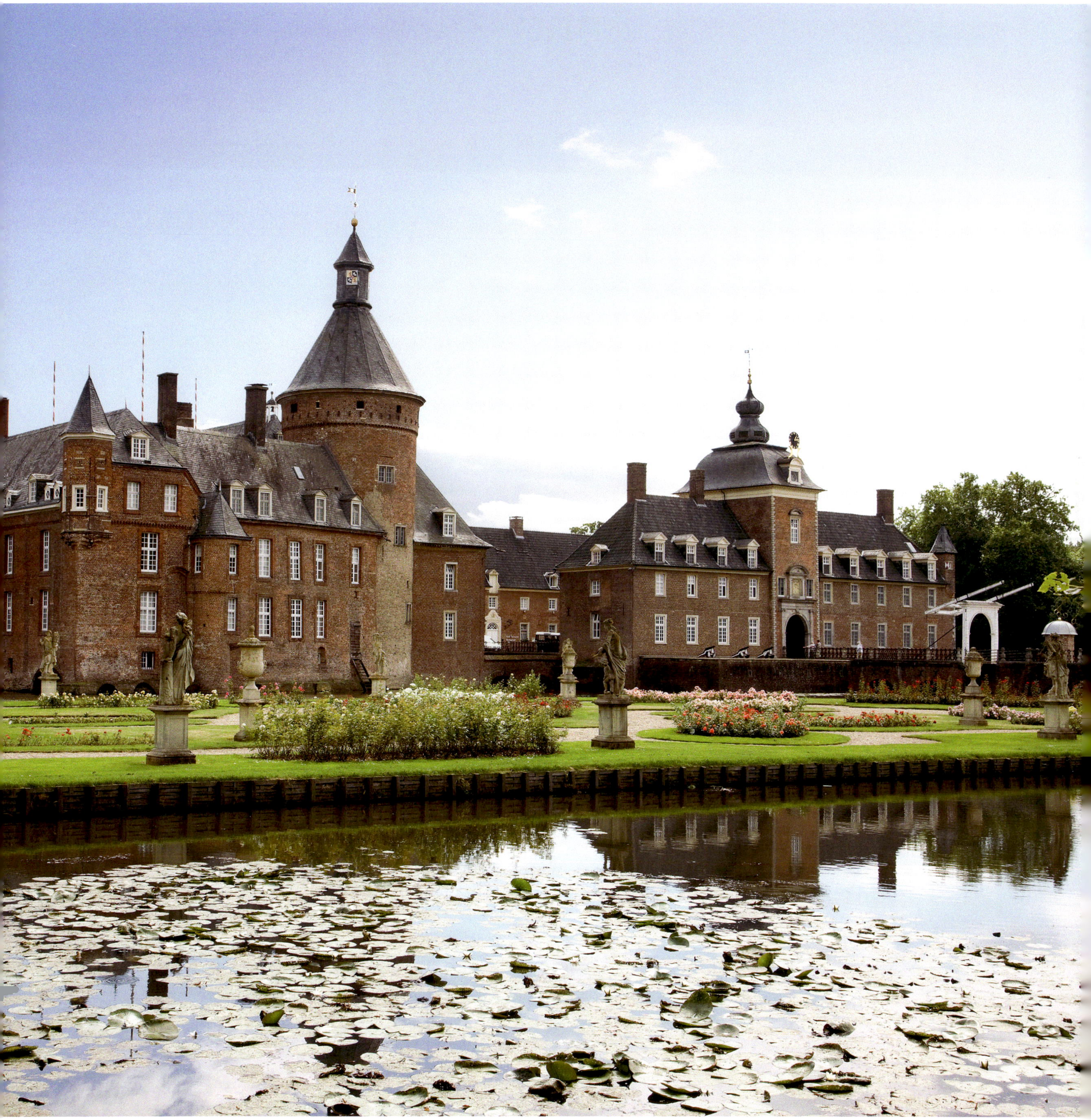

sive art collections were extended and the main library equipped to hold 8000 historical volumes.

The Second World War brought massive damage to both castle and park. Restoration started in the 1960s, and since that time Wasserburg Anholt has fulfilled a double function as hotel and museum. With its art collections, library and archives, as well as the castle park, "Swiss Anholt" fauna biotope, and golf course, the ensemble offers a wealth of tourist attractions and is a popular destination for day excursions.

Billiard room

Knights' room

Prince's apartment

Arolsen Palace
A residence steeped in family history

Arolsen Palace, the splendid Baroque residence of the Princes of Waldeck and Pyrmont, lies in the small town of Bad Arolsen in the north of the Waldecker Land between Kassel and Paderborn. Built on the site of a medieval abbey, the 18th century palace is still the princely family home.

Founded in 1131, Aroldessen Abbey passed into the ownership of the counts of Waldeck during the post-Reformation process of secularization. It had already been converted into a Renaissance castle in the 1530s, but when Count Friedrich Anton Ulrich von Waldeck (1676–1728) was elevated to the rank of imperial prince, his need for accommodation appropriate to that rank resulted in the demolition of the Renaissance building in 1710 and its replacement with a palace on the model of Versailles – an impressive three-wing ensemble with a classically restrained façade, designed by master builder Julius Ludwig Rothweil. But Prince Friedrich Anton Ulrich's ambitions went further: he had the town of Arolsen planned in the Baroque manner on the drawing board to match his residence, which stood at its focal point.

Since 1720 the Baroque palace has been the seat of the House of Waldeck and Pyrmont. As it was never destroyed, it remains an important witness to the successive generations that have left their mark on it. The interior was only finished in the 19th century, and the entire ensemble was restored and renovated between 1984 and 2009. Today it is probably more complete than ever before.

Part of the palace is open to the public. Guided tours of the *corps de logis* introduce visitors to the architectural, artistic and family history captured by these highly authentic rooms, with their paintings by various masters of the Tischbein dynasty, furniture by the Kaulbachs of Arolsen, and sculptures by Christian-Daniel Rauch and Alexander Trippel. The unique setting of the "Steinerne Saal" – a garden hall with stucco by Andrea Gallasini – comes into its own for concerts and other festal occasions, and ground floor rooms

Looking across the countryard to the *corps de logis* of the Arolsen Palace.

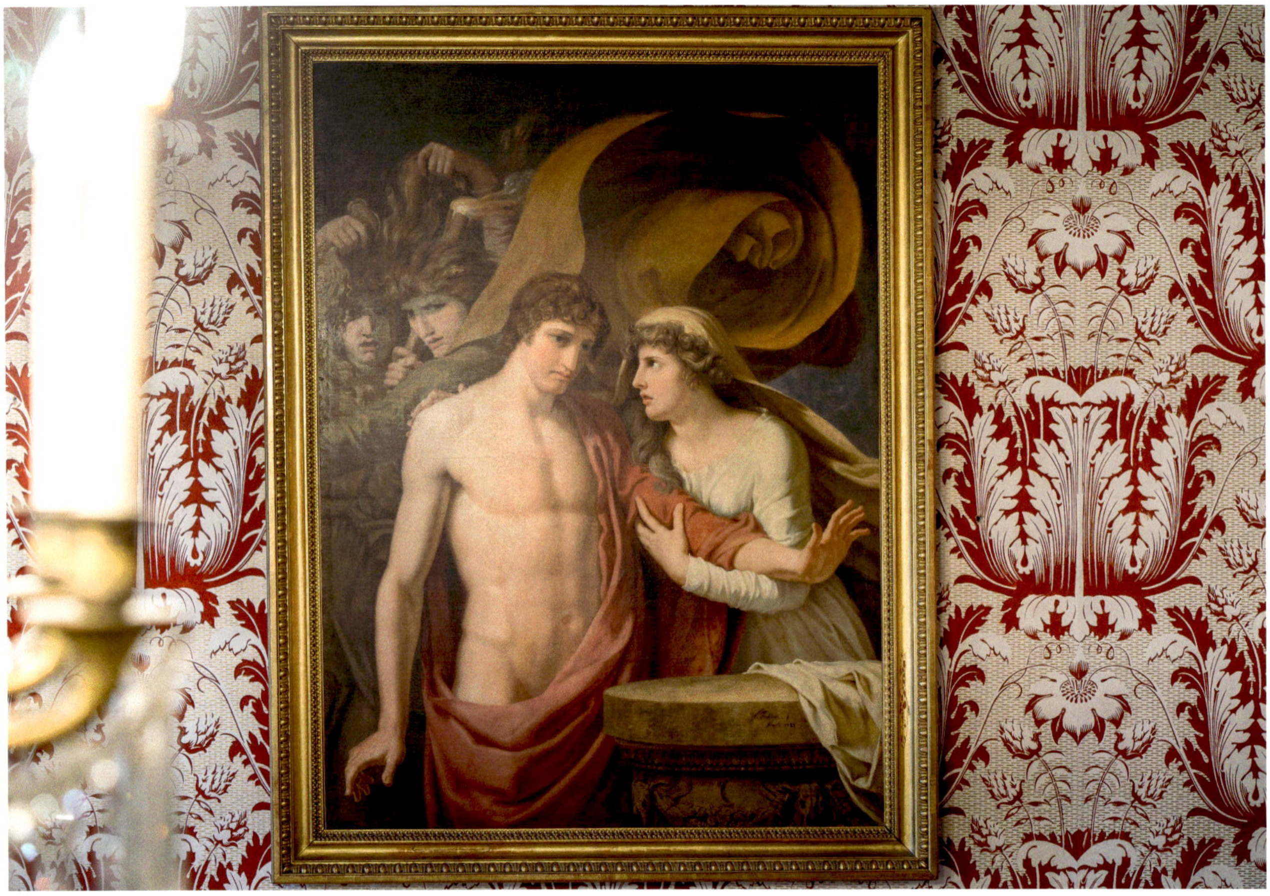

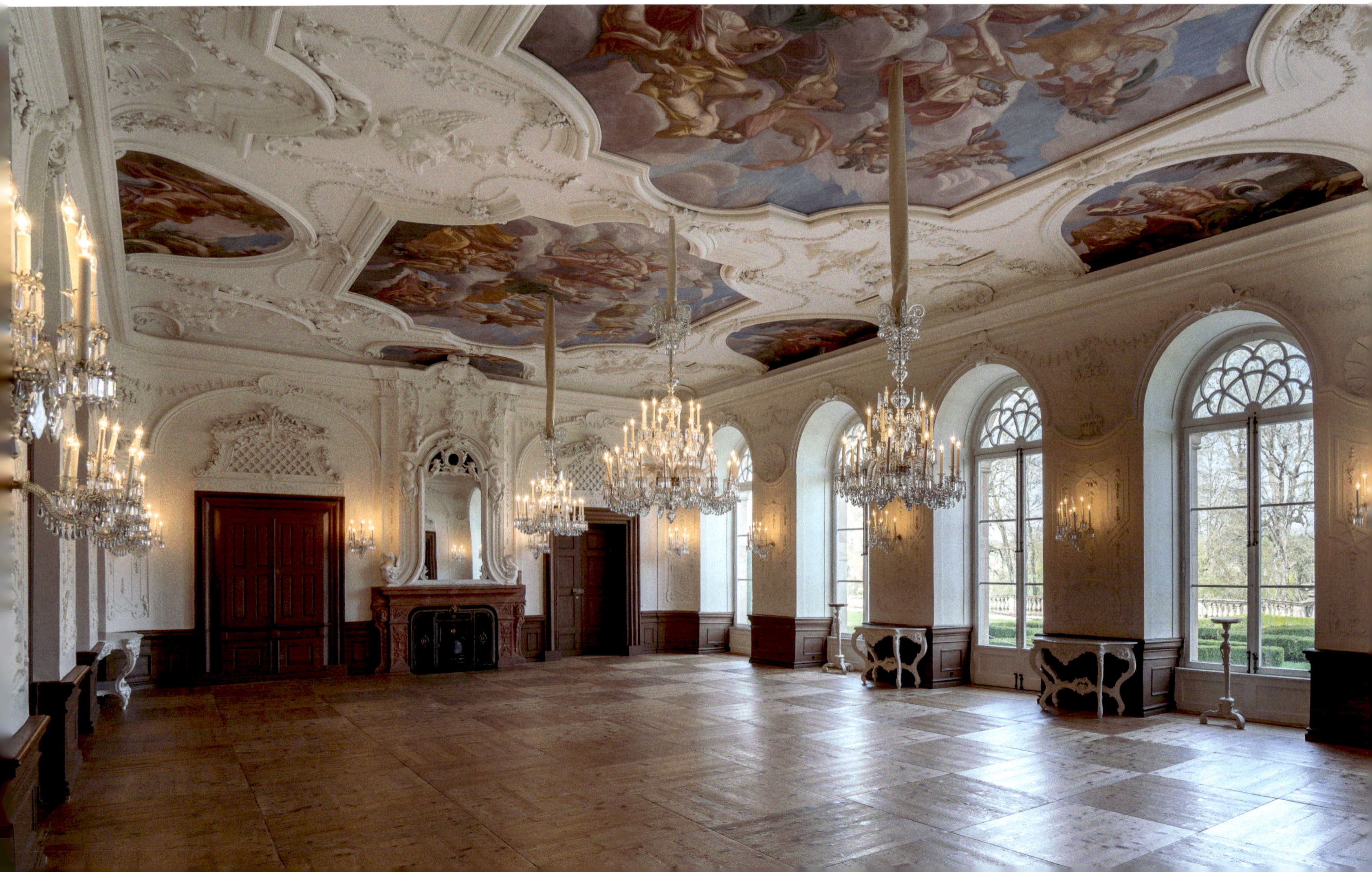

Orestes and Iphigenia, by William Tischbein

"Steinerner Saal" with stucco by Andrea Gallasini and ceiling frescoes by Carlo Ludovico Castelli

White Hall with ancestral gallery

Bust of Goethe as a Greek poet, by Alexander Trippel

feature a permanent exhibition on Waldeck hunting and military history. The Palace Chapel has seen such historic events as the marriage of Princess Emma of Waldeck and Pyrmont to King Willem III of the Netherlands. Today it – and other rooms also steeped in history – can be booked for weddings and events.

The west wing contains the Prince of Waldeck's Court Library, with some 35,000 volumes, more than 1000 maps, charts and plans, 500 works with copperplate engravings and several thousand more individual prints. Bad Arolsen Museum also uses rooms here for temporary exhibitions.

Bad Homburg Castle and Park

Seat of the landgraves of Hesse-Homburg and summer residence of the German emperors

Bad Homburg Castle as it is today was built from 1679 in the Early Baroque style. The white tower shows, however, that the history of what was then still called Friedrichsburg goes back to the Middle Ages. The former keep is the only remaining visible fragment of the 11th-century hilltop castle whose demolition Landgrave Friedrich II ordered with a view to replacing it with a modern residential complex. Clustered around two courtyards, the Baroque ensemble was until 1866 the official residence of the landgraves of Hesse-Homburg and after that the summer residence of the German emperors.

The interior provides an insight into the courtly domestic culture of both periods. Alongside the Baroque sequences, the rooms of the so-called English wing represent a high point of noble décor and furnishings. Prepared for Landgravine Elizabeth, a daughter of the English monarch George III, the wing reveals her liking for English furniture combined with the contemporary Biedermeier style. Of special interest is the dining room with its splendid wall and ceiling paintings. The appeal of the domestic apartments lies above all, however, in the landgravine's valuable art collection, which also features her own work.

The royal wing contains the only authentic imperial apartments in a German palace that still retain their original form. After extensive renovation they will be reopened in spring 2021, presenting the taste of the last German imperial couple in pristine glory. A tour of the palace's 18 rooms includes the study, bedrooms, bathrooms and dressing rooms of Kaiser Wilhelm II and Kaiserin Auguste Viktoria. A unique feature is the telephone room, which demonstrates the state of technical progress at the turn of the twentieth century.

Bad Homburg Castle is set in an extensive park that combines various epochs of horticultural and landscaping art. Contemporary with the landgraves' residence is the Baroque upper garden with the orangery, while the great cedars planted there came to Bad Homburg in 1818 as a wedding present for Landgravine Elizabeth. Through a bosquet one reaches the lower garden, laid down in the 1770s as a landscaped park in the English style. A walk around the lake reveals a number of typical architectonic elements, like the historic

Bad Homburg Castle with upper garden and part of the park

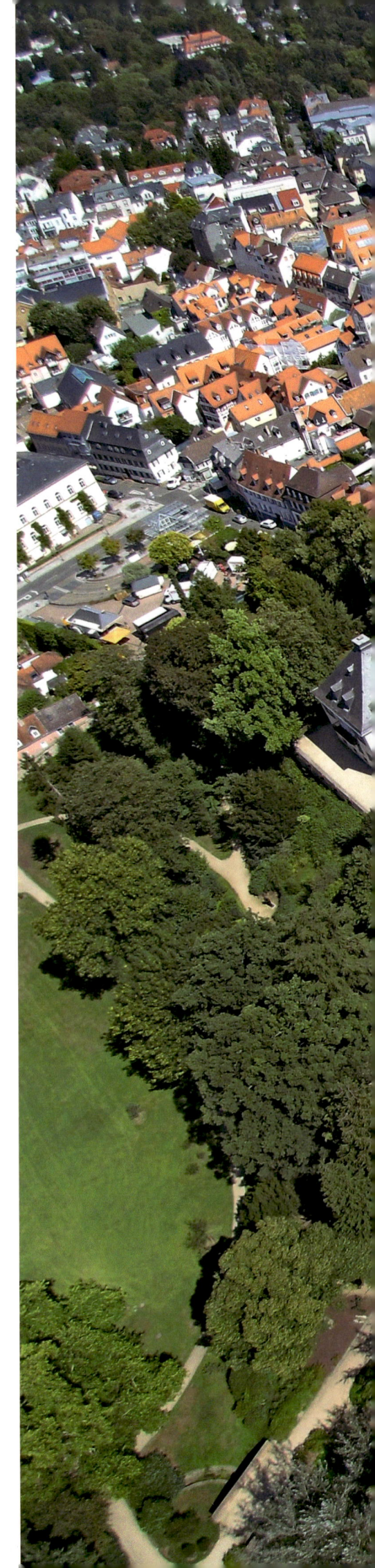

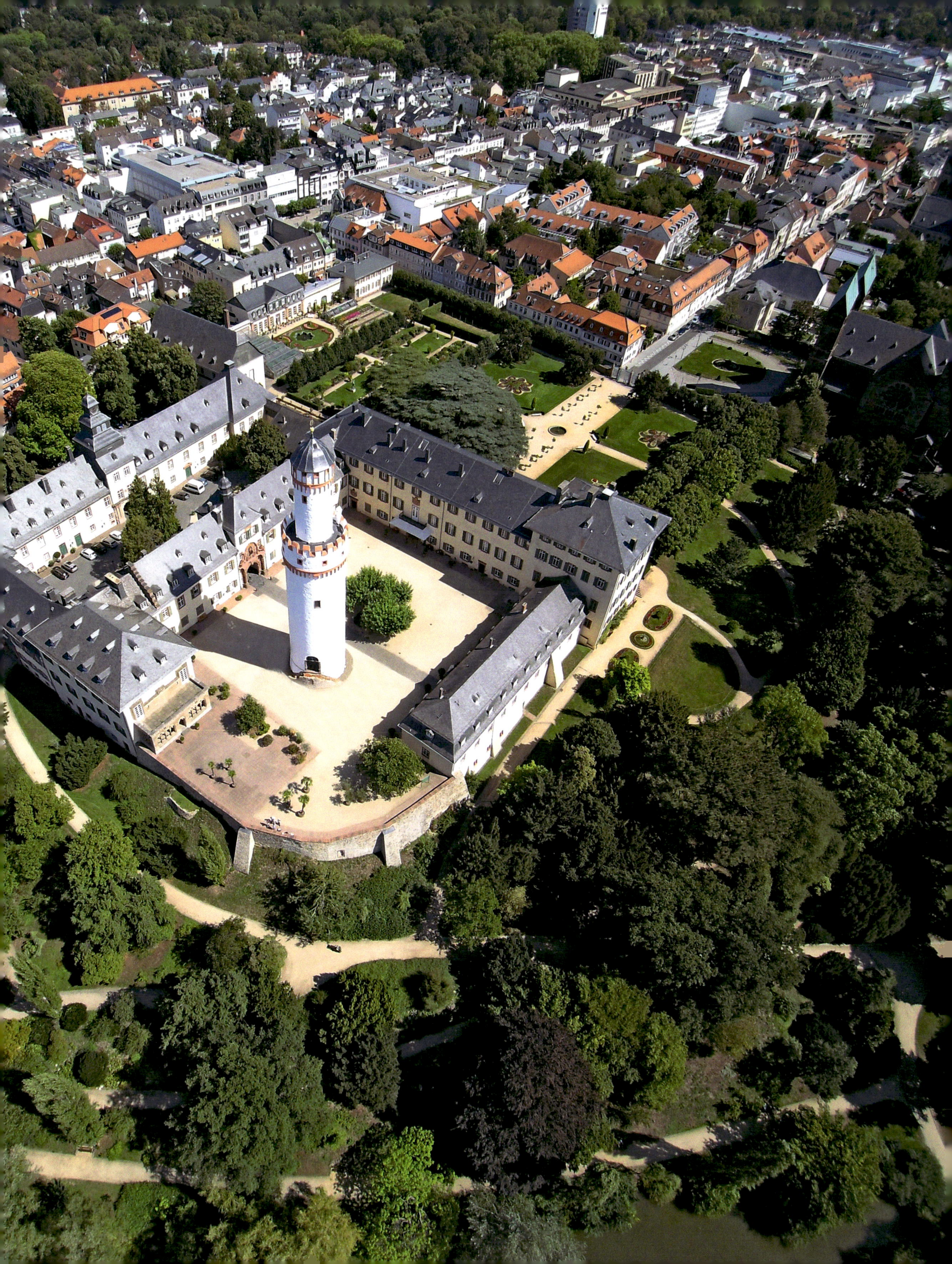

pinewood avenue, over ten kilometres in length, which links a number of other gardens, or the Master's Orchard, or again the so-called Fantasy with the Temple of Pomona, all of which invite the visitor to pause for a moment's rest.

Dowager apartment of Landgravine Elizabeth in the English wing

Visible from afar: the white tower in the upper courtyard

Belvedere Castle and Park

A floral paradise at the gates of Weimar

Belvedere Castle, the former hideaway of the Weimar court and one of the many *maisons de plaisance* built by Ernst August, Duke of Saxe-Weimar (1688–1748), lies amid broad parks and gardens at the end of a long Baroque avenue some 3 kilometres from the City of Weimar.

In essence, the country mansion derives from a hunting lodge lavishly extended by the Duke when he became sole ruler in 1728. Wider than it is deep, the building was furnished with a tall central lantern equipped with a gallery from which the leisured society of the time had "a fine view" of the surrounding forests with their abundant game and venison. From here one could also see the ducal residence in Weimar. Embellished with cavaliers' houses to the side, and with an orangery, stable block and richly stocked menagerie, the complex displayed all the features of a contemporary absolutist court residence.

Even after the death of Duke Ernst August, Weimar court society under Duke Ernst August II Constantin and Duchess Anna Amalia still frequently withdrew to Belvedere, although with the duchy facing a financial crisis the extravagance of the premises soon had to be compromised. The menagerie was largely abandoned, but the orangery was retained and even expanded with the construction of the Long House. With its valuable collection of exotic trees – oranges and other citrus fruits, dates and laurels, cypresses and figs – it is in fact one of the few German orangeries to have been in continuous use for almost 300 years. It still contains some valuable historical individuals, myrtle trees, for example, and one particular cypress, but at the same time the focus of the collection remains on classical orangery cultivars.

New life came to Belvedere in 1804, when Duke Carl August gave his newly-wed son and heir Carl Friedrich and his young bride – the Tsar's daughter Maria Pawlowna (1786–1859) – the use of the castle as their residence. In 1811 they transformed the Baroque park into a landscaped garden, with twisting paths leading through the valley of the Possenbach to pretty arbours like the Mooshütte, Rosenberceau, Four Scholars' Clearing, Rose Bower or Great Fountain. Until his death in 1828, Carl August retained the right to use the orangery and gardening facilities, and these became – with the keen involvement of Goethe – a centre of botanical studies. It was in this context that the Duke laid down the botanical garden to the south of the Long House.

In Belvedere Castle Park

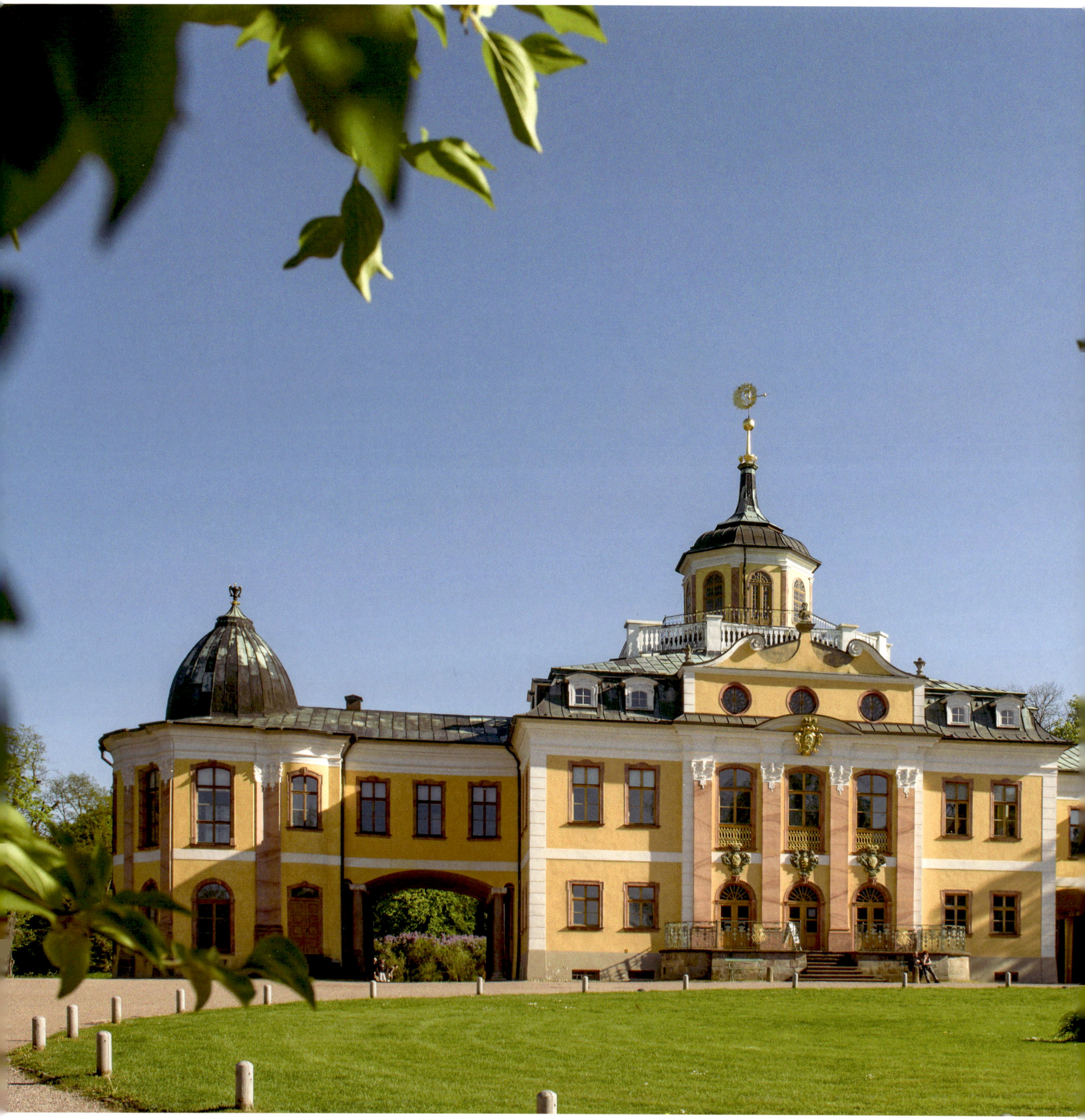

A visit to Belvedere Castle takes one back to an era before Weimar Classicism. Inside the castle is a museum of applied art displaying products from two centuries, especially the Rococo and the courtly culture of the early 18th century.

Belvedere Castle

Orangery in Belvedere Castle Park

Benrath Palace

Most beautiful palace on the Rhine

Benrath Palace and its park lie immediately on the right bank of the Rhine in the Benrath district of Düsseldorf. Elements of the old palace, with its bygone glory, unite with the new building and park to create a striking artistic synthesis.

Benrath's history of noble architecture goes back to the Middle Ages, but we have little information about the buildings from that time. In the mid-17th century an impressive waterside castle, "Old Benrath Palace", was erected. Parts of this building – the gatehouses and remnants of the south and north wings – have survived, in the latter case (the orangery) with some rich interior fittings and decorations that count among the outstanding artistic products of the 17th century Rhineland. These include an original staircase, some fine stucco work and fireplaces,

Palace ensemble from the north

Benrath Palace in Düsseldorf

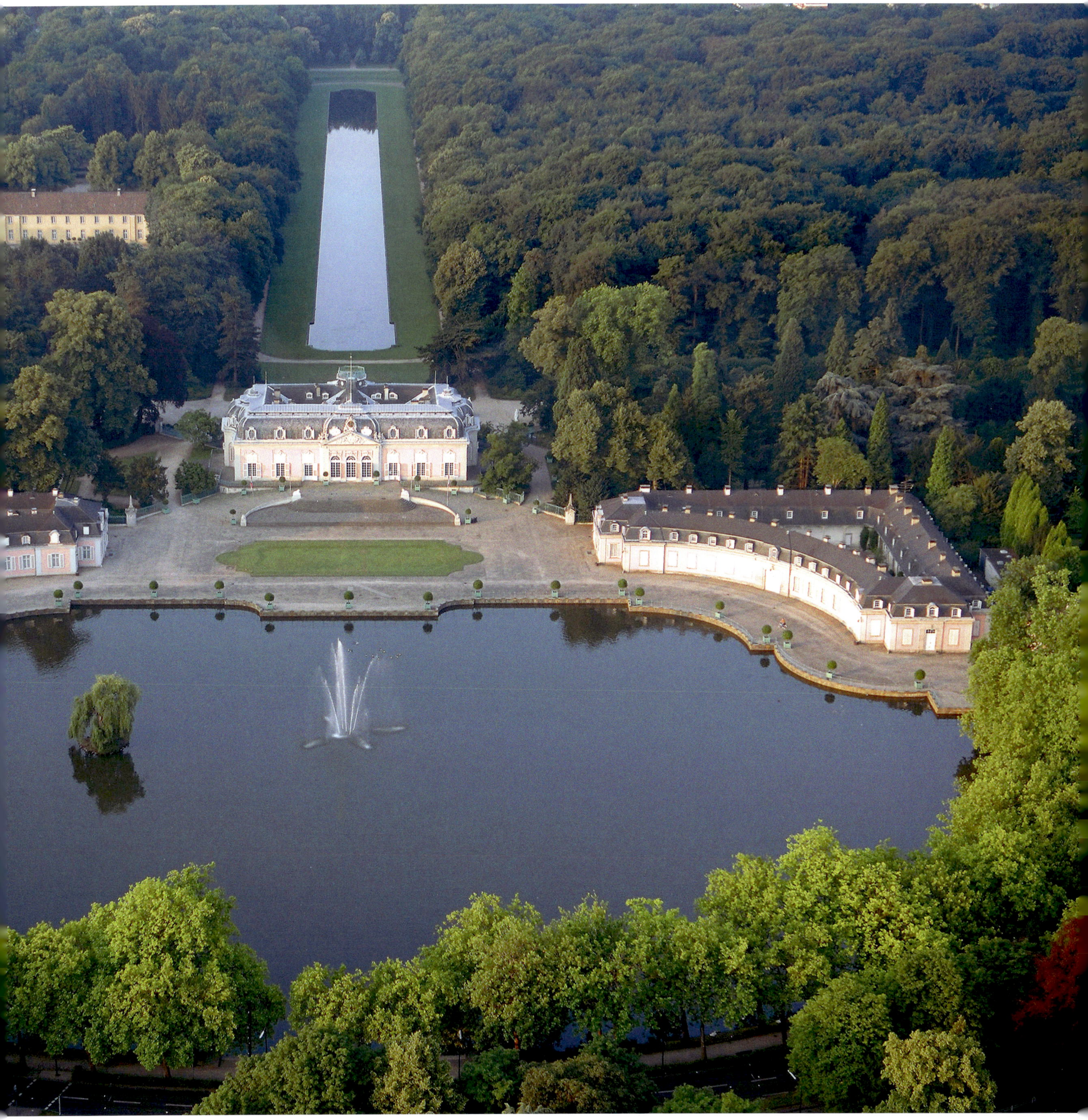

and a cycle of paintings illustrating the relations between the genders in the light of classical mythology.

In 1755, Elector and Count Palatine Carl Theodor and his wife, Electress Elisabeth Auguste, resolved to replace his old *maison de plaisance* in Düsseldorf with a new and more fashionable building. By 1770 his Palatine architectural director, Nicolas de Pigage, had created an ensemble of palace, park, gardens, paths and water basins that formed a perfect artistic unity. The underlying spatial principle of the electoral couple's summer residence was that of a graduated theatrical *mise en scène* of opulently adorned buildings in an artistically designed natural environment.

Inside, as well as the splendid domed hall, the *corps de logis* has two master apartments on the *bel étage* and four guest apartments on the upper floor.

The origins of the 60 hectare (c. 150 acre) park lie in the 17th century. Between the garden façade of the palace and the long sunken mirror of the water basin, the terrace serves as the axial hub for the park's three main sightlines. Now, as in the 18th century, it holds in summer an array of laurel plants in tubs. Most of the park is taken up by a large square bosquet intersected starwise by four long paths terminating in ponds or clearings – visual closures that afford ever-varying perspectives and turning points for the visitor. To the left and right of the *corps de logis* the private gardens of the electoral couple form an immediate extension of their apartments into the grounds of the palace.

Owned today by the (state capital) City of Düsseldorf, Benrath Palace, with its three museums – *Corps de logis*, Museum of European Garden Art, and Museum of Natural History – as well as the museum shop and café, is administered by the Benrath Palace and Park Foundation.

Domed Hall in the *corps de logis*

Bentheim Castle
A journey into history

Set on a 90 metre-high spur of the Teutoburg Forest, Bentheim Castle is Lower Saxony's biggest hilltop fortress. Even from afar the great sandstone stronghold defines the silhouette of Bad Bentheim, a historic spa town on the Dutch border.

Bentheim first occurs in records of 1020, when Count Otto of Northeim was named as master of that estate. A leading Saxon nobleman, he had in 1061 been granted the duchy of Bavaria by Empress Agnes. The first mention of the House of Bentheim occurs in a deed of 1154 issued by the bishop of Münster. The founder of the present-day line of Bentheim-Steinfurt was Eberwin IV of Götterswick, who in 1421 inherited the title of count from the Dutch line of the counts of Bentheim, who had no male heir.

Like most other German castles, Bentheim was subject to changing fortunes. Disputed inheritance and divisions of the property, coupled with economic mismanagement, the ravages of the Thirty Years' War, and military occupations, led to the county being pledged as security, and in 1753 to its loss as an independent polity. While other rulers were demolishing their medieval castles to make way for splendid Baroque palaces, the Bentheims simply lacked the money for such extravagance – which is why the medieval and Early Modern structure of Bentheim Castle has been preserved so well.

However, in the 19th century the House of Bentheim flourished anew, and the castle was duly extended in the historicist style. Most of the complex was opened to the public in 1993, a small part being reserved to the family of Hereditary Prince Carl Ferdinand of Bentheim and Steinfurt, in whose hands the management of the castle complex now lies.

History comes alive behind the five-and-a-half-metre thick walls between Knights' Hall, Powder Tower and Torture Chamber. The Gothic Church of St. Catherine and the 30 metre-high keep convey an impression of life in the Middle Ages, while the neo-Gothic Kronenburg contains finely worked examples of the castle's typical sandstone. The reception rooms – for example the Ernst-August-Salon – are notable for their historical furnishings. The famous Early Romanesque stone crucifix known as the "Herrgott (Lord God) of Bentheim", together with an exhibition

Aerial view of Bentheim Castle

of historical coaches, complete the visitor's tour of discovery. A permanent exhibition – "The World of Alchemy" – in the round tower reconstructs a 17th century chemical laboratory, where visitors can experience first-hand how alchemists of bygone centuries strove to find ways of making gold.

Ernst August Salon, used today for weddings

Arcade room

Bedroom of Queen Emma of the Netherlands

Staircase in Kronenburg

Cannon on the battlements

31

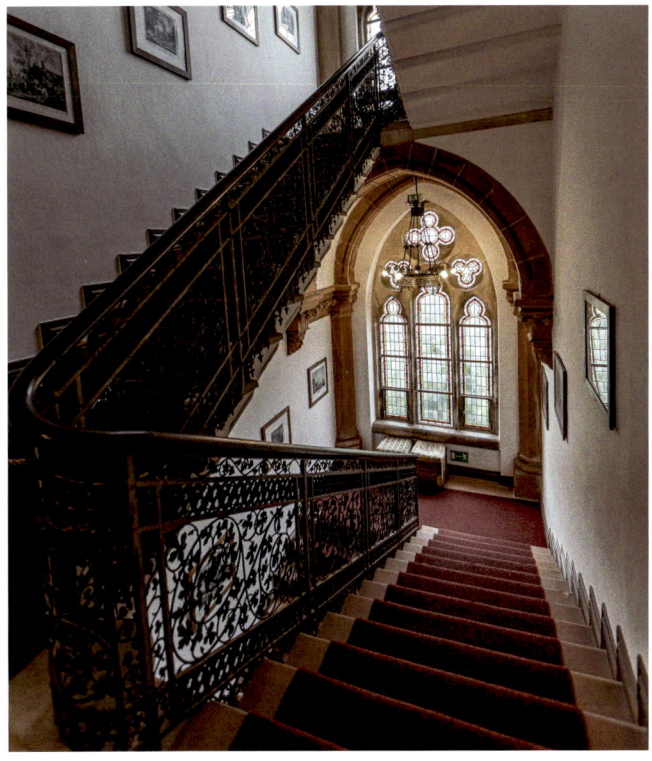

Bothmer House

A piece of England in Mecklenburg

A jewel of Baroque brick architecture, Bothmer House owes its existence to the adventurous career of Hans Caspar, Count Bothmer (1656–1732). At its zenith, this took him to London, where he lived in the legendary number 10, Downing Street. It was from there that, in 1726, he commissioned the magnificent house and estate bordering the village of Klütz, 4 kilometres from the Baltic coast. His architect, Johann Friedrich Künnecke, was bold enough to prophesy that people would remember Count Bothmer by his house "as long as stone is called stone".

And Künnecke has proven right. For close on 300 years, the irresistible charm of the ensemble has kept its founder's name alive in the memory. So near the seaside, the house draws many visitors, not only for the beauty of the newly restored rooms in the main house, but also for its modern exhibition, which relates Count Hans Caspar's fairytale life and the construction of the house under the motif of his personal motto "respice finem" ("consider the end"). Modelled on an English country mansion, Bothmer House housed the Count's descendants until 1945. After the war it was used as an old people's home; only in 2015 was it reopened, after extensive refurbishment, as a cultural centre and museum.

Surrounded on the Dutch model by channels of water, house and park blend impressively into the Mecklenburg landscape, creating an island of idyllic peace. Bothmer House has for many years also served as a verdant background for concerts, drawing enthusiastic audiences in their thousands. Bothmer's unique avenue of lime-trees, the Festonallee, is one of Mecklenburg's most popular photographic motifs. Approaching the house along the 270 metres of this partly sunken path, one sees at first only the central building; the closely planted trees cut off the view to either side. But, with every step, the view broadens, until opening out onto the front terrace it embraces the entire majestic ensemble in a masterly Baroque *mise en scène*. Over the centuries nothing has been lost of this impact – a reward for visitors at every season.

The Orangery Café and Restaurant welcomes museum visitors and excursionists and offers generous facilities for private celebrations, conferences and weddings – an ideal platform for memorable occasions.

Bothmer House – a jewel of Baroque brick architecture

270 metres long, the Festonallee gives an impressive step-by-step view of Bothmer House.

33

A modern museum at Bothmer House relates the adventurous career of Hans Caspar, Count Bothmer.

The extensive park is an invitation to linger and relax.

Branitz Palace and Park
Prince Pückler's masterpiece and refuge

Prussia's one and only dandy, celebrated 19th century bestselling author, adventurer in orient and occident, brilliant centrepiece of German society and legendary connoisseur of beauty in every dimension, Prince Hermann von Pückler-Muskau (1785–1871) was a progressive man of his century, poised between absolutism and democracy, a clever self-promoter who lent his name to an ice-cream specialty known to this day, and above all a garden landscape designer of international repute.

In Branitz the "Green Prince", as he was known, created from 1845 onward an artistic synthesis of landscaped estate and garden, architecture and interior design that would stand as his ultimate masterpiece and serve him as retirement residence. To this day the great house is the centrepiece of an immense cultural landscape, a reflection of Pückler's idiosyncratic journeying through life: "If you want to know me," he said, "know my garden: my garden is my heart."

Extending over more than 600 hectares (almost 1500 acres) south of Cottbus in Lower Lusatia (Branden-

Lake pyramid and tumulus – Prince Pückler's burial place

burg), Branitz Park was landscaped into zones on the English model. Thus the "ornamental farm" was created with ordered zones of woodland, meadows and cultivated fields, an idealized conjunction of horticultural art and agricultural use. This so-called "outer park" is accessed via a drive that leads unobtrusively through scene after scene of the Prince's landscape: fine views, decorative buildings and beauties of nature alternating like pearls on a necklace.

The "inner park" is a more intensive creation, a work that involved considerable physical landscaping to create attractive reliefs with artificial lakes and stands of trees planted to define and emphasize the view. Here one also finds the singular green pyramids Pückler erected as reminiscences of his years travelling in the East. One of these, the lake pyramid, is his burial tumulus and now the iconic landmark of Branitz Park.

At the heart of the Prince's pleasure ground, surrounded by ornate flowerbeds, trees and sculptures, stands the Baroque family seat, refurbished to the Prince's sumptuous taste in the years after 1845. From the music room – with the instrument on which Clara Schumann played – to the important Pückler-Callenberg library, the salons and the oriental rooms, the visitor gains an insight into the Prince's exalted lifestyle. With its art collections and travel souvenirs, its richly coloured wall coverings and opulent materials, as well as its splendid parkland vistas, Schloss Branitz reveals the masterly qualities that made it Pückler's secluded home and the expression of his heart.

Further high-points are the historical glasshouses with the pineapple house and the permanent exhibition entitled "Masters of Landscape – Prince Pückler and Carl Blechen". Born in Cottbus, Blechen (1798–1840) was among the 19th century's most important landscape painters; Branitz holds one of the largest collections of his works.

The ensemble of Schloss Branitz with its surrounding pleasure grounds

The breakfast salon

The park smithy

Upper house with lion statues

Terrace with main entrance on the east of the house

37

Bückeburg Palace
Living tradition

On the edge of the North German plain, a good 60 kilometres west of Hanover, the 700 year-old palace of Schloss Bückeburg lies amid water-filled moats in the broad reaches of a landscaped park. In earlier centuries the seat of the independent principality of Schaumburg-Lippe, it has, since the abdication of that dynasty as rulers in 1918, been the family's private home.

Initially constructed in 1307 by Count Adolf VI zu Holstein-Schaumburg as a moated fortress, the schloss was transformed in the early 17th century by Count (later Prince) Ernst of that line into a palatial Renaissance residence to which he transferred his seat from Stadthagen. Over the following 400 years both house and park were continually extended. In 1925 parts of the complex were opened to the public, a development eagerly promoted by the present owner, Alexander, Prince of Schaumburg-Lippe, a keen art collector and music lover.

A tour of Schloss Bückeburg takes one through the centuries. The inner courtyard is largely unchanged from the original shape it had in 1562. The chapel, also part of the Late Medieval complex, was a mere 40 years later lavishly refurbished in the Mannerist style. Like the Golden Salon, it is a splendid product of the years under the art-loving Prince Ernst. In the pure Baroque idiom, the White Salon, with stucco ceilings,

Two styles, Renaissance and Baroque, blend into harmony in Obernkirch sandstone.

The idyllic site, where the Weser Hills meet the North German plain, draws thousands of visitors every year.

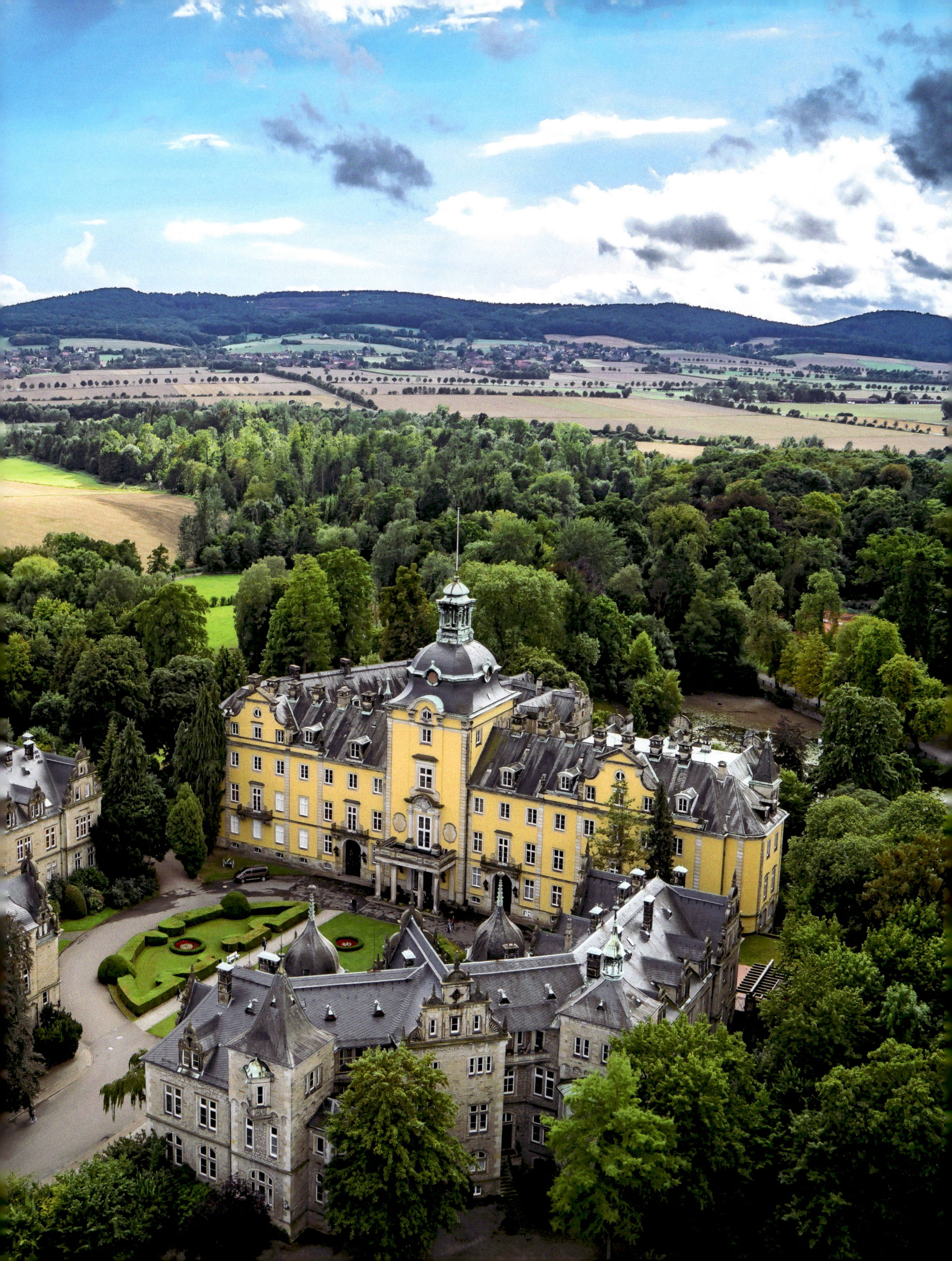

chandeliers and soft colours, conveys a sense of festal joy. Some 200 years later the imposing two-storey Great Hall was created as a reflection of the Rococo Age – but one that from the start was lit and heated electrically.

Far from ending at the palace gate, the more than 300 year-old cultural identity of Schloss Bückeburg extends into the park, where every tree and bush has been planted with care and yet evokes a sense of uncontrived naturalness. Laid down initially in the 1560s, the grounds were completely redesigned in 1732, and again generously enlarged and redesigned in the course of the 19th and 20th centuries. The sculptures on the schloss bridge are copies of works by Adrian de Vries (1621) now in Berlin's Bode Museum. The Mausoleum (1911–16) is striking not only for the brilliant white limestone of its walls, but also for a 42 metre-high dome glistening with millions of golden enamelled mosaic stones. The court riding school that flourished from 1609 until 1787 was revived in 2004; its exhibition shows six different epochs of European equestrianism.

Some 40 kilometres from Bückeburg, in the middle of the so-called "Steinhuder Sea" and only accessible by boat is another aspect of the former principality: Wilhelmstein Fortress. Built within the territories of the ruling family in 1765 as an impregnable refuge in an emergency, it later seved as a prison. In the 19th century Biedermeier Age it was already a tourist attraction.

Built in 1896, the neo-Baroque stateroom is used for events of many different kinds.

Celle Castle

A noble residence with a living history

Celle possesses one of Lower Saxony's finest examples of the German *Schloss*. Enclosed within the city ensemble, which has itself been preserved essentially intact, Celle Castle presents a unique topography. With an architectural history that reaches back to the 12th century, it was until 1705 the residence of the Guelphs, Europe's oldest still existing princely line, and for almost 300 years from 1433 that of the dukes of Brunswick-Lüneburg. The transformation of the original fortress into a stately home was gradual; its definitive phase came around 1670 with the addition of the wings that turned the castle into the quadrangular ensemble we know today – a fitting residence for a ducal family. In the 19th century Celle became the summer residence of the Hanoverian kings.

One of the most striking elements of the castle is the chapel. Consecrated in 1485, it was decorated shortly after the Reformation with a magnificent programmatic sequence of reliefs and paintings. With its combination of princely pomp and artistic quality, Celle Castle chapel is a key witness to the culture of the Reformation period in Germany.

The museum in the north and east wings conveys the history and significance of the castle's inhabitants with vivid immediacy. Even a late medieval banqueting hall awakens to new life with a modern presentation. With their fine stucco decoration, paintings and furniture, the Early Baroque state rooms of the last duke form an architectonic high point. Three spectacular gifts from the same period testify to the castle's bygone significance: two imposing gilded silver drinking cups and a table fountain are part of a unique Europe-

Aerial view of the quadrangle of Celle Castle (1660–1670)

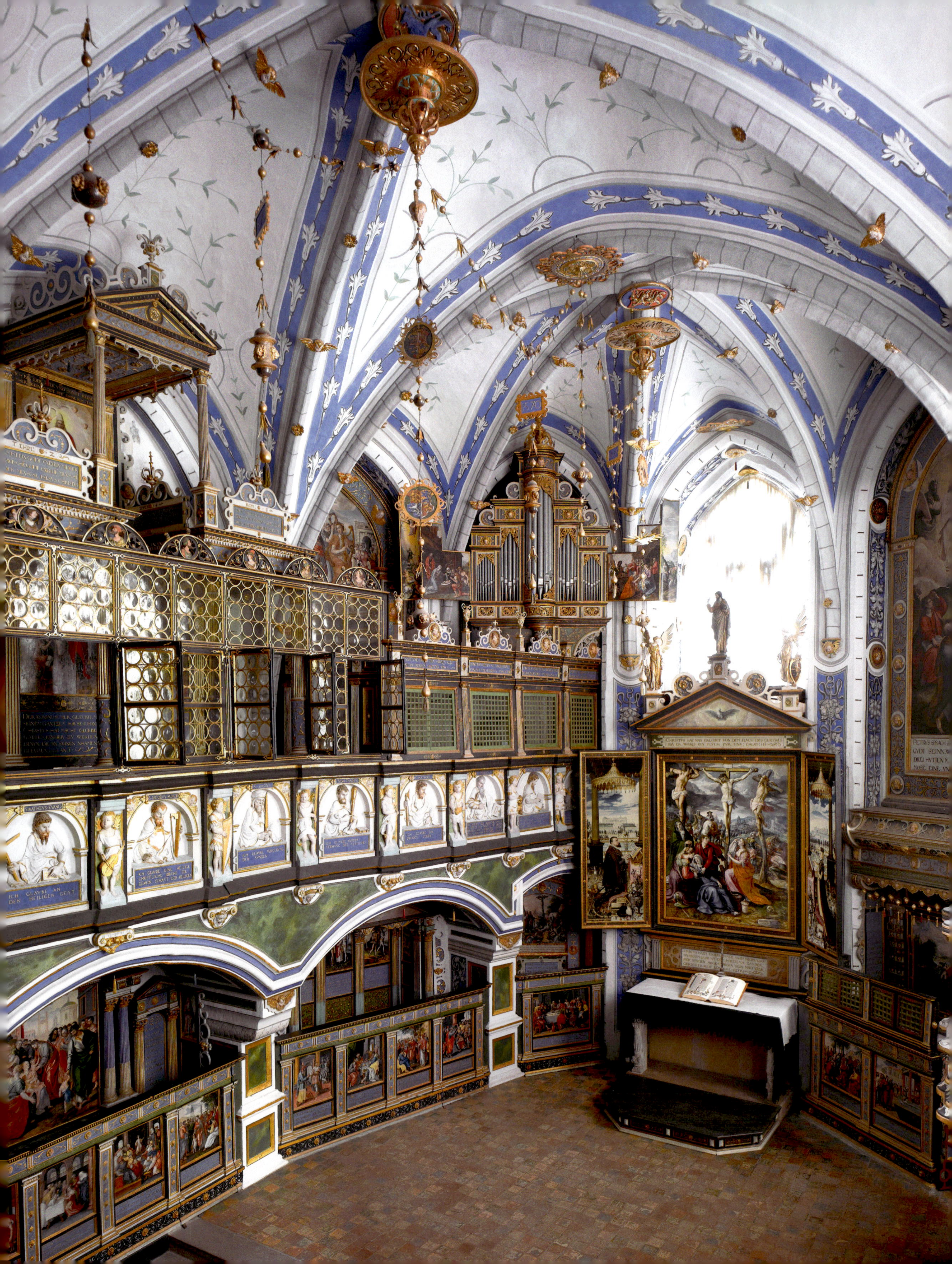

an collection. Also from the 1670s, the castle theatre is one of Europe's oldest Baroque court theatres. The former state rooms of Queen Caroline Mathilde, exiled to Celle in the 18th century, illustrate the era of personal union of the Hanoverian and British crowns (1714–1837).

As well as a variety of guided tours, the museum offers a unique attraction conceived especially for children. Colourful furnishings designed with loving attention to detail enable them to discover and experience with all their senses the life and culture of a Baroque residence. The innovative concept brought the museum a special award in 2009.

The richly appointed Court Chapel is an artistic synthesis of the Reformation period.

The Prince's bedroom

43

Cochem Imperial Castle
A fairytale castle on the Moselle – a dream come true

Perched on a mighty outcrop of rock high above the town of Cochem on the River Moselle, the imperial Castle, with its many turrets, oriels and battlements, presents a delightful view. It is the river's biggest hilltop castle.

Built around 1000 CE by Count Palatine Ezzo, son of Hermann Pusillius, Cochem Castle is first named in title deeds in 1051, when Richeza – eldest daughter of Count Ezzo and former queen of Poland – transferred its ownership to her nephew, Count Palatine Heinrich I. Cochem remained associated with the County Palatine even after later disputes in which the House of Ezzo lost its hereditary claim to that title.

This finally occurred in 1151, when King Konrad III occupied the castle with a garrison of knights and repossessed it as a terminated fiefdom. Cochem, therefore, already became an imperial castle in the Hohenstaufen era. When, in the course of the War of the Palatine Succession (Nine Years' War), the French troops of Louis XIV (the "Sun King") overran the Rhineland and Moselle, the castle was occupied, set on fire and, on May 19, 1689, blown up with a charge set deep beneath it in the hill. In the same year almost the entire town of Cochem was razed by the French.

For nearly 200 years afterwards Cochem Castle stood in ruins. Then, in 1868, the Berlin merchant (and later commercial privy counsellor) Louis

View of the Moselle Valley from the castle balcony

Cochem Imperial Castle

Dining Hall

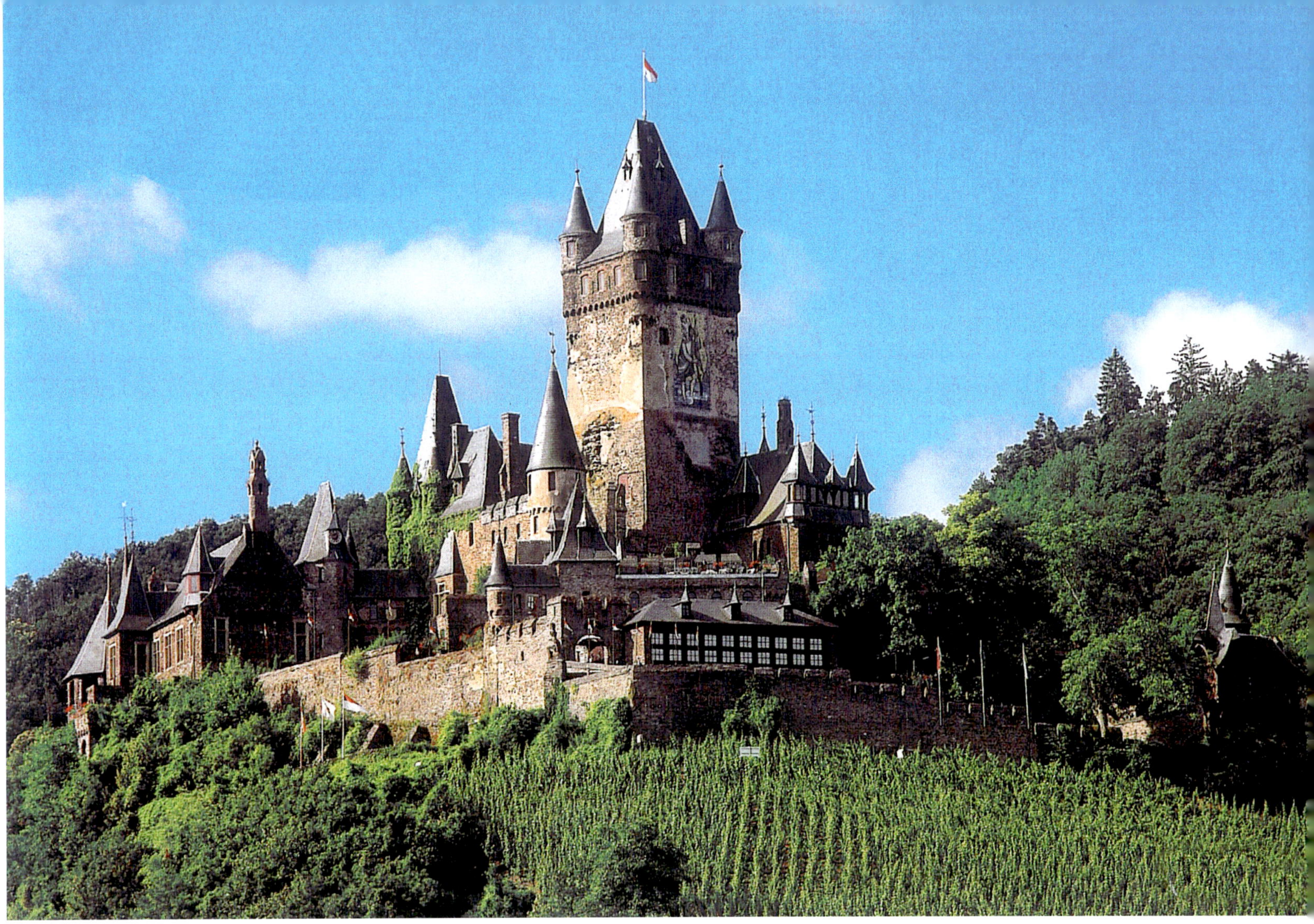

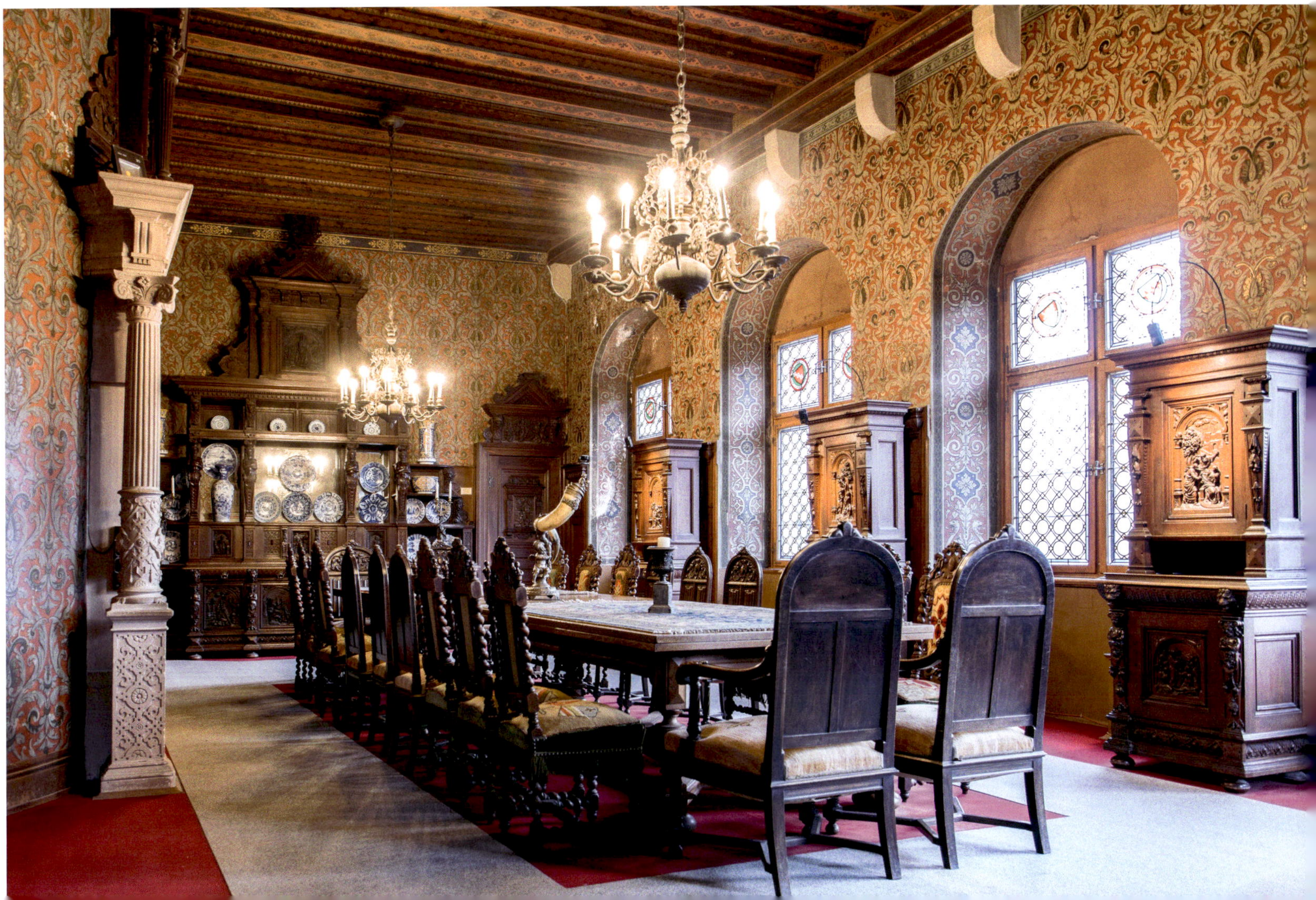

Ravené bought it for 300 gold marks. He had it completely rebuilt in the neo-Gothic style beloved of 19th century Romanticism, incorporating whatever remained of the Late Gothic buildings. The Ravenés used the castle as their summer residence.

In 1943 the castle was sold to the German Reich. Since 1978 it has belonged to the town of Cochem. As a popular destination for outings and excursions, it offers guided tours in several languages from mid-March until early November, including special tours for younger visitors – for example in costume or through the punishment cell with its absorbing instruments. The venerable castle chapel provides a stylish setting for civil weddings, and at weekends the Knights' Dinner offers a memorable experience in its ancient vaulted cellars under the heading "An Allsorts of Pranking and Disportment".

Rose courtyard with clock tower

Fireplace in Knights' Hall

A niche in the Bower

Dennenlohe Castle – House and Park

An English garden paradise in the centre of Franconia

Nestled between woods and meadows on the western edge of the Franconian lakeland, around 10 kilometres (c. 6 miles) distant from the small town of Gunzenhausen, lies one of Southern Germany's finest Baroque ensembles, Dennenlohe Castle. The estate covers 26 hectares (c. 64 acre) of landscape park and gardens, which are constantly extended and improved by the owners. Recognised as a botanical garden, these include a masterfully integrated private lake, as well as the biggest collection of rhododendrons in the South of Germany. Above all for its gardens, Dennenlohe Castle demands attention.

First mentioned in records dating as far back as 1167, the estate itself is 900 years old. However, its history properly begins in 1711, with the purchase of the noble lands by Paul Martin Eichler von Auritz and his brothers. They were responsible for the construction (between 1734 and 1750) of the house as and outbuildings. In 1773 Baron Fries bought the property together with "24 orange trees in oak tubs ... with many fruits ... 30 rosemary bushes ... 70 pots of carnations ... 5 Indian fig trees ... 4 dwarf fig trees ... 2 pomegranate trees in pots ... etc." The park was already a garden paradise at that time, a circumstance from which the most famous of all German garden designers, Prince Hermann von Pückler-Muskau, profited. His wife, Lucie von Hardenberg, had previously been married to Dennenlohe's former owner, Karl Theodor von Pappenheim. As well as a substantial dowry for the enhancement of Pückler's gardens in Muskau, she brought many ideas from the Franconian park with her to her new home in Upper Lusatia. In the mid-19th century Dennenlohe Castle was acquired by the Süsskind family, one of whose descendants, Baron Robert Andreas Gottlieb von Süsskind, starting in 1978, has given the gardens and rhododendron park their present form. Since 1990 Baron von Süsskind has spent almost every day tending to his garden, planting 99 percent of its plants and collecting and laying every stone with his own hands.

The castle park has three distinct areas: the rhododendron park (open daily), whose diversity of plants has qualified it for official recognition as a "botanical garden"; the constantly expanding landscape park – a traditional patchwork of cultivated and wild growth; and lastly, the family's private

Dennenlohe Castle is a rectangular baroque ensemble.

47

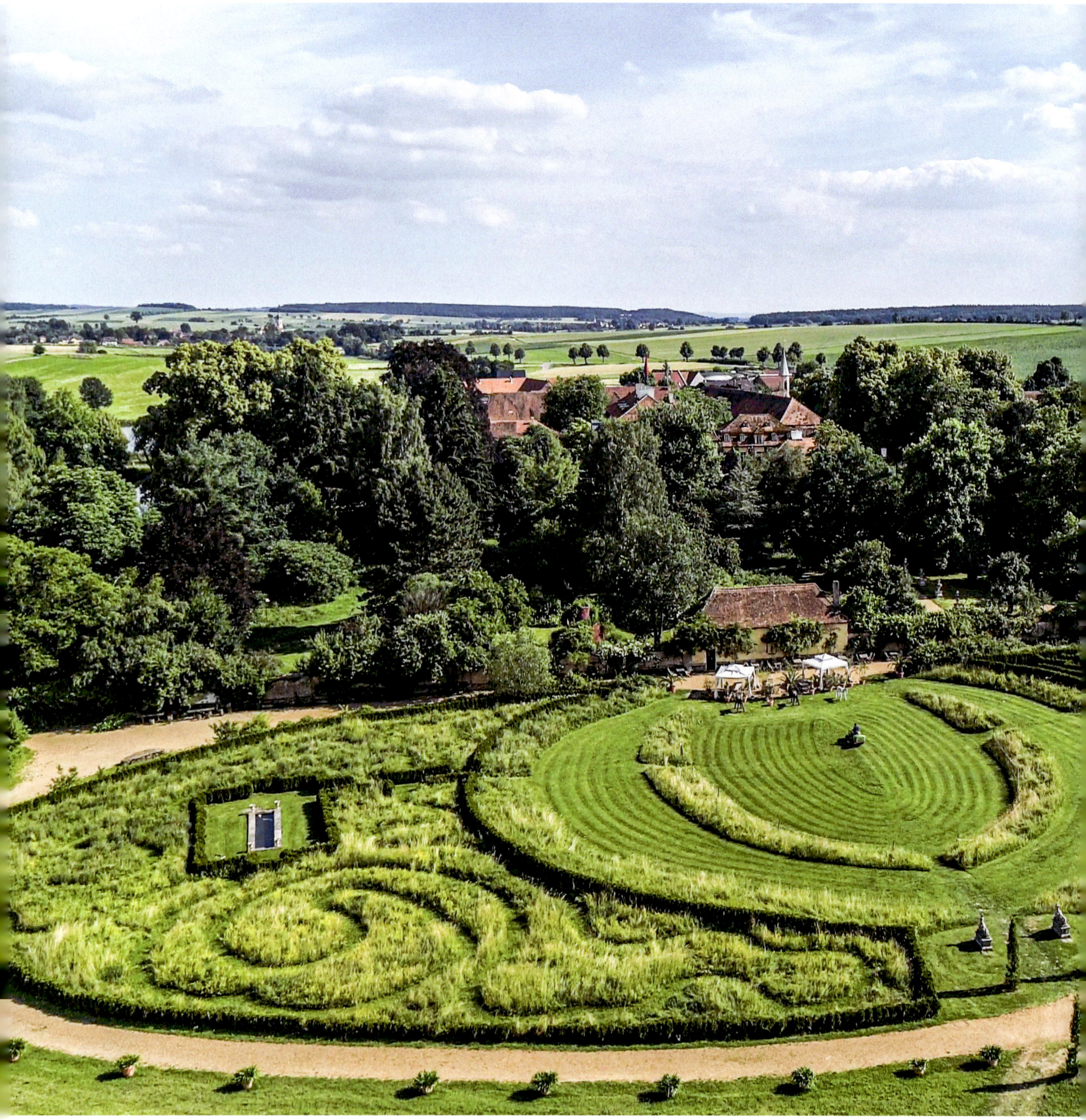

garden, which is only open to the public on special days.

A further unique feature of Dennenlohe is Germany's first international garden library, which, starting in 2013, contains all the books submitted and selected for the German and European garden book awards – events initiated and planned by Robert and Sabine von Süsskind.

Finally, a visit to the classic car museum in the manor house, the restaurant in the former stables, the café in the orangery, the flower and souvenir shop in the old pigsties, the art gallery in the historic riding hall, or the European garden photo award exhibition in the former alcohol distillery completes the Dennenlohe experience.

Labyrinth and maze encircling the Sphinx Garden in front of the Orangery Café

The Moon Gate in the park frames the entrance to another world ...

49

Detmold Castle
Seat of the counts and princes zur Lippe

Detmold Castle forms the historical heart of the old city of Detmold. Still the home of the princely family, the castle was built in the style of the so-called Weser Renaissance. With its "English Garden" and museum, it draws visitors from far beyond the borders of the East-Westphalian region of Lippe.

Detmold Castle – exterior view

Inner courtyard

Between 1230 and 1265 Bernhard III zur Lippe built a fortress on the site of the present castle. This 13th century building was sacked in 1447 in the Feud of Soest but, remarkably, its keep has come down intact and still forms the south-eastern corner of the castle façade. After 1472, under Bernhard VII zur Lippe, the fortress was rebuilt and its defences greatly strengthened with ramparts, moats, and bastions furnished with cannons. The family has resided there since that time. Between 1535 and 1551 Count Bernhard VIII zur Lippe had the buildings converted into a Renaissance castle by the Swabian master-builder Jörg Unkair and his successor Cord Tönnis. Under Count Friedrich Adolf zur Lippe (1667–1718) the exterior of the castle was restyled and the interior rooms magnificently refurbished in the Baroque fashion. Finally in 1789, to celebrate the elevation of the House of Lippe to princely rank, the gardens were landscaped in the English manner and terminated with the Marstall (formal stable block).

Since the early 20th century, twelve rooms in the castle have served as a museum, open every day to visitors, who can in this authentic environment learn something of the family's eventful history. Among the treasures in the Red Salon are Baroque works by the Hamburg-born court painter Hans Hinrich Rundt (1660–1759). Especially famous are eight monumental tapestries from the Brussels manufactory of Jan Frans van den Hecke. Woven in the 1670s, they are based on scenes from the life of Alexander the Great by the French court painter Charles Le Brun.

The neo-Renaissance Ancestral Hall, completed in 1882 by the Munich architect Lorenz Gedon, contains the family portrait gallery. Among the paintings is a portrait of Princess Pauline (1769–1820), who for 18 years acted as regent over the State of Lippe. By joining the Confederation of the Rhine, she suc-

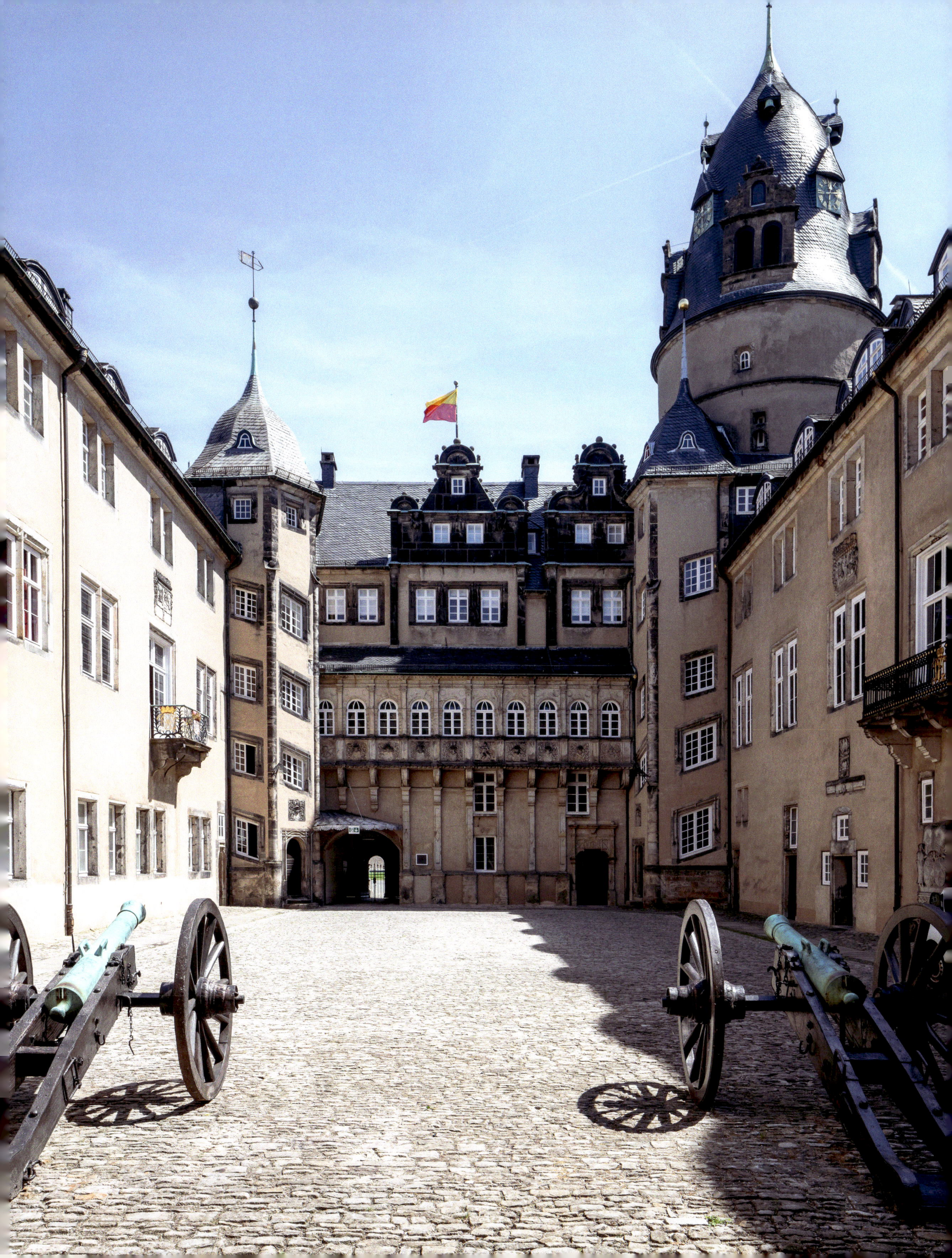

ceeded in keeping Lippe as an autonomous state under Napoleon – an independence that continued, despite the abdication of Leopold IV, the last ruling prince, in November 1918, right through to 1947. The castle remained through all these events in the possession of the family, who still live there today, and who continue to play an active role in the social, cultural and political life of the region.

Red Salon

Ancestral Hall

Dornburg Castles – a Triad of Stately Homes

Gardens with views

A few kilometres north of Jena the limestone scarp of the Saale Valley is crowned with vineyards. Here, perched on the valley crest, stand three historical houses and gardens that together became the summer residence of the Grand Duke of Saxe-Weimar. Defining the landscape, the "Dornburg castles" are known familiarly as the "balcony of Thuringia".

The picturesque ensemble began with a medieval fortress on the site of the present-day Old Castle. Rebuilt in the 16th century, this was the first step in the development that turned Dornburg into a secondary residence of the Ernestine branch of the House of Wettin. The 18th century Rococo *maison de plaisance* formed a playful counterpart to the Old Castle, and the triple estate was completed in the early 19th century with the purchase of the Renaissance schloss at the southern end of the scarp. From 1870 onwards the ensemble was woven into a unity by Grand Duke Carl Alexander, under whose aegis Dornburg became an embodiment of dynastic memory.

The Old Castle at the north-eastern end of the rocky plateau retains its Romanesque keep, Great Hall and other remnants of a medieval stronghold. Destroyed in 1451 in the Saxon Fratricidal War, it was rebuilt from 1560 to 1574 as a residential schloss; from this era date the imposing beamed ceilings and fragments of wall painting preserved in the small Emperor's Hall. The colourful Rococo schloss next door was built between 1736 and 1741 to plans by the leading Baroque architect Gottfried Heinrich Krohne as the country hideaway of Duke Ernst August I of Saxe-Weimar. It reflects three distinct stylistic phases. The *bel étage*, with the marbled stucco of the formal reception room and virtuoso ceilings, dates from the origins of the house under Ernst August; the colourful adjoining apartments and their furniture are from the Neoclassical era of Carl August; and on the ground floor the impact of the 19th century is evident, for example, in the dining room, which was fitted out

Dornburg Castles overlooking the Valley of the Saale

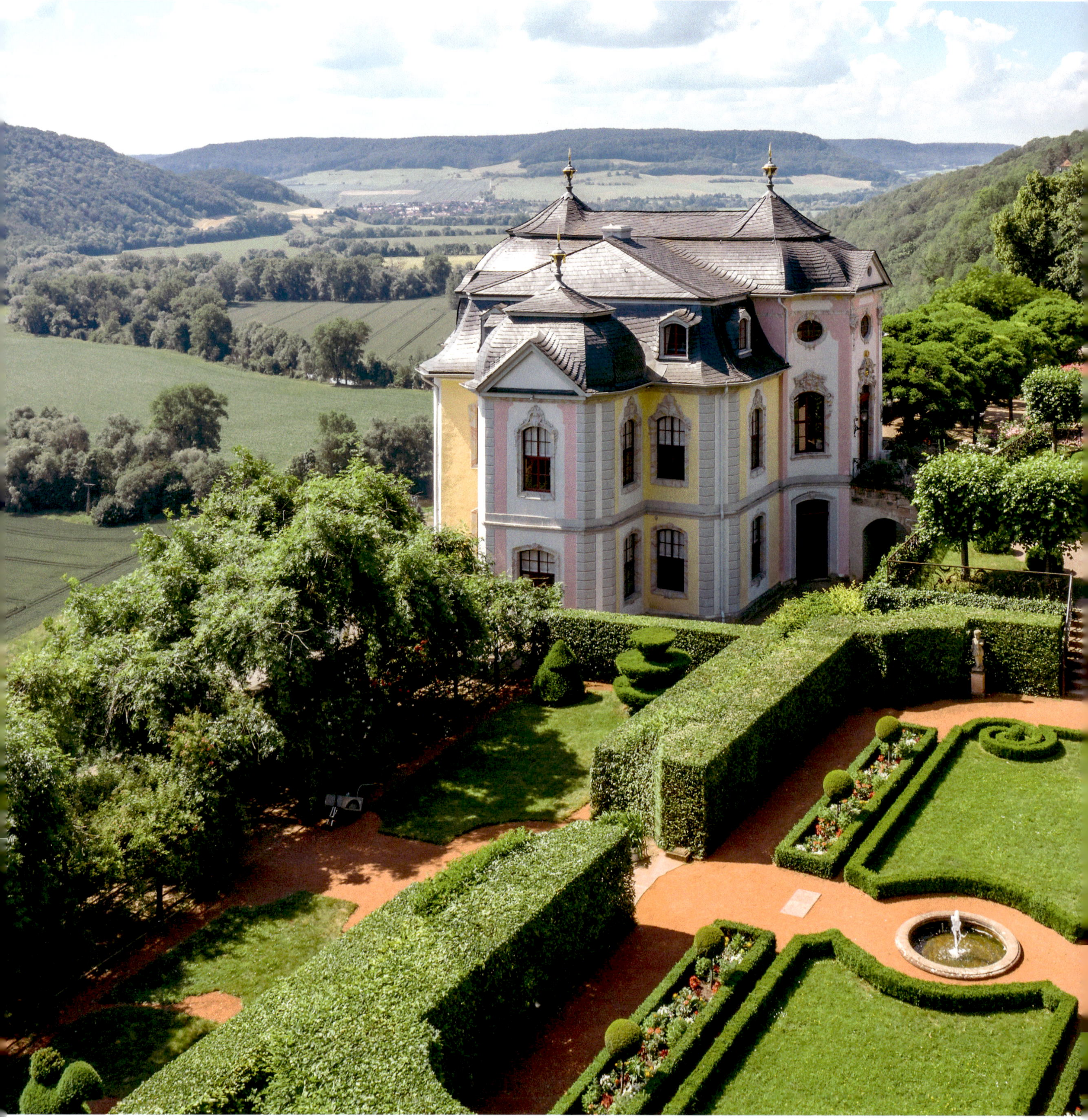

in 1875 by Carl Alexander with Neo-Baroque furniture and valuable porcelain.

The Renaissance mansion, built c. 1540 at the south-west end of the plateau as the centre of a former knightly estate, received its present form in the early 17th century. In 1826–27 Grand Duke Carl August made it – with appropriate changes – his residence. Three rooms on the upper floor hold memories of Goethe, who stayed here for several weeks in 1828, drawing inspiration for his poetry and taking a keen interest in wine growing. Much admired by Goethe, and regularly visited by Grand Duke Carl Alexander when the roses were in bloom, the Dornburg gardens are striking not only for their unusual position on the crest of the escarpment – and hence their terraced paths – but also for their wealth of different forms. Each complete in themselves, the geometrically patterned gardens of the Rococo schloss, the adjoining landscaped garden to the south-west, the vineyards overlooking the valley, and the grassed orchard garden at the Old Castle are at the same time intimately linked.

Rococo schloss with terraced garden

Formal reception room in the Rococo schloss

Dresden Zwinger
Home of world-famous artworks

At the heart of Saxony's state capital, the Dresden Zwinger is one of Germany's best-known Baroque ensembles, and along with the Frauenkirche the city's most famous architectural monument. Its museums are renowned the world over, and it provides a splendid stage for both musical and theatrical performances.

Commissioned by Elector Augustus the Strong as a venue for court festivities, the Dresden Zwinger was created at the beginning of the 18th century by the Baroque architect Mattheus Daniel Poeppelmann and the sculptor Balthasar Permoser. Poeppelmann's famous copperplate engraving of his plans has been preserved down to the present day.

The Wall and Glockenspiel Pavilions at the mid-point of the two curved galleries, the four corner pavilions, and the Long Gallery with the Crown Gate at its centre form three sides of a rectangular courtyard resplendent with lawns and fountains. Completing the symmetrical arrangement, the northern side of the courtyard is bounded by the Semper Wing. The Dresden Zwinger takes its name from its situation on the outer bailey (German *Zwinger*) of the ancient city fortifications – the space between inner and outer walls designed to enclose and overpower an encroaching enemy.

In 1709 Augustus the Strong commissioned Poeppelmann, his master builder, to construct a winter conservatory in the garden of the Dresden Zwinger for his collection of several hundred Italian orange trees and tub plants. The result was one of Germany's finest orangeries, which in due course became the setting for the Elector's festivities. As such, its purpose was by no means only court entertainment – it

A group of putti on the balustrade of the Nymphs' Bath in the Dresden Zwinger

Glockenspiel Pavilion. Made of genuine Meissen porcelain, the porcelain glockenspiel plays well-known melodies.

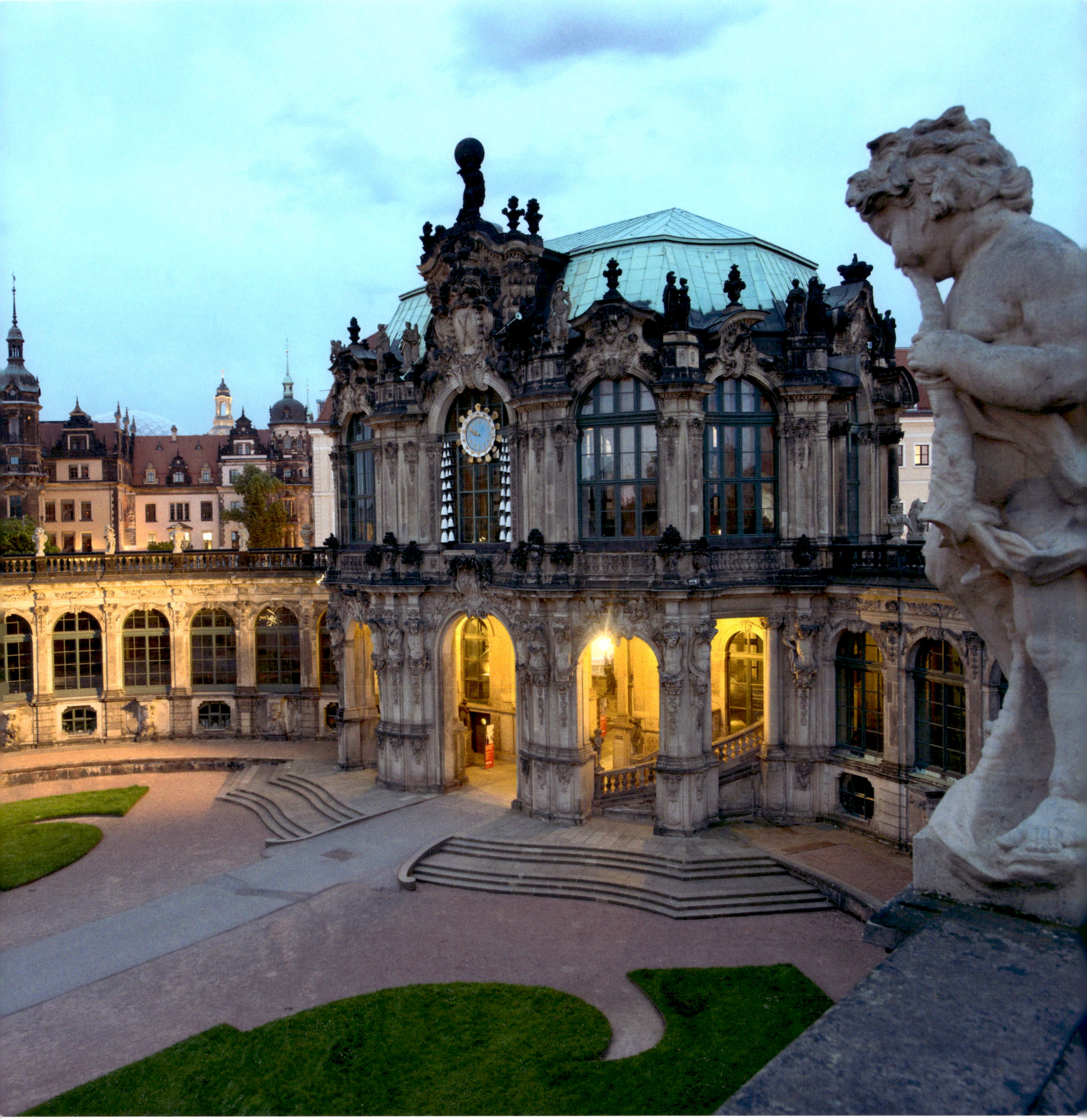

was also called upon to incorporate the Prince's power and display his wealth. Today some 80 trees once again give the Dresden Zwinger the Mediterranean flair that was so dear to Augustus the Strong.

In 1712 the Long Gallery was built and in 1714 the Crown Gate. The Dresden Zwinger was formally inaugurated in 1719 on the occasion of the marriage of Augustus' son, the young Prince-Elector Frederick Augustus II, with Maria Josepha of Austria, daughter of the Habsburg emperor. The buildings were finally completed for his father's magnificent collections in 1728. The Allied bombing of Dresden in February 1945 almost entirely destroyed the Zwinger. Reconstruction already started in 1945, and parts of the complex were reopened in 1960.

Today the impressive sandstone building contains world-famous collections, as well as individual artistic masterpieces. Pre-eminent in the Old Masters Picture Gallery is Raphael's *Sistine Madonna*, while the vast range of Chinese, Japanese and Meissen porcelain derives immediately from Augustus the Strong's passion as a collector. The oldest museum in the Dresden Zwinger, however, is the Royal Cabinet of Mathematical and Physical Instruments, which today harbours one of the world's most important historical collections of scientific instruments.

Crown Gate with view of the symmetrical interior courtyard containing the French Pavilion and Marble Hall (l.) and German Pavilion (r.)

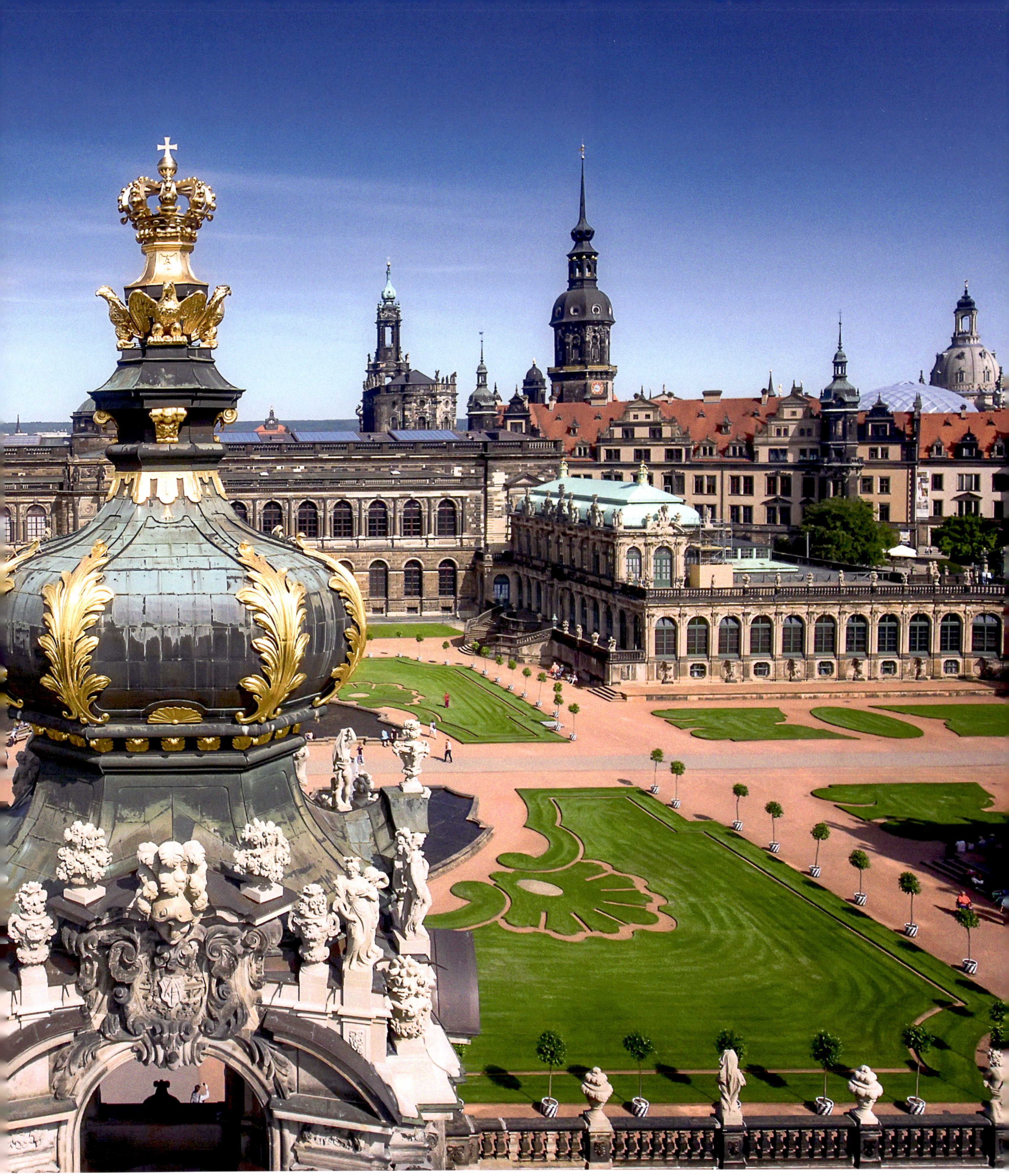

Dyck Castle
Architectural, garden and landscape culture through the centuries

Surrounded by water and set in a magnificent historical park, Dyck Castle is an important cultural and natural monument of the Rhineland. For more than 900 years, the estate was owned by the zu Salm-Reifferscheidt-Dyck family. A foundation was established in 1999 to manage Dyck as a centre for garden design and landscape culture, presenting its visitors with the carefully restored castle and chapel, orangery peninsula, outbuildings and estate yards, as well as with the historic park surrounding the castle. Here the contemporary park and gardens of the old nursery form a balanced contrast with the Dycker Feld.

Already in 1094, a simple fortified complex provided the centre of what is still recognizable as the cultural landscape known locally as the "Dycker Ländchen". Severely damaged in the Thirty Years' War, the original complex was replaced by the Early Baroque castle and further extended in the late 18th century into a stately Rococo residence. The ensemble of rooms accessible to the public features finely papered walls, ceiling paintings and stucco work, as well as exhibits illustrating the history of the castle and its family. These are complemented by displays (both permanent and temporary) of rare books in the castle library. Photo enthusiasts will delight in "Gartenfokus" – an annually changing exhibition of contemporary large-format garden photography.

Landscaped in the English manner, the picturesque c. 53 hectare (c. 130 acre) park was painstakingly restored at the beginning of the present century to its original state. Here, shady avenues and twisting woodland tracks lead past stretches of water to broad meadows and gently rising hills with stands of trees or solitary majestic specimens, some dating from the 18th century. The park was laid down between 1820 and 1835 in the spirit of the Enlightenment by the passionate botanist and plant collector Prince Joseph zu Salm-Reifferscheidt-Dyck, who commissioned the Scottish garden architect Thomas Blaikie to enact his plans. Among the colourful seasonal highlights of the gardens is one of Germany's biggest collections of hydrangeas, with 350 species drawn from across the globe.

A contrast to the historical park is formed by the thematically ordered model gardens in the horticultural section in the old nursery at the park entrance. Here, show gardens designed

Baroque bridge

Dyck Castle viewed from the park

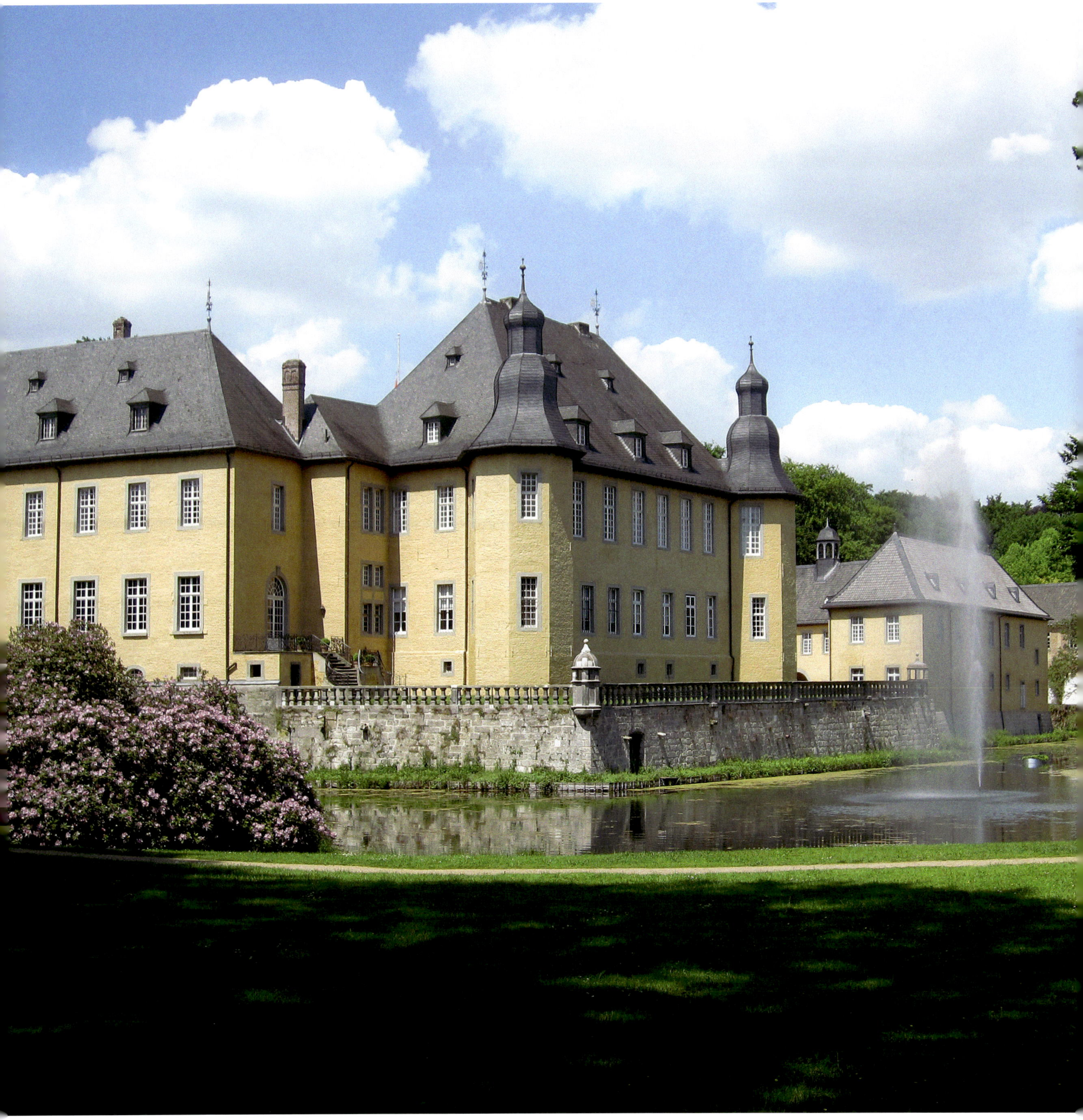

by landscape and garden architects provide tips and ideas for visitors' domestic plots. Complementing these along a 200 year-old avenue of edible chestnut between the castle and the Convent of St. Nicholas, the 24 hectare (60 acre) Dycker Feld presents large-scale landscape architecture in a striking display of close-cropped lanes and avenues cut through a sea of Chinese silvergrass.

East wing viewed from
the Tea House garden

Orangery terrace with the Prince
Joseph botanical collection

View along the main axis of the landscaped
"English Garden" towards the lime-tree roundel

62

Eberbach Monastery

From medieval economic powerhouse to modern secular institution

If, as the Romantic author Heinrich von Kleist once reflected, the Rheingau was created from a poet's dream, then how much more must this be true of its most famous landmark, the former Cistercian monastery of Eberbach, near Eltville on the Rhine. Situated at the mouth of the Kisselbach Valley and protected by the encircling Taunus hills and vineyard slopes, the walled monastery is one of Europe's oldest church buildings, renowned for its unique architectonic ensemble of Romanesque, Gothic and Baroque elements.

According to legend, Abbot Bernard of Clairvaux sought out this spot for the foundation of a new monastic house in 1135, when he visited the idyllic valley with Archbishop Adalbert I of Mainz. On that occasion a wild boar is said to have appeared; the animal sprang three times across the Kisselbach stream and then drew an outline of the future monastery in the earth with its tusks. Bernard interpreted this as a divine sign and in 1136 sent twelve of his monks under Abbot Ruthard of Clairvaux to Eberbach.

With its extensive lands and the flourishing vineyards and wine-making business developed by the monks, Eberbach Monastery became one of the order's largest and most important houses. In 1803 the monastery was dissolved in the course of Napoleonic secularization. Thanks, however, to careful reutilization, the complex has – despite some structural changes – remained largely intact to the present day. It has become a popular destination for tourists and one of Europe's prime venues for events, including the outstanding concerts of the Rheingau Music Festival, which attract thousands of visitors every year. As a rare example of an almost perfectly preserved medieval monastery, Eberbach was chosen as the location for the masterly film version of Umberto Eco's best-seller *The Name of the Rose*.

Another aspect of the Cistercian heritage still preserved today is the

Prelate's garden with abbot's garden house

tradition of wine-making and the cultivation of vineyards. Over the good 100 kilometres between the Hessische Bergstrasse wine region and Assmannshausen on the Rhine, the monastery owns more than 250 hectares (c. 625 acres) of extremely valuable and widely varying vineyards – the basis for its subtly faceted wines. The different situations of the vines and the meticulous care with which the grapes are treated in the Steinberg and Assmannshausen cellars make for wines – both still and sparkling – of great individual character. The annual vintage of the former Cistercian monastery amounts to 2.5 million bottles, making Eberbach the biggest winery in Germany.

Listed as a unique cultural monument, the estate complex is managed and maintained on energy-efficient principles by the Eberbach Monastery Foundation, a non-profit organization established in 1998. The foundation also promotes cultural projects and opens the buildings and grounds to visitors from across the globe.

Choir and transept of the basilica viewed from the orangery

North aisle of the Romanesque basilica

North and west cloisters

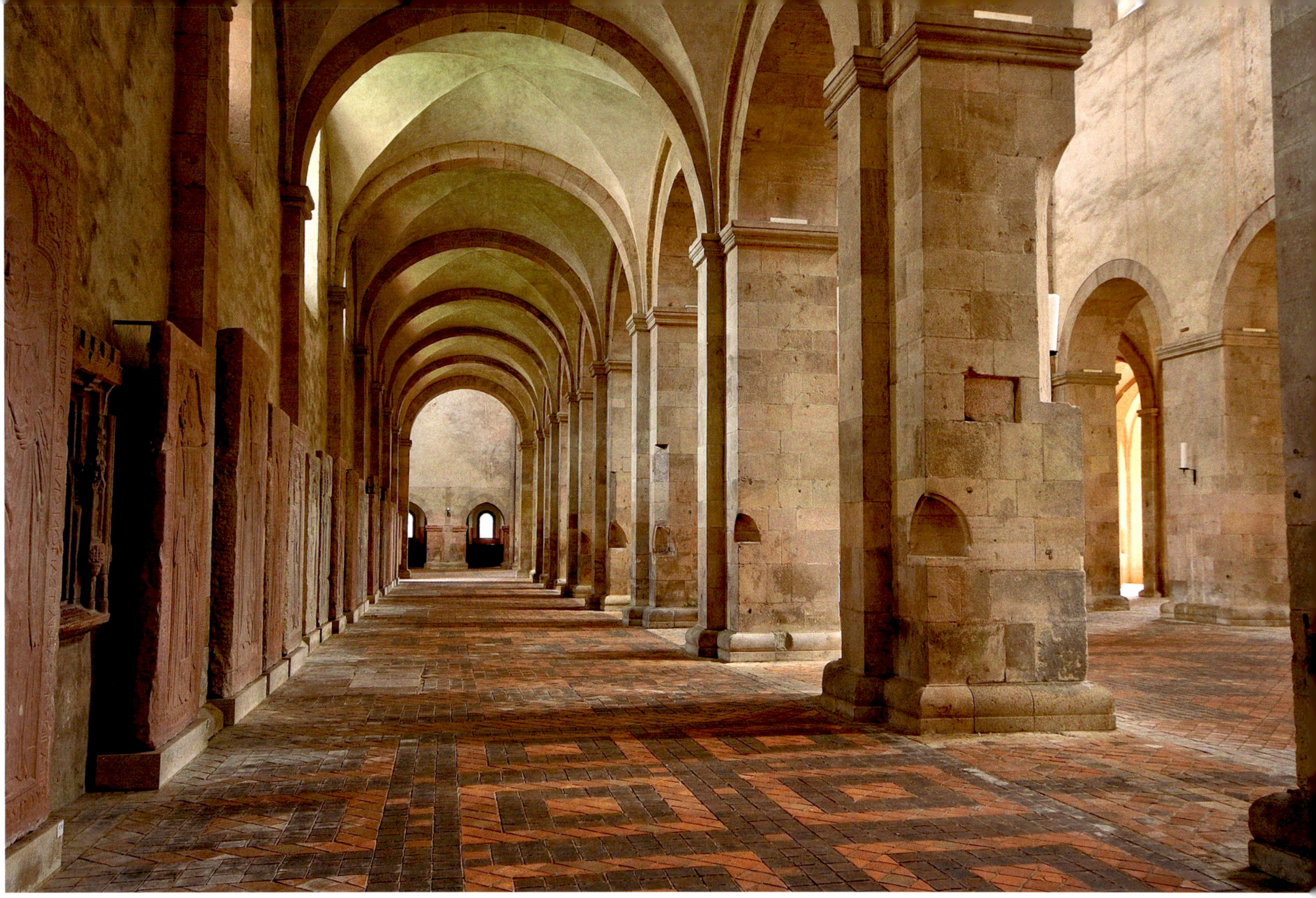

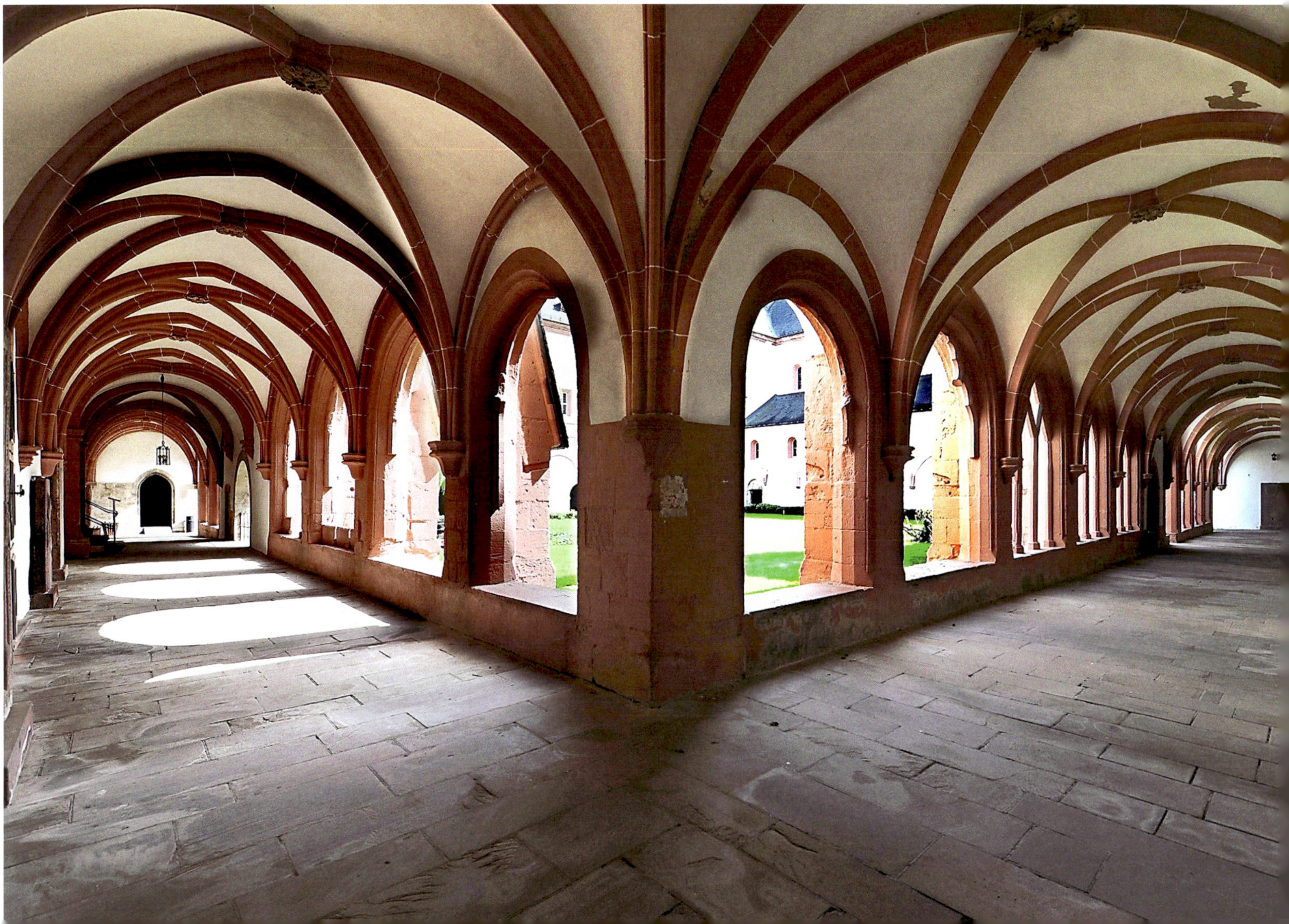

Ehrenbreitstein Fortress

From military stronghold to cultural forefront

Visible from afar, Ehrenbreitstein Fortress dominates the confluence of the Rhine and Moselle. Standing 118 metres above the Rhine and only approachable from one side, it was constructed by Prussian military architects between 1817 and 1828 to replace the earlier Baroque fort of the Electorate of Trier destroyed in 1804. Ehrenbreitstein was the most modern military stronghold of its day, the mainstay of the defensive ring around Koblenz and the Deutsches Eck. As such it combines the complex functionality of "neo-Prussian defensive architecture" with Neoclassical aesthetic elements.

From a bird's eye view the dimensions and complexity of the fortress are evident. It covers the entire headland, which on three sides is bounded by sheer cliffs. Hence the main ramparts are on the more vulnerable north side, where they form a tiered zigzag of bulwarks, trenches and concealed artillery emplacements more than 300 metres across. It was reckoned that 1500 men and 80 cannons could hold the position for half a year.

The Prussians were not the first to exploit the topographical advantages of this headland. Traces of small defensive settlement go back to the Bronze Age: Celts, Romans and medieval warlords left their mark on the land, and from the 12th century onwards the Archbishop-Elector of Trier continually expanded the fortifications. By the early 16th century these formed a regular citadel. As the safest place in the archbishopric, Ehrenbreitstein was chosen to house the Holy Tunic, Trier's most sacred relic, and at times the archbishop himself resided here.

Generations of artists and tourists from across the globe have been fascinated by the view of Ehrenbreitstein from the left bank of the Rhine. Combining functions of military efficiency and state representation, it soon acquired considerable aesthetic and historical value, and it was these qualities – given the fact that by the end of the First

Inner courtyard

View from the south-west

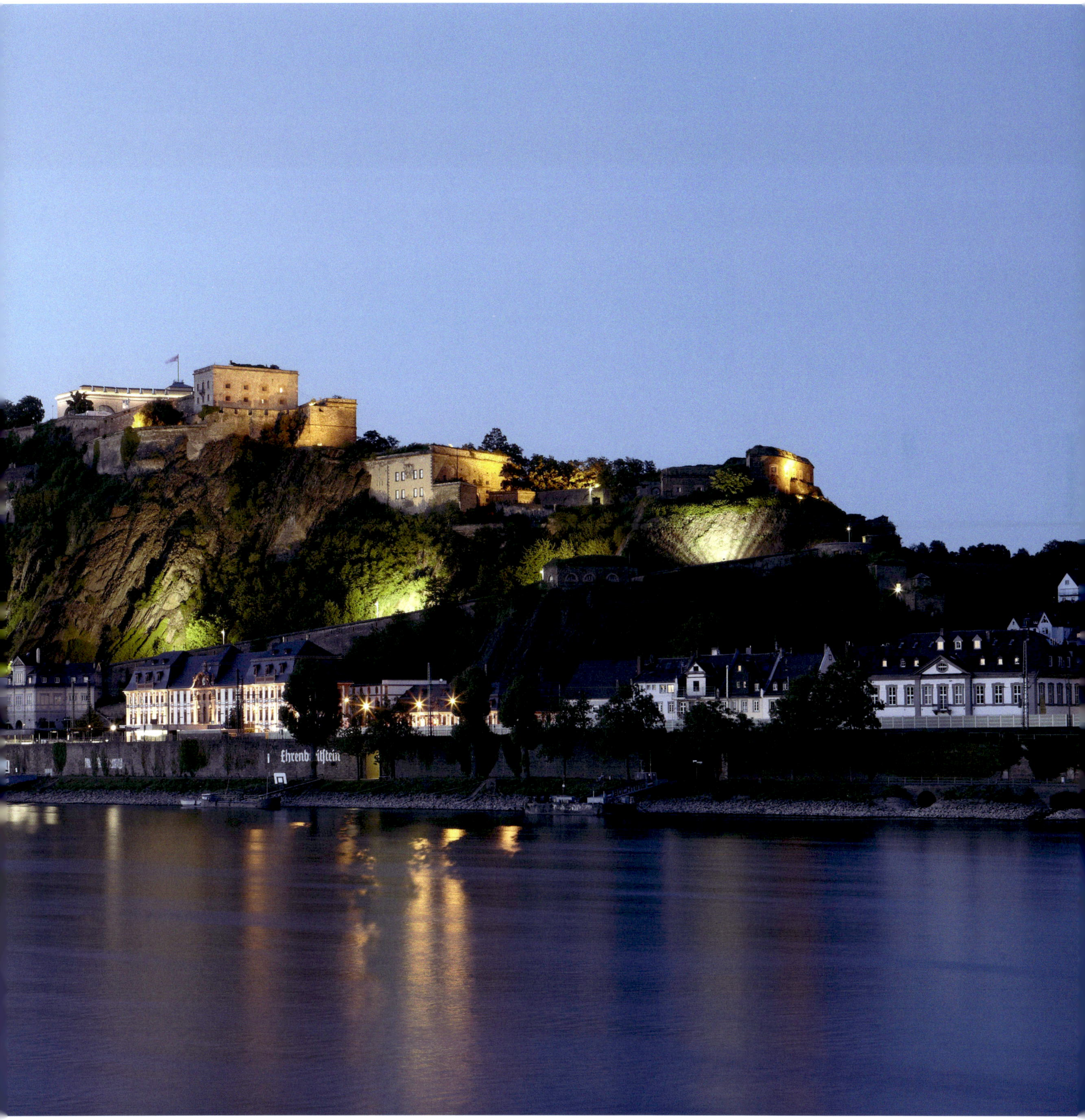

World War it was also a military relic – that saved it in 1922 from demolition as ordered by the Treaty of Versailles.

Today Ehrenbreitstein is a cultural stronghold – since 2002 an integral part of the UNESCO World Heritage Site of the Upper Middle Rhine Valley. As well as the Koblenz State Museum, Archaeological Office and Castles Administration, it also houses the Rhineland-Palatinate Historical Photographic Collection. Four buildings provide space for exhibitions both large and small. A comprehensive year-round programme of events with appropriate gastronomic highlights provides visitors with a range of entirely peaceful opportunities to take by storm a fortress whose impregnability was in Prussian days never put to the test.

Ehrenbreitstein Fortress with Koblenz and the Deutsches Eck in the background

Eltz Castle

Nine centuries of German family history

Inner courtyard, Kempenich House

Perched in the midst of untarnished nature on a rocky spur in a side arm of the Lower Moselle Valley, Eltz Castle has for more than 850 years been the seat of the Eltz family. Its medieval tradition, unique architecture and picturesque setting make it the very epitome of the German knightly castle.

With William Turner, Eltz Castle became the symbol of Romantic yearning; Victor Hugo described it as "tall, powerful and uncanny"; for Katherine Macquoid it was "a fairytale in stone"; and for the historian Georg Dehio simply "the castle as such". For more than 30 years its image decorated Germany's 500 mark note – a homage to the country's cultural heritage and knightly tradition.

An imperial deed of 1157 bears the seal of Rudolf von Eltz, the founder of the noble house of the Counts zu Eltz. In 1268 three lines of that dynasty established a *Ganerbschaft* (joint inheritance) which endured successfully for five and a half centuries. The combination of physical circumstances and family constellation, with three families sharing the property, explains the eight residential towers that define the unique architecture of Eltz Castle. Of these families, the Eltz-Rodendorf line died out in 1780 and the Eltz-Rübenachs gave up their inheritance in 1815. Since then the Counts of Eltz-Kempenich have been sole masters of Eltz Castle.

The castle took 500 years to build. It is based (literally) on Rudolf's original fortified dwelling of the 1150s. The upper tiers, and Kempenich and Rodendorf apartments, followed between 1200 and 1300. The six-storey high Rübenach house dates from 1311; between 1442 and 1444 it was raised a further two storeys. The High Gothic Rodendorf house was completed in 1520. Around 1660 the addition of the castle gate and timber-framing on the Kempenich house gave the premises their present-day appearance.

The fact that Eltz has always been lived in by the same family accounts for the existence there of apartments that still possess their complete original historical furnishings – for example the armoury, with the oldest recorded cannon bolt, Lower Rübenach Hall with the Cranach Madonna, the bed-chamber with its Burgundian decoration, Knights' Hall with its armour from the time of Emperor Maximilian I (early 16th century), the nursery with the oldest extant painted bed, the Banner Hall with its elaborate Gothic vault, and the Rodendorf kitchen with utensils dating back 500 years.

In 1980 the armoury and treasury were opened to the public. Among the items on display are an important collection of goldsmiths' work and ivory carving, as well as jousting and fighting weapons, rare porcelain and glass, and other articles belonging to the Electors and wider Eltz family.

Complementing its unique blend of fairytale buildings and magnificent natural setting, Burg Eltz offers forest trails for every taste and age – for example the incomparable Eltzer Burg Panorama Track, awarded the 2013 prize for Germany's most beautiful *Wanderweg*. And afterwards one can relax in one of the castle's two comfortable taverns.

P. 71: Gothic boudoir

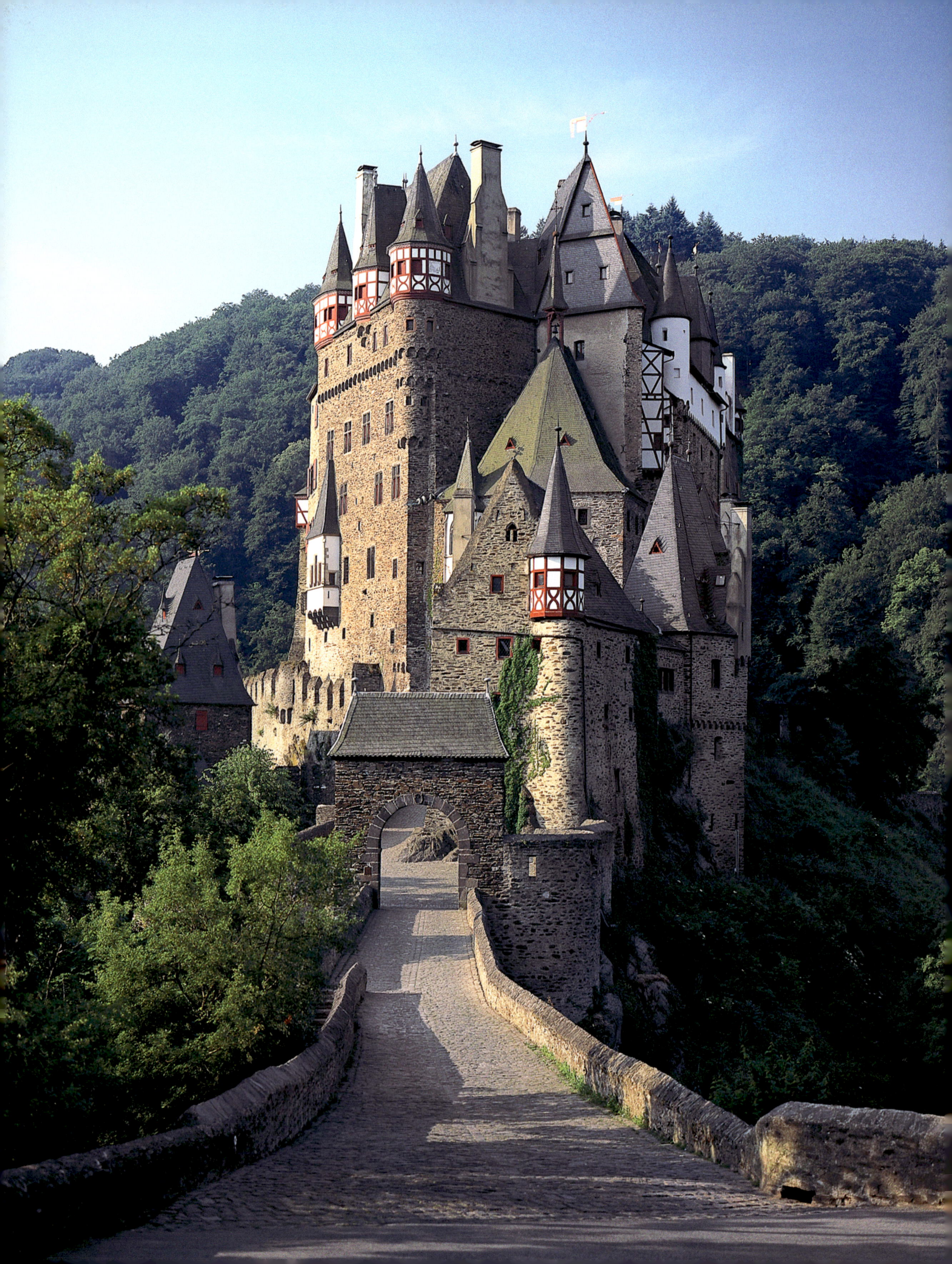

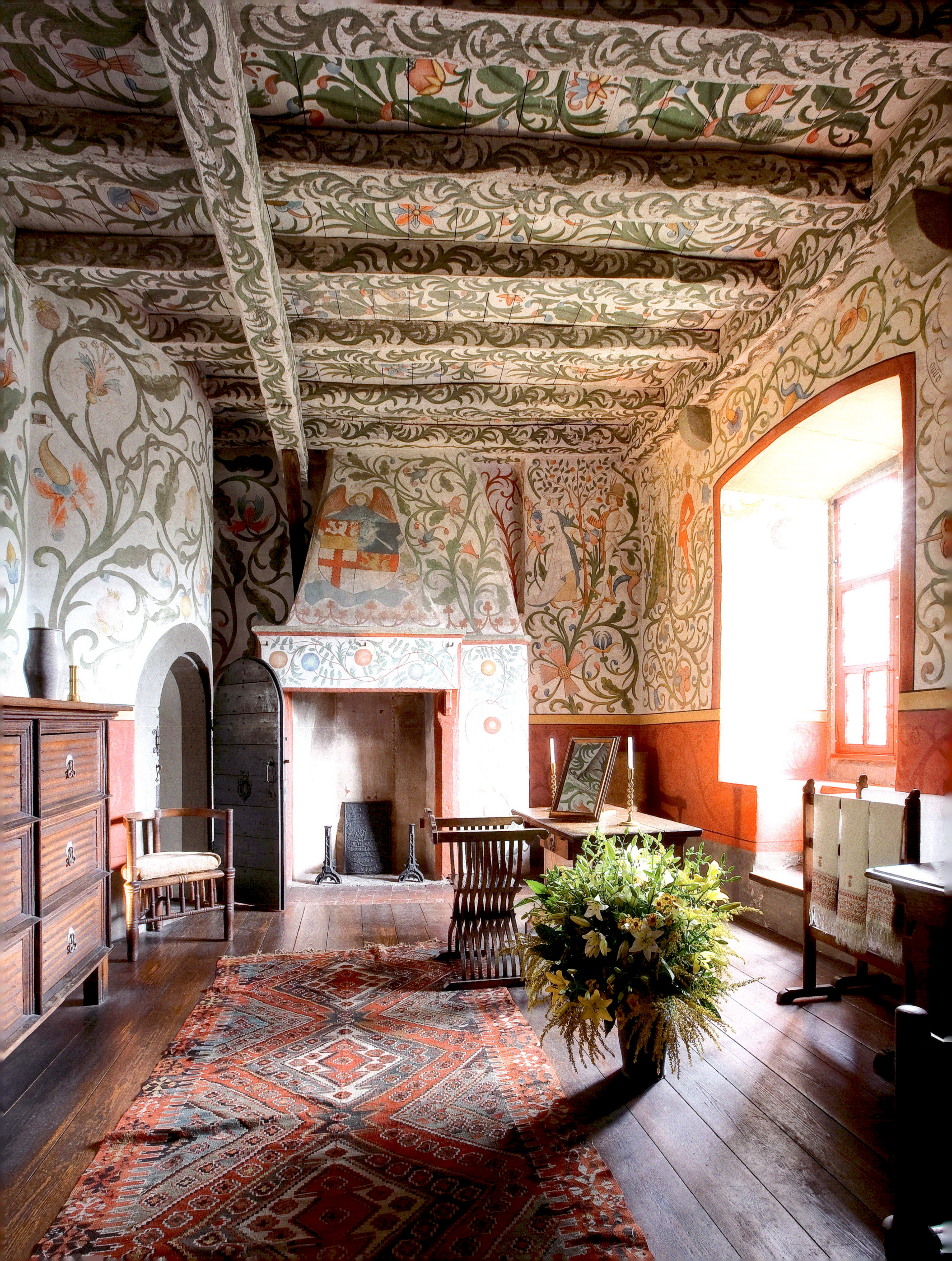

St. Emmeram's Palace, Regensburg

From Benedictine abbey to stately home of the Princes of Thurn and Taxis

The south wing of St. Emmeram's Palace, built between 1883 and 1888

For more than 350 years the princely house of Thurn and Taxis directed the postal services of Central and Western Europe. In 1748 Prince Alexander Ferdinand, on his appointment as First Commissioner – the emperor's personal representative at the Perpetual Diet of Regensburg – transferred the family seat from Frankfurt to the city on the Danube, where the ancient dynasty remained after the demise of the Holy Roman Empire and the cessation of their postal monopoly. Since 1812 the princes have resided in the secularized buildings of the former Benedictine Abbey of St. Emmeram.

Originally an imperial foundation, the abbey possesses one of the most impressive Romanesque-Gothic cloisters in Germany, its oldest parts dating from the 11th, its most recent from the 14th century. The Romanesque Chapter Hall, the magnificent group of windows in the Early Gothic north wing, and the splendid Benedict Portal from the first half of the 13th century still convey the solemn tranquillity of this unique monument. Between 1835 and 1843 Prince Maximilian Karl had a burial vault and chapel built in the cloister garden. Designed by the Prince's architectural counsellor, Victor Keim, it represents the earliest and most important princely mausoleum of German Historicism and still serves as the last resting place of members of the Thurn and Taxis family.

Conversion of the secularized abbey into a stately home began in 1816, with many of the Rococo fittings and furnishings of the family's former Frankfurt residence being put to new use in Regensburg. Between 1883 and 1888 the architect Max Schultze built the 165 metre long neo-Rococo south wing as the family's new living quarters. Visitors have access to the cloisters and to noble rooms in the south and east wings,

The ballroom (c. 1720), originally from the Thurn and Taxis' Frankfurt palace, was reinstalled in St. Emmeram in 1890.

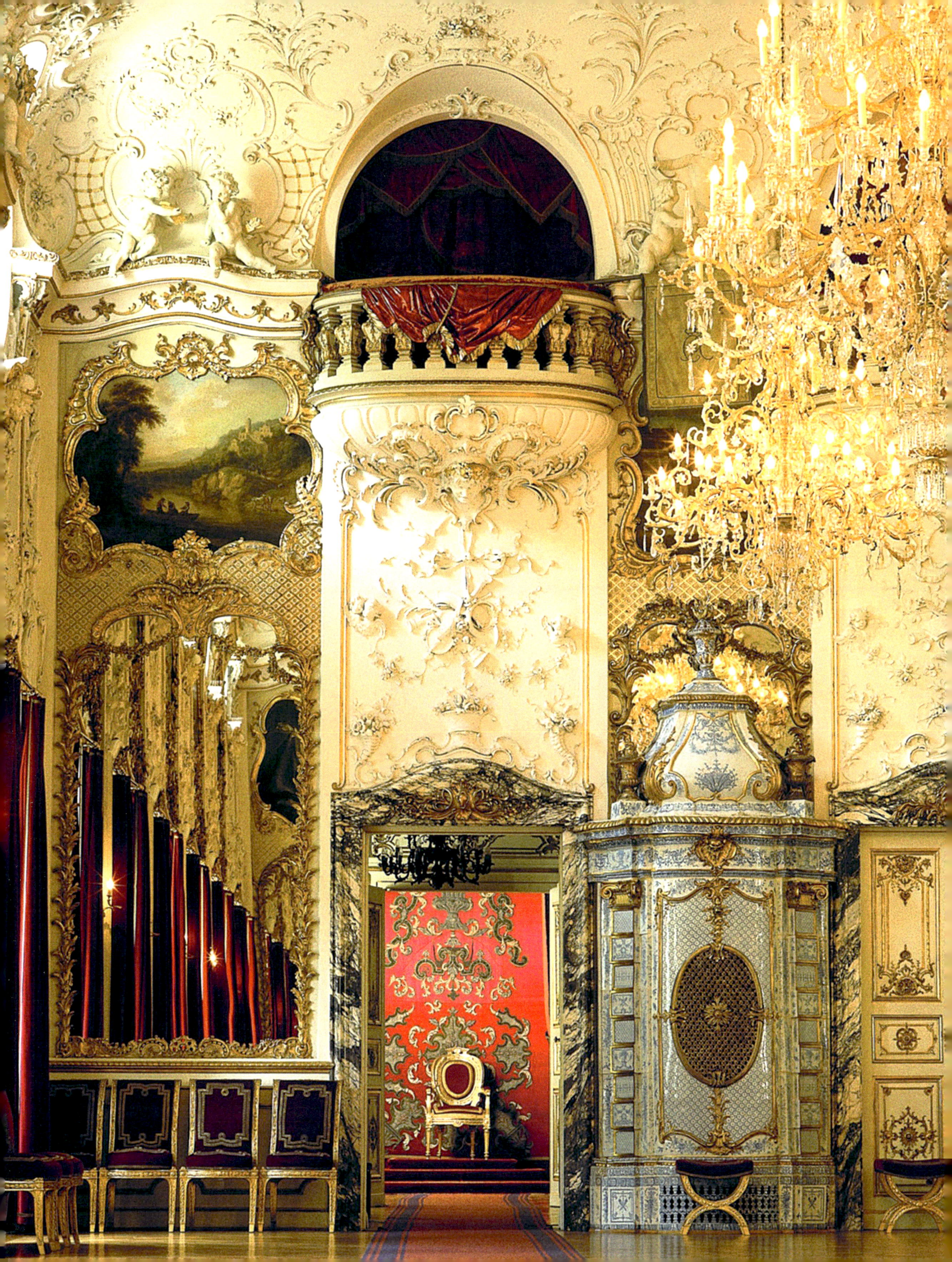

including the ballroom, throne room and various salons, the house chapel and winter garden (indoor conservatory), and the marble staircase.

Erected in 1829–1832 by master builder Jean-Baptiste Métivier, the princely stables contain not only the horse-box wings but also the 600 square metre riding hall with sculptures by Ludwig von Schwanthaler. With its extensive collection of coaches, sleighs, palanquins and open sedan chairs from the 18th and 19th centuries, the stable museum ranks with any in Europe.

Since 1998, the north stalls of the neo-Classical former stables have housed the princely treasury, now a branch of the Bavarian National Museum. Among the outstanding artworks from the family's collections exhibited here are valuable items of furniture, fine porcelain, precious snuff boxes, exclusive weapons, and selected gold and silver artefacts from leading European workshops. Schloss St. Emmeram's Palace takes the visitor on a journey into the brilliant world of one of Europe's leading noble dynasties.

The Silver Room, completed in 1873, is modelled on Schloss Nymphenburg's Amalienburg interiors.

The west wing of the cloisters, with the Benedict Portal, dates from the 13th century.

Schloss Fasanerie (The Pheasantry)

The most beautiful Baroque palace in the State of Hesse

Some seven kilometres south of Fulda, on a gentle rise surrounded by superb woodlands and fertile fields, stands Hesse's finest Baroque residence. The extensive ensemble conveys to the modern visitor a vital impression of an 18th century prince's country seat, complete with agricultural buildings, parkland and important collections from the era of courtly residential culture.

Around 1740, Amand von Buseck, Bishop-Elector of Fulda, had Schloss Fasanerie built just outside the gates of the city as a house worthy of his rank. After the Napoleonic secularization and the subsequent Congress of Vienna (1816), the premises passed to the Elector of Hesse-Kassel, and Wilhelm II of that house had the interior redecorated in Neoclassical style. Until 1918 the house served as the Elector's summer residence; after the Second World War Landgrave Philipp of Hesse turned it into a museum in which he presented the family's collections of art and *objets d'art* to the public.

Today, Schloss Fasanerie's rooms exhibit a wealth of high quality 18th and 19th century furniture and furnishings. The north wing, where many of the original stucco ceilings are still intact, is dedicated to Baroque applied art, and the south wing to the 19th century, with items of Empire furniture along with valuable clocks and gilded bronze work – pieces taken from several electoral residences in Kassel. Here, late 19th century furnishings form the final chapter in a developmental history covering almost 180 years of courtly living: a history in which each room has its own definition and atmosphere, where fixtures and furniture create such a balanced whole that one feels one could simply move in and start living.

Kept in separate exhibition rooms is the Fasanerie's collection of porcelain: pieces of inestimable worth from every leading manufactory in Europe, among them Meissen, Sèvres, Berlin and Copenhagen. Furthermore, the Fasanerie has one of the country's most valuable private collections of ancient art and offers a special annual exhibition in the former bath house.

Schloss Fasanerie is set in a historic park that forms an integral part of the heritage-protected ensemble. Elector Wilhelm II of Hesse-Kassel had the park landscaped in the English manner, and still today it offers the visitor the charms of a well-maintained early 19th century estate. Finally, a restaurant with a spacious southern terrace, along with one of the region's best beer gardens, provides all one needs to round off a visit.

Main staircase

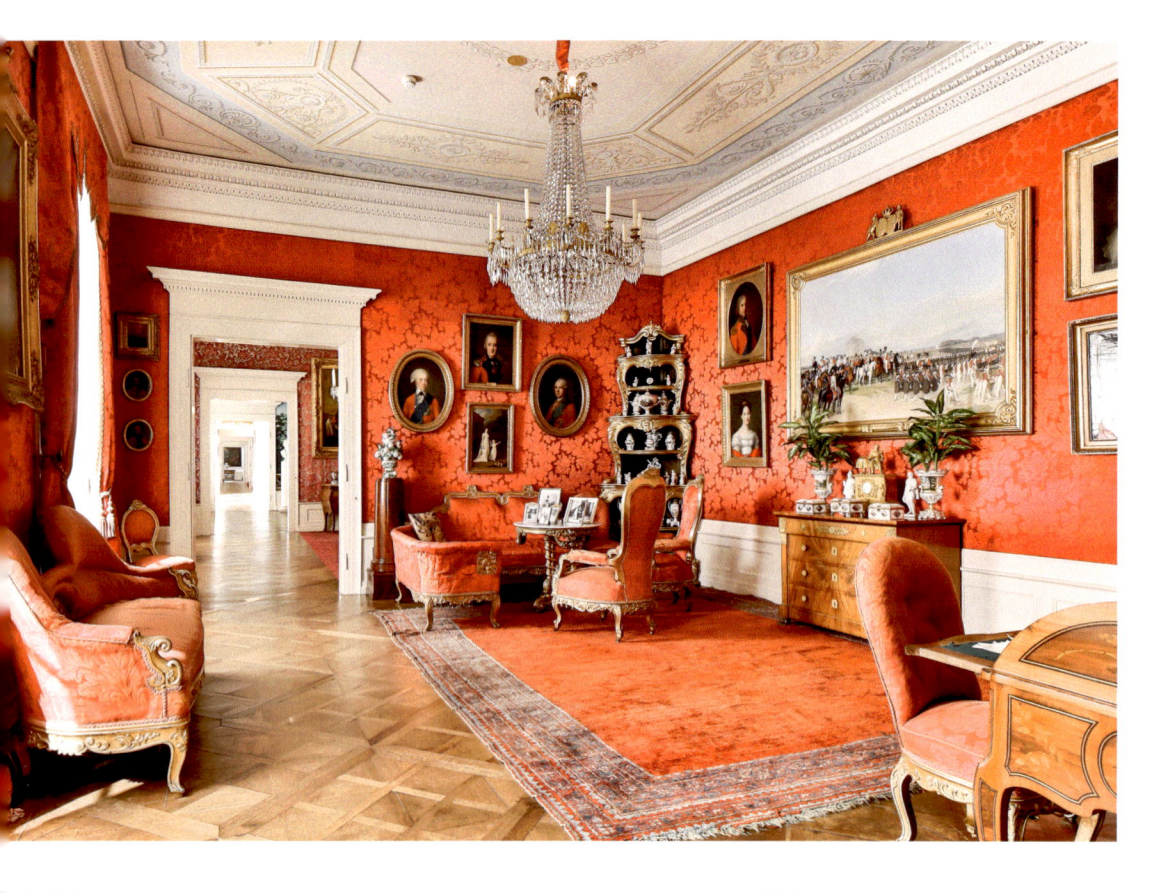

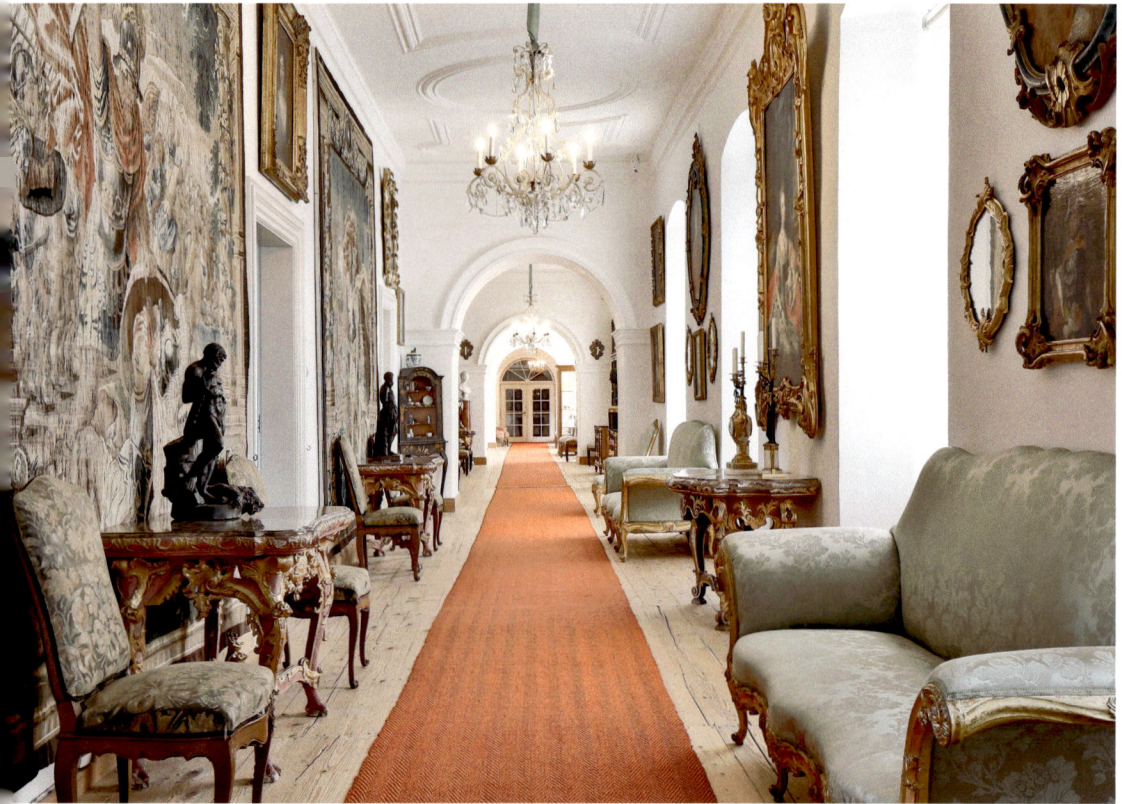

Danish drawing room in the south wing

Baroque furnishings in the north wing

View from the garden side

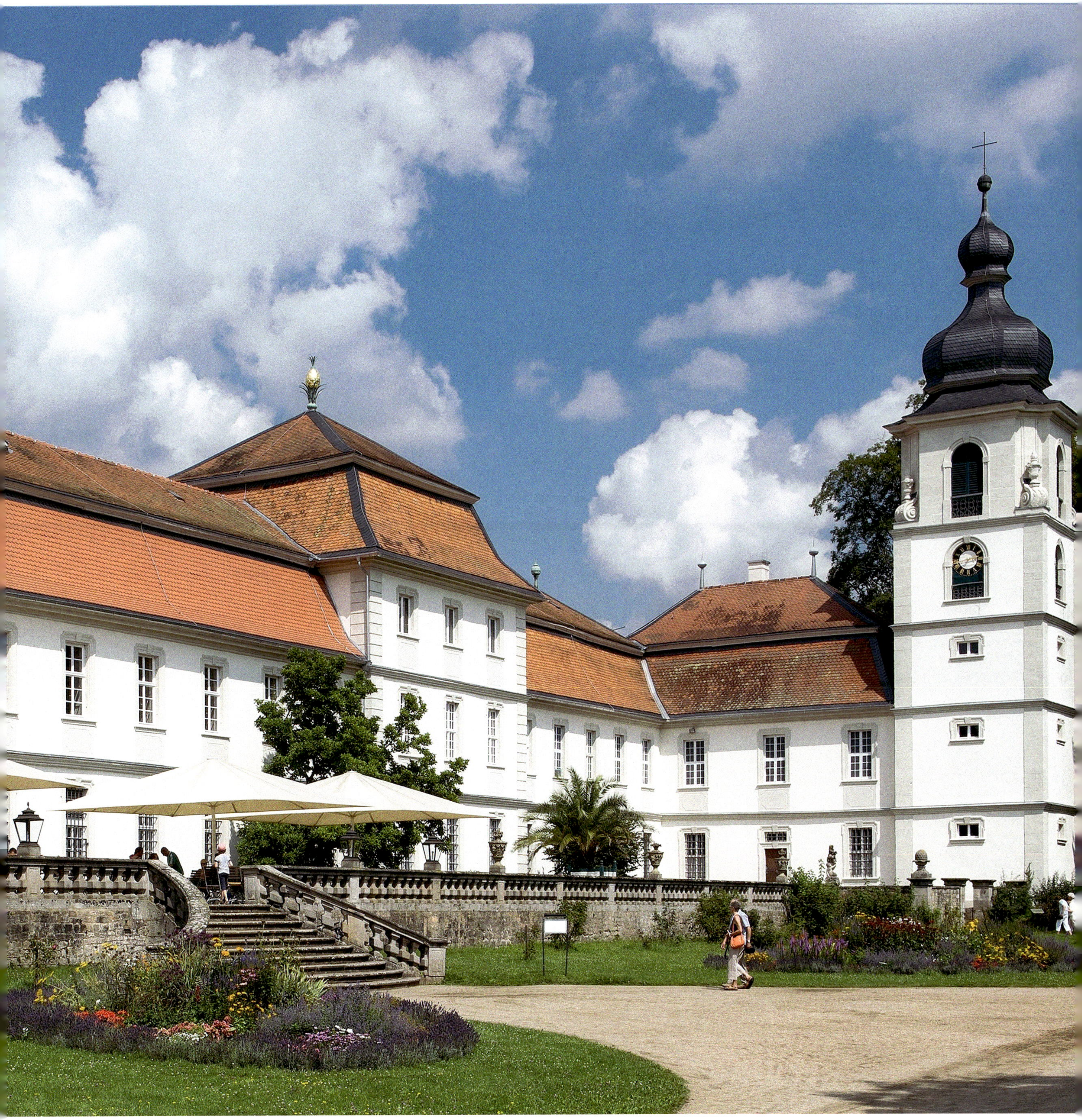

Friedenstein Castle

The Baroque Universe of Gotha

Take the Gotha exit on the A4 autobahn in Thuringia, and there's a time-warp in store for you. Rising in the distance, the imposing twin towers of Friedenstein Castle will already have come into view. They are part of a vast Early Baroque residence set at the centre of an extensive park, an ensemble – more recently renamed "The Baroque Universe of Gotha" – which contains, among other notable elements, the ducal museum (to the south of the palace) and the orangery. The historical apartments, the Baroque Ekhof theatre, and the unique collections of art, as well as objects of natural and cultural interest, enable the visitor for a few hours to leave the present-day world behind and enter a long bygone age.

The story of Friedenstein Castle begins amid the turmoil of the Thirty Years' War, when in 1640 Ernest I (the Pious) of Saxe-Gotha chose Gotha as his official residence. In a mere eleven years this devoutly Protestant Duke erected Germany's biggest Early Baroque palace. Its name, "Friedenstein" (literally "stone of peace"), expressed his intention to inaugurate a new, peaceful era.

The ducal residence soon became the birthplace of important political, as well as artistic and cultural innovations. The mortar was scarcely dry when Ernest I installed an art gallery, launch-

Ernest the Pious built Friedenstein Castle in a mere eleven years (1643–1654).

Banqueting Hall with stucco ceiling by Giovanni Caroveri

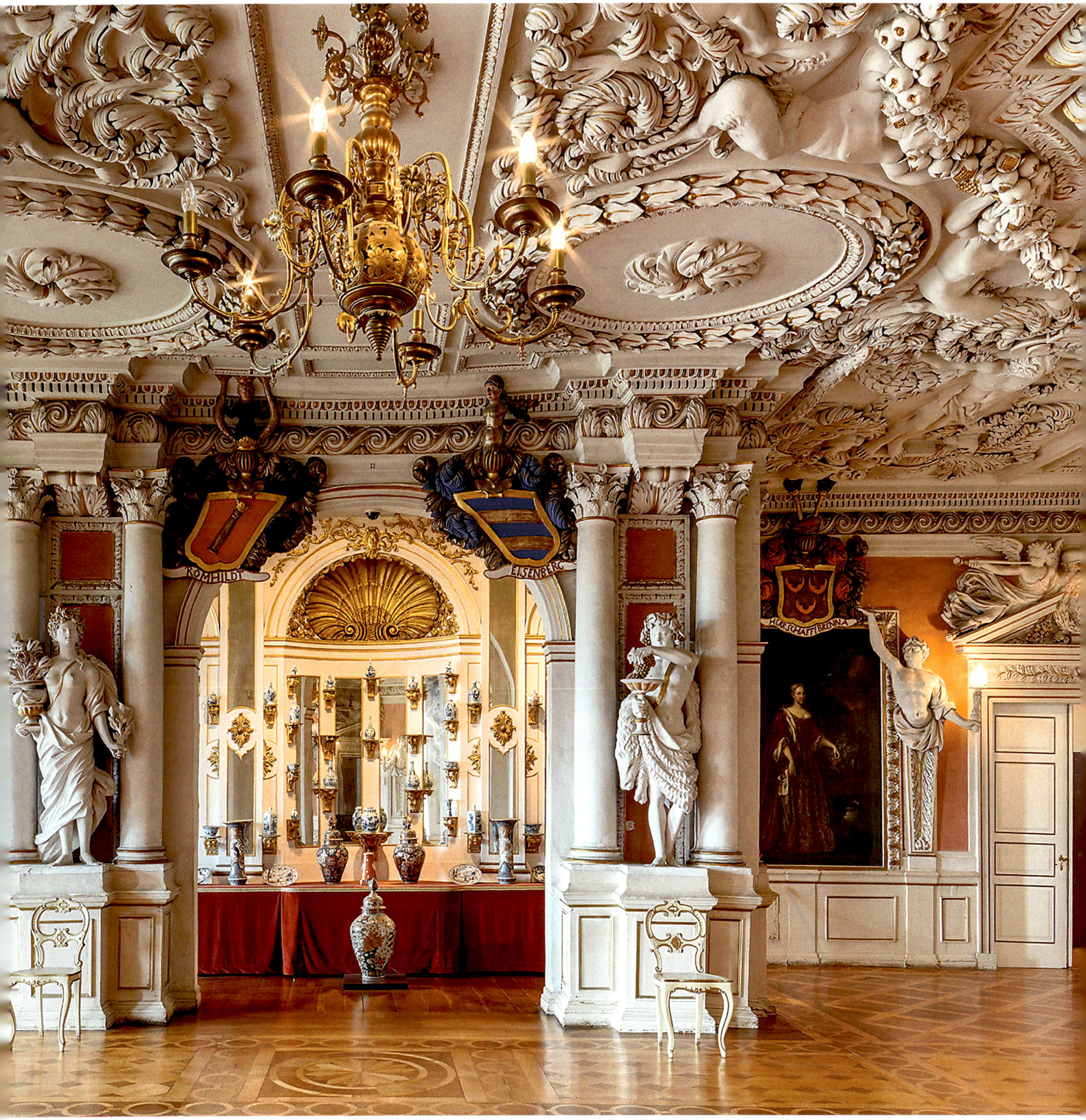
ROMHILDT
EISENBERG
HERRSCHAFFT BRENNA

ing a tradition followed by almost all his successors, each of whom added his own characteristic touch to the collections. Word of this spread far and wide, drawing such figures as Goethe, Voltaire, Frederick the Great and even Napoleon to the court of Gotha.

Today the Friedenstein ensemble has three museums, the Schloss Museum, the Natural History Museum, and the Historical Museum. The palace apartments are as unique as the collections are various, ranging as they do from gilded elephants and Nautilus cups to an original hat of Napoleon's to astronomical instruments and a mounted tiger. A particular gem can be found in the west tower: the Baroque Ekhof theatre, one of the few in the world with still functioning stage machinery from the 17th century.

Exiting the palace courtyard by the south gate, the visitor is confronted by a splendid building in the classical style: the ducal museum erected by Ernest II of Saxe-Coburg and Gotha and opened in 1879. After extensive refurbishment, the building – itself a work of art – now houses an important exhibition of art from antiquity to the Modern period.

Returning to the A4 autobahn, the traveller may wonder at the melee of images left behind by Gotha's "Baroque Universe", where paintings by Cranach, Rubens and Caspar David Friedrich vie with sculptures by Jean-Antoine Houdon, to say nothing of Japanese lacquer-work, Egyptian mummies, and Chinese porcelain. Or what about those strangely fascinating cork models?

Friedenstein Castle's art gallery and "Cabinet of Curiosities"

The Ekhof Theatre – a unique example of Baroque stage technology

"Fürstenlager" State Park, Bensheim-Auerbach

Idyllic village on the Bergstrasse

As if painted by an artist, a cluster of houses snuggles into a valley between steep woods, meadows and vineyards. Situated 23 kilometres south of Darmstadt, the village forms the heart of a 46 hectare (c. 115 acre) landscaped park stretching across the foothills of the Odenwald on the Bergstrasse: "Fürstenlager" (Princes' Camp) State Park in Bensheim-Auerbach.

The complex that served the landgraves of Hesse-Darmstadt, and later the grand dukes of Hesse and by Rhine, as permanent summer residence was built in three phases between 1783 and 1810. An avenue of ancient lime and plane trees leads to a group of timber-frame buildings whose exteriors, rendered and whitewashed over wattle and daub, have scarcely changed since that time: the guard-house, the stables, the cavalier's house, the princes' and ladies' quarters, and the guesthouse (dated 1810), which now contains exhibition rooms as well as a registrar's office, and the picturesque linen store, now a little shop and information bureau. The only fully two-storey building in the village is the manor house, which stands at the foot of a long meadow with one of Germany's oldest sequoias and other arboreal rarities.

The charming houses with their prettily shuttered dormer windows are set around the Gesundbrunnen, the "Fountain of Youth". The discovery of a source of mineral water here in the early 18th century led to the development of the park as a spa, at first only with facilities for isolated visits, until in 1790 Landgrave Ludwig X made the Auerbach "Fürstenlager" his regular summer seat, extending and adding buildings in appropriately munificent style.

As Aloys Schreiber put it in his popular "Handbook for Travellers Along the Rhine" (1818), the whole area around this great manor house "has been transformed with the lightly helping hand of art into a Romantic park". Paths were cut and vistas opened along the steeply wooded hillsides, broad meadows and vineyards were laid down and numerous small architectonic features introduced. A bark-lined hermitage, an Asian-looking birdcage, a grotto, a tea house and a temple of friendship are interspersed with resting places, urns, monuments and memorials in a landscape where enchanting views open across vineyards, fields and meadows dotted with fruit trees and grazing

The village lies at the centre of the former Grand Ducal summer retreat on the Bergstrasse.

VON LUDWIG UND EMIL

sheep. Visible from afar, tall Lombardy poplars line the hillside paths, conveying a touch of the Arcadian south. The impression is that of an "ornamental farm" in which the boundaries between the park and the surrounding cultural landscape are intentionally blurred and the church towers of the neighbouring villages, as well as nearby Schloss Auerbach, are integrated into a systematically artistic perspective.

Temple of Friendship dedicated by the princes Ludwig and Emil to their mother, Grand Duchess Luise

View across the vineyard to the avenue of poplars

The village in the centre of the park

Glücksburg Castle
Home to "Europe's father-in-law"

Glücksburg Castle is among Europe's most important lakeside castles. Situated on the Flensburger Förde, close to the Danish border, it has, with its unique position and its trademark corner towers, become a striking emblem of the State of Schleswig-Holstein.

The Renaissance castle was built between 1582 and 1587 by Duke Johann the Younger of Schleswig-Holstein-Sonderburg on the grounds of a former Cistercian monastery, the so-called Rude Kloster. It takes its name from the Duke's motto, "Gott gebe Glück mit Frieden" ("May God Grant Happiness with Peace"), whose initial letters "GGGMF" are inscribed on the coat of arms above the castle's entrance. Master builder Nikolaus Karies joined three formally identical structures into a single entity and set a tower at each corner of the almost square ground plan. In contrast to most castles built close to or surrounded by water, Glücksburg is set on granite rather than on wooden pile foundations.

At the death of Duke Johann, the duchy was divided between his heirs. The castle and its estates were bequeathed to his son Philipp, who founded the elder line of Schleswig-Holstein-Sonderburg-Glücksburg. Five generations of that family lived at Glücksburg before the line died out in 1779. In 1825 the castle and ducal title passed to the younger Glücksburg line of Friedrich Wilhelm of Schleswig-Holstein-Sonderburg-Beck. Today the castle is owned by the Schloss Glücksburg Foundation, established by the ducal family to maintain the unique cultural heritage of the castle and park and make it accessible to the public. The ducal family, some of whose members still live on the premises, set store on sustaining the discernibly personal character of the house and its history.

Of especial interest is the European dimension of this history, exemplified in Christian IX, King of Denmark from 1863, who spent part of his childhood

The castle garden and the orangery are right next to the castle island.

The island was created by flooding the former monastery grounds and building a dam to form the castle lake.

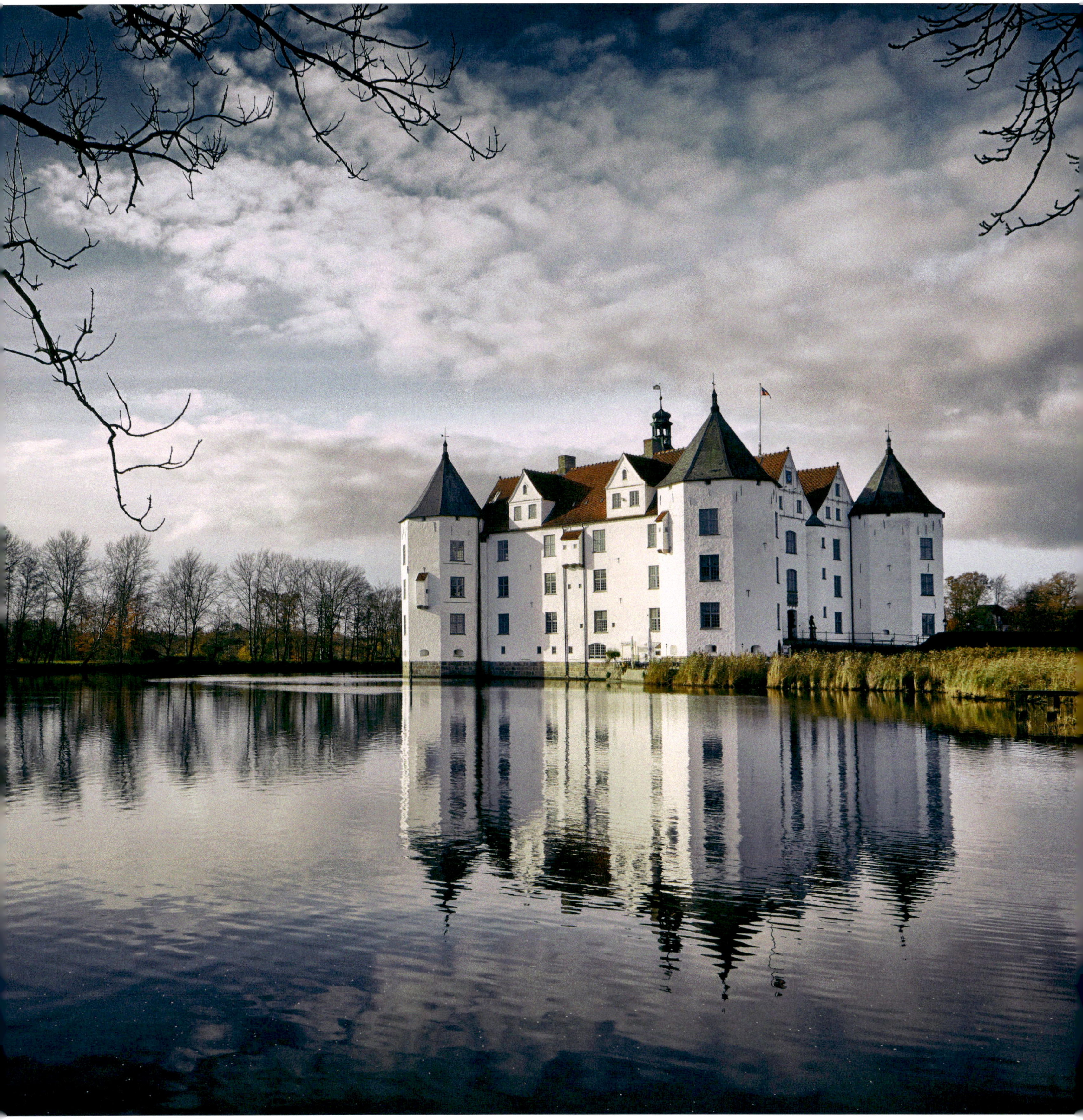

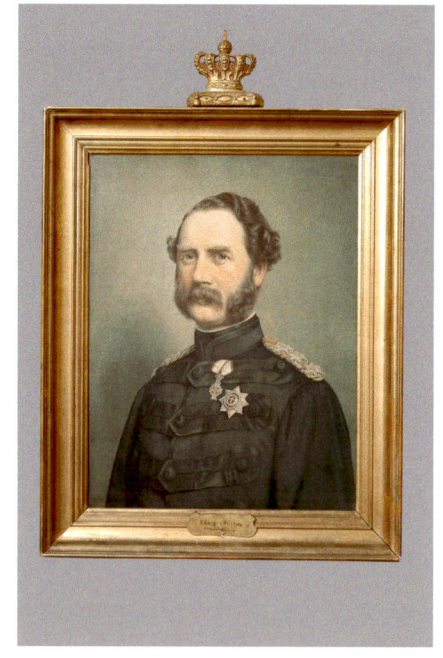

and youth at Glücksburg. The marriage of his six children into leading European noble houses earned him the sobriquet "father-in-law of Europe".

The castle is open to the public daily from May to October, with a wide range of items of interest for every age group, among them some valuable 17th- and 18th-century tapestries given as presents to the house in accordance with ancient tradition. For those seeking a longer stay, two comfortably and stylishly furnished apartments in the castle courtyard make ideal holiday accommodation.

Dress up like a princess or a prince? Take part in a guided tour especially for children? Visit a fairytale exhibition and do and see many more things? No problem at all: Glücksburg Castle caters for the needs of our little guests.

Christian IX, forefather of the Glücksburg line, from which even today the Danish kings and queens are descended.

86

Granitz Hunting Lodge
Rügen's crown

High on the 107 metre-tall Tempelberg, surrounded by one of the island of Rügen's most densely forested areas, stands the noble hunting lodge of Granitz. A uniformly light-coloured building in so-called Norman style, the schloss was commissioned in 1837 by Prince Wilhelm Malte I zu Putbus. Designed by Karl Friedrich Schinkel, its 38 metre-high central tower is a symbol, visible from afar, of the power and glory of that line.

For visitors to the popular Baltic island, a trip to Granitz will be among their most memorable experiences, for the princely hunting lodge is more than just a historical building. Its elegant salons, trophy collections and imposing Marble Hall convey an immediate impression of the house in its original condition, while modern museum media with audio scenes, models and installations provide complementary information in a variety of modes. Classical concerts, moonlight walks through the beech woods, and individually styled weddings regularly bring new life to the unique location.

The house's permanent exhibition presents a fascinating picture of its eventful history, and of the life and times of its founder, Prince Wilhelm Malte I. Halls that once witnessed banquets of venison and *bombes glacées*, where noble guests told tales of adventure in distant lands, resound today with the call of the hunting horn and signals of the chase. Among other items happily restored to their original place – and now displayed in a new exhibition – are some recently rediscovered embroideries from the ladies' salon long given up as lost. Furniture in the shape of golden ropes on the one hand, and letters of tender affection on the other, bring the social round of the island aristocracy to life for every visitor – and the house dachshund Waldi will be only too willing to act as guide for excited children and adults alike.

The former hunting lodge of the princes of Rügen is today one of the island's most popular tourist destinations.

The high-point of every visit, in the true sense of the word, and a regional trademark, is the tower. The 154 filigree cast-iron steps of its spiral staircase are held not by a central core but by the inner tower wall, making ascent and descent something of a trial of nerves – but one rewarded with a breathtaking panoramic view of Rügen from the platform at the top. From this point, 144 metres above sea level, one looks across the salt marshes to Cape Arkona, and to Putbus, Stralsund and Greifswald – even as far as Kołobrzeg (Kolberg) on the Polish Baltic.

Crowning the Tempelberg, Granitz Hunting Lodge is surrounded by a 1000 hectare (c. 2500 acre) forest.

Countless trophies testify to the successes of the princely hunt.

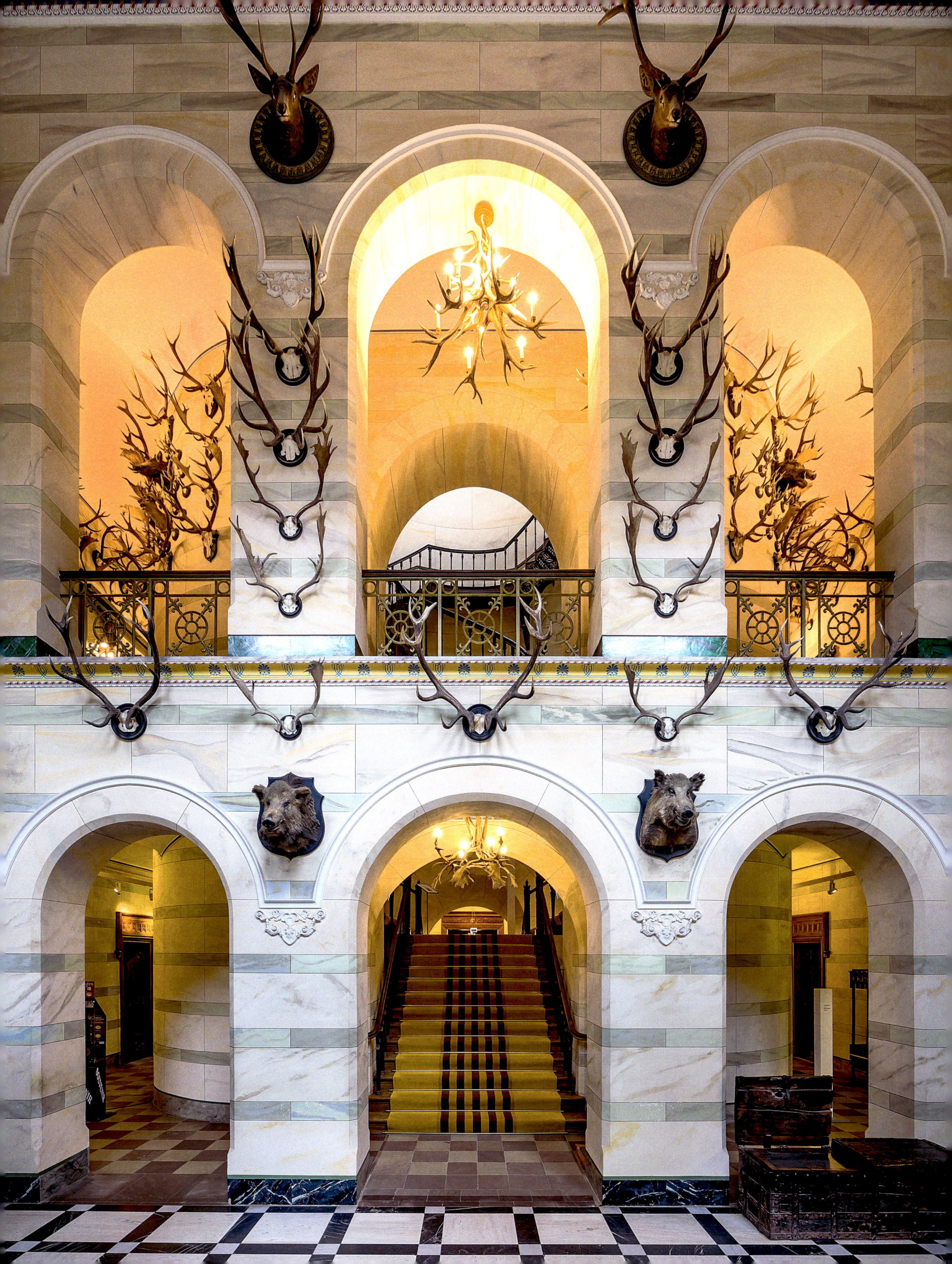

Greiz – Summer Palace and Princely Park

Art and nature in harmony

Set below the majestic upper castle in a great landscaped park with broad meadowlands and rich plantations, the summer residence in Greiz is a treasure-trove of art – and at times of a distinctly earthy humour. Among the possessions of the Reuss family displayed here is a collection of graphics ranging from historical prints to modern caricatures. Completed in 1769 as a seasonal retreat by the then Count (later Prince) Heinrich XI of the Elder Line of Reuss, the mansion radiates the freshness of summer. After a disastrous flood in 1800, the original garden was extended and redesigned in the course of the 19th century to cover the entire floodplain of the Elster.

Built on the site of an earlier building – a small summer palace with a Baroque *jardin de plaisance* – the summer residence was planned during the Prince's journey through France and reflects contemporary French architectural style. It is one of Thuringia's earliest Neoclassical buildings. With its (later upgraded) interior, it was an expression of the recent elevation of the Elder Line of Reuss from the rank of count to that of *Reichsfürst* (imperial prince).

On the ground floor of the mansion is the garden room. Decorated entirely in white with stucco gardening implements and bouquets of flowers, as well as musical instruments and theatre masks – summer entertainments included concerts and theatrical performances – it was used in winter as a suitable shelter for orangery plants. On the first floor, to the east and west of the banqueting hall, are the former apartments of the Prince and Princess. In the

Pleasure ground

Summer residence and flower garden

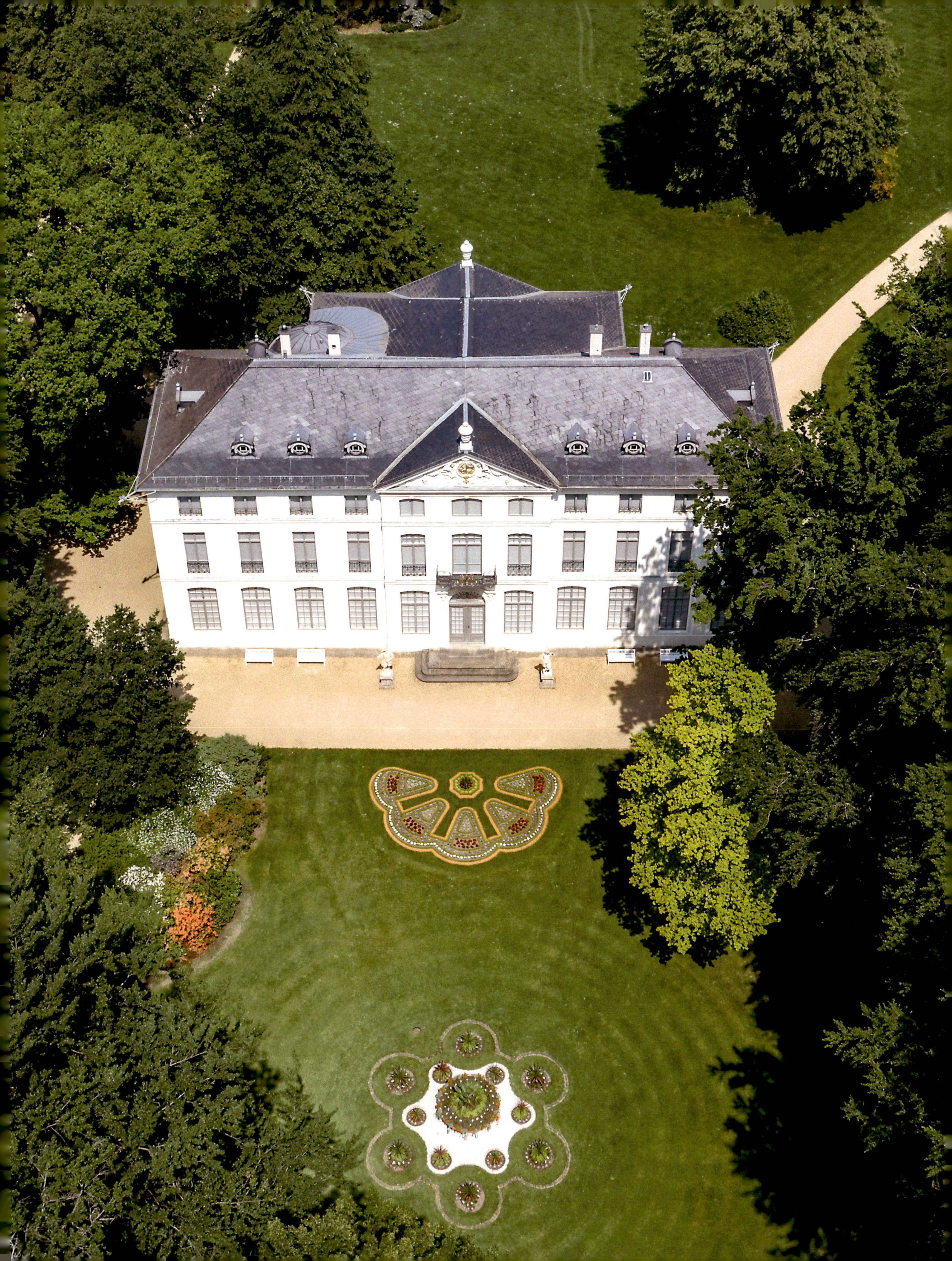

reception rooms the state collection of books and copperplate prints presents its holdings in varying exhibitions.

The first steps towards a landscaped park were already taken in the 18th century to the north-east of the mansion. Later, the pinetum, a plantation of foreign conifers, was established there. The systematic landscaping of the park began in 1873 under the direction of Rudolph Reinecken to plans by the Pückler pupil Carl-Eduard Petzold. Next to the mansion were a flower garden and pleasure ground – intensively cultivated areas with blossoming plants and trees. Already encircled by a pathway, the rush pond was now upgraded with planted islets and a curving shoreline. The northern part of the park is dominated by wide meadowlands with a natural diversity of plant life interspersed with picturesque stands of woodland arranged to provide alternating near and distant views. Ancient trees, some more than 200 years old, still show the trajectory of avenues that once ran through the water meadows to the north of the park. The fame of Greiz's princely park rests, among other things, on its unusual botanical wealth.

Exhibition in the Prince's apartments

Hambach Castle
Cradle of German democracy

On the eastern edge of the Palatine Forest, close to the culturally important cities of Speyer, Heidelberg and Worms, Hambach Castle is a living centre of democratic history and one of the Rhineland-Palatinate's most attractive tourist destinations.

For the first time ever, the Hambach Festival ("Hambacher Fest") of May 1832 united almost 30,000 people beneath the black, red and gold on the Kastanienberg near Neustadt. That legendary meeting has been regarded as the birth of German democracy ever since. With the Paulskirche (St. Paul's Church) in Frankfurt and the Reichstag in Berlin, Hambach Castle is honoured as one of the key sites of German democratic history. The words "Long live every people that breaks its chains", with which Philipp Jakob Siebenpfeiffer almost two centuries ago ended his impassioned plea for unity and freedom, have lost none of their burning relevance.

Because of its important cultural and historical role for Europe, Hambach Castle was awarded the European Heritage Label in 2015 – a signal of the European Commission's recognition of the castle as symbolizing the struggle for civic freedoms, and hence of its importance for all who subscribe to the ideals of equality, democracy and tolerance.

This legacy still lives on today. The impressive exhibition "Up! Up to the castle!" – a multimedia hands-on recreation of events around the Hambach Festival ("Hambacher Fest") of 1832 – invites visitors to experience with immediacy the origins, history and development of German democracy up to the present day. A key exhibit is the original flag of 1832 in the national colours of the Federal Republic of Germany: black, red and gold. Guided tours and workshops for every age offer more intensive engagement with democracy as a societal structure and way of life. From 2006 to 2020 rebuilding and modernization measures in the entire castle complex have created barrier-free access. Two new buildings, Restaurant 1832 and Visitors' House, blend harmoniously into the historical structure, and the exterior has been partly reshaped and furnished with a new lighting con-

Hambach Castle with the new "Restaurant 1832"

Concert and events hall

cept, providing excellent conditions for the castle's broad cultural programme. This ranges from classical concerts to children's theatre, and from drama and political cabaret to serious political discussion. Private events, weddings and conferences also enjoy an unforgettable setting in these walls, where rooms of classic beauty convey an atmosphere steeped in Hambach's unique history.

Hambach Castle – where living history and multi-faceted culture combine in a breathtaking panorama at the heart of the Palatinate.

Panorama terrace

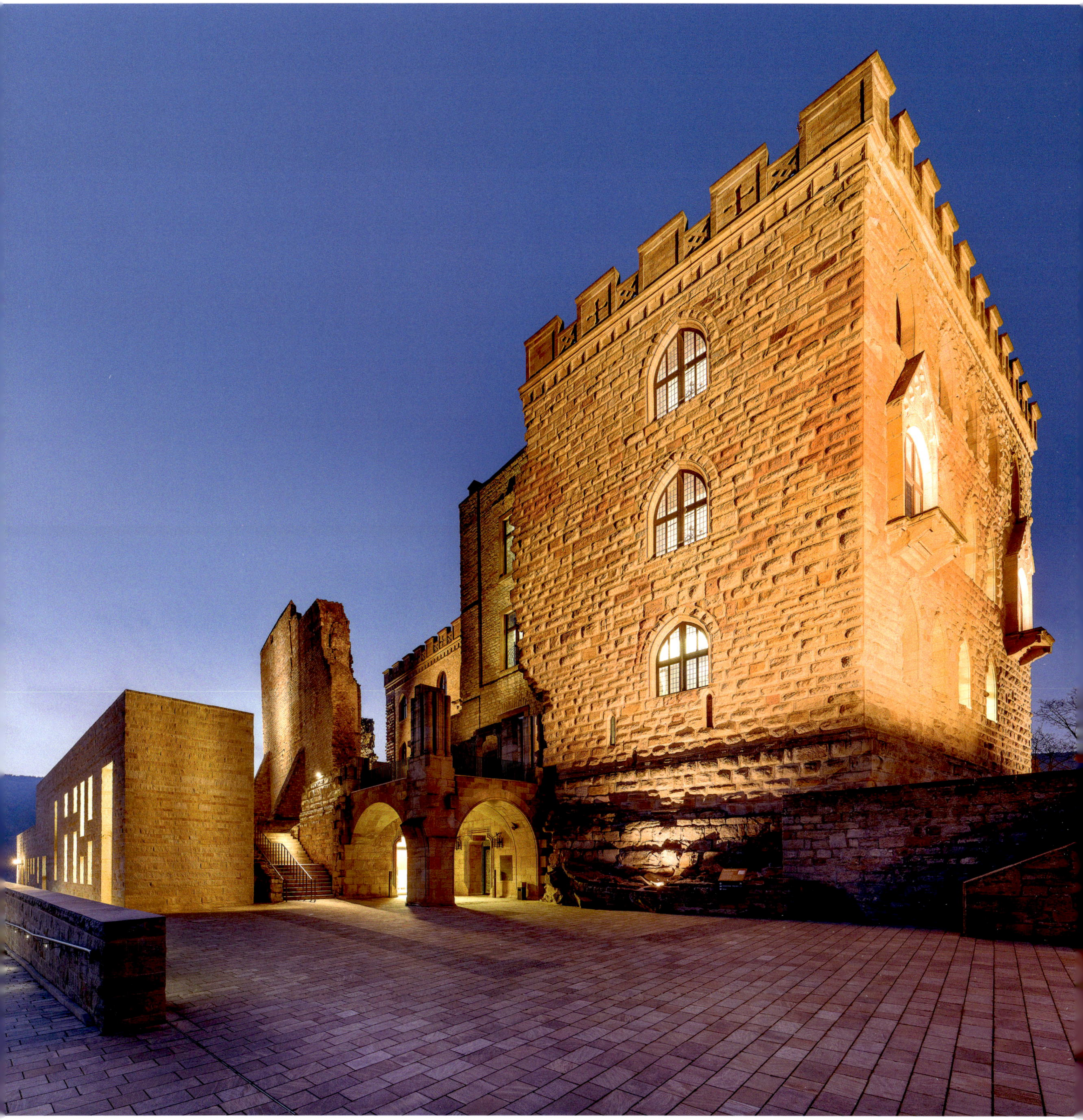

Hämelschenburg Castle
An authentic fairytale castle

Hämelschenburg Castle with the Renaissance church and Tithe Barn

In the Weser Hill Country between the towns of Hameln and Bad Pyrmont stands an imposing stately home, Hämelschenburg Castle. The castle with the adjacent gardens, farm buildings, watermill and church form an intact Renaissance ensemble, which is encircled by pastures, farmland, and an extensive forest. For five centuries the family has strived to preserve the castle with its abundant sandstone ornamentation, and today the property is managed according to the principle of sustainability. Hämelschenburg Castle is one of the finest examples of Weser Renaissance architecture in northern Germany.

In 1437 the Guelph Duke Otto of Brunswick and Lüneburg granted Wilken Klencke the fief of Hämelschenburg, which has remained in the hands of the family ever since. In 1563 Germany's first freestanding Lutheran church was built at the centre of the estate. Between 1583 and 1613 Jürgen Klencke and his wife Anna von Holle added the farm buildings and mill. They completed the ensemble with the erection of the moated castle, a work of art built to demonstrate the owner's wealth and independent power. Originally two wings of this majestic building housed a court of justice, the hall of knights, a brewery, stables, servants' quarters, storerooms and a large kitchen. The south wing served as living quarters for the family. In the 1890s the functional aspects of the north and middle wings were abandoned to add stately rooms on the ground floor and an abundance of guest rooms. The entire building was modernized with plumbing and electricity. In addition to the 15th century walled garden below the castle, a landscaped park was created behind it in the mid-19th century and a pyramid-shaped mausoleum built there for the family in 1855. The grandeur of the castle and the courage of its occupants kept it from destruction during Europe's numerous wars.

In 1973 guided tours through the historic rooms made the castle and its collections of art available to the public. The historic rooms on the ground floor of the castle contain precious furnishings and paintings, stoves and fireplaces, as well as porcelain, glass and weapon collections that bear the imprint of many different styles, tastes and generations.

Originally the castle provided hospitality to pilgrims and the needy. Today the farm buildings house a visitor's centre and café looking onto the decorative southern façade of the castle. Pathways lead through the walled garden to the old watermill, a modern hydroelectric plant and handicraft workshops. Trakehner horses from the nearby Langels stud farm graze in the meadows. The castle is located on the pilgrim route between Loccum and Volkenroda, as well as on the Weser Hill Trail and the Weser Cycle Path.

Medieval garden with church and castle

Café with view of the south façade

**P. 98:
Grand Hall**

Charlotte's Hall – used for wedding ceremonies

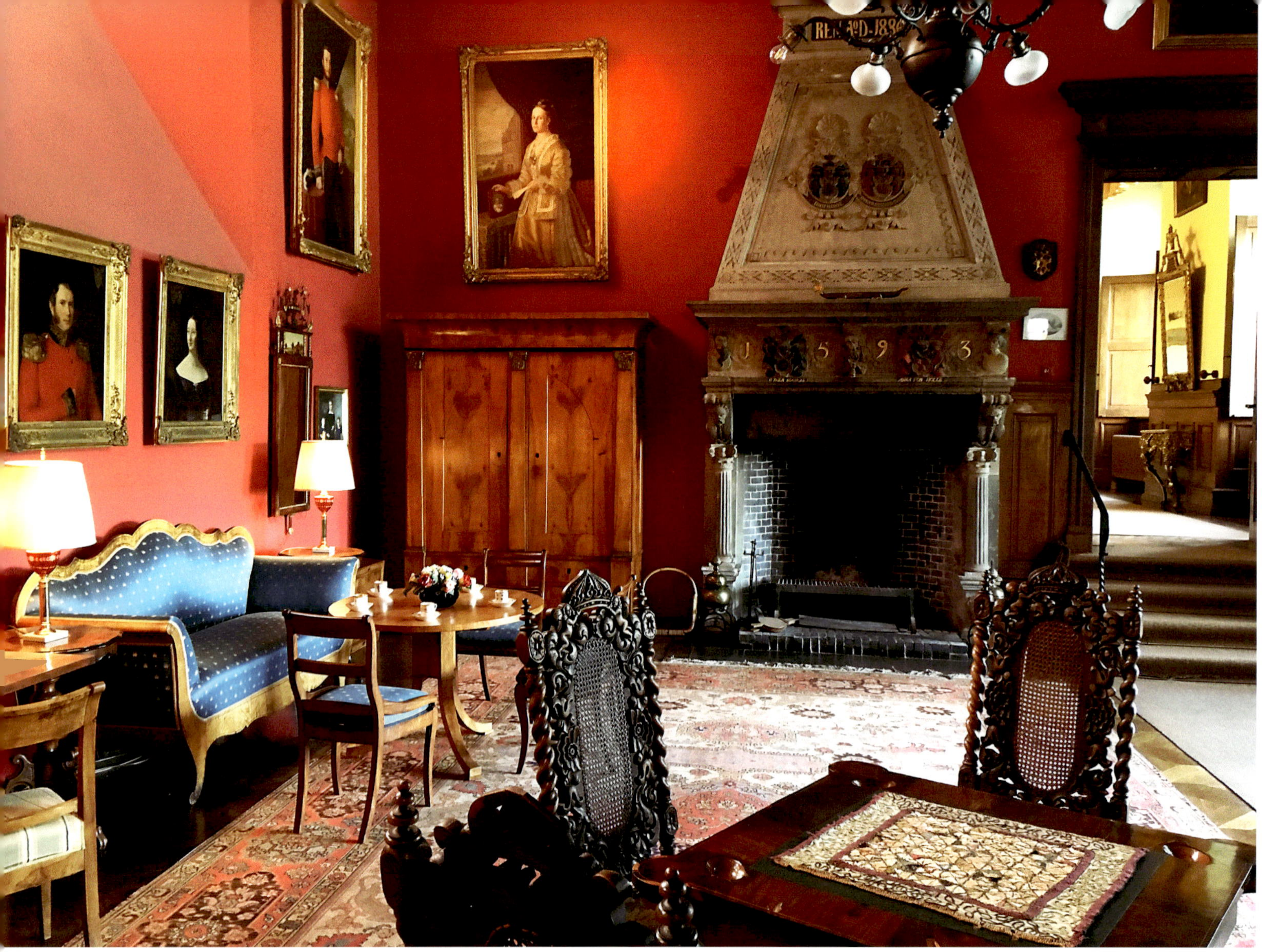
1 5 9 3

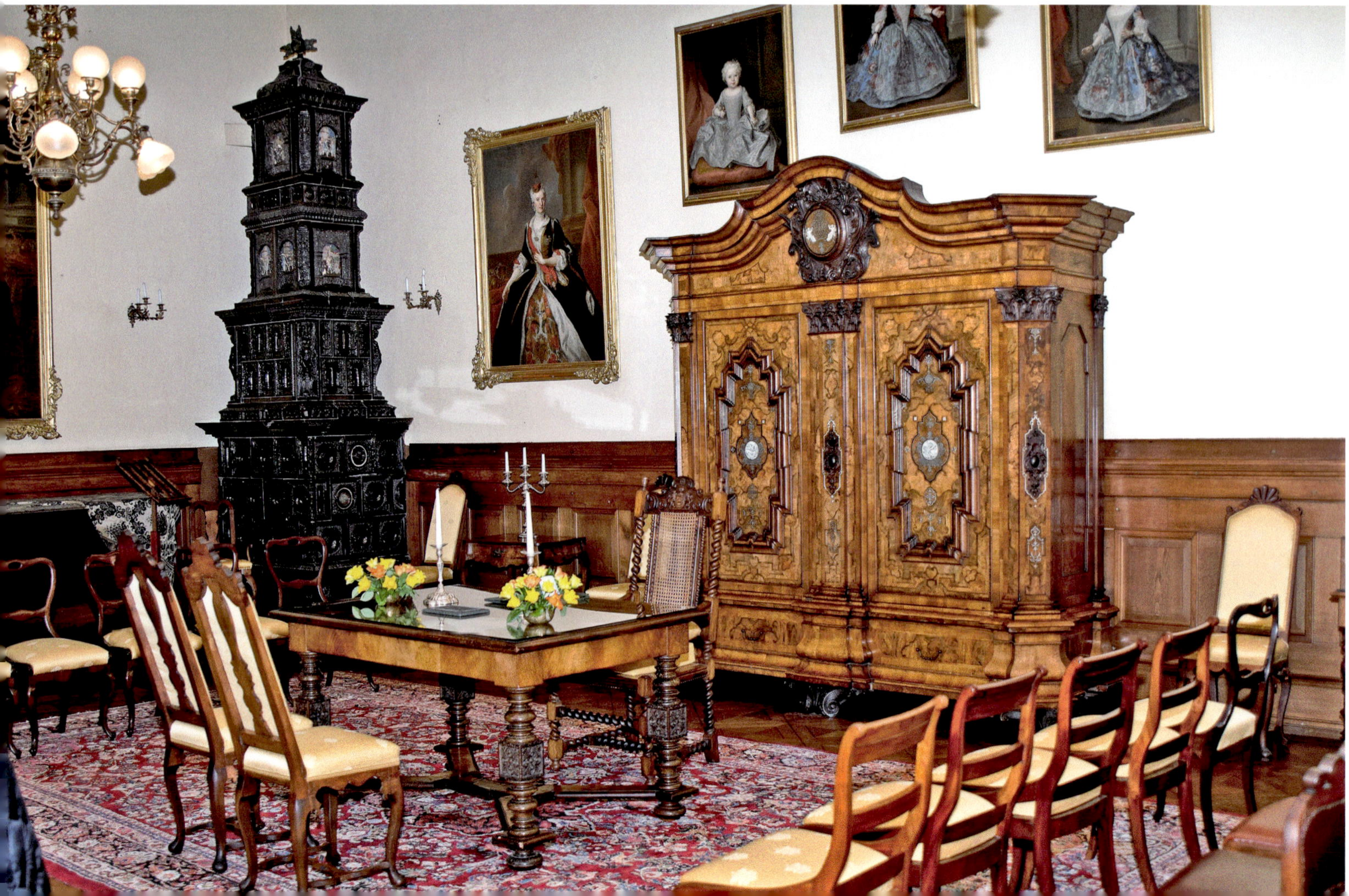

State Park Hanau-Wilhelmsbad

From quarry to fashionable spa

Alongside Wörlitz in Saxony-Anhalt, Hanau's Wilhelmsbad is one of Germany's earliest landscaped parks. Established close to his Hanau residence by Count Wilhelm IX (1743–1821), ruler of Hanau and hereditary Prince of Hesse-Kassel, the park is directly accessed from the town's main promenade, with the Late Baroque buildings that mark its one-time status as a fashionable spa. Wilhelmsbad Park features a variety of planted areas, complemented on the one hand with islands in an artificially dammed stream, once navigable by gondola, and on the other with a scattering of decorative buildings strategically placed to enhance the atmosphere of this "Garden of Sensibility".

A broad open ground in front of the promenade contrasts with a shady bosquet where a network of narrow paths leads beneath native trees and marshy thickets across a deer meadow and valley clearing into the natural landscape. On the other side of the spa buildings the park once featured a "green arcade", a hilly area of pathways and woods, lawns and fruit trees.

The noble watering place came into being in two phases between 1777 and 1781, when mineral springs were found in a former basalt quarry. Largely the work of the engineer and master builder Franz Ludwig von Cancrin (1738–1816), the spa was initially simply called Guter Brunnen ("Good Spring"), but its name was changed in 1779 to Wilhelmsbad in honour of Count Wilhelm. Until 1785, when Wilhelm left to rule as landgrave in Kassel, Hanau's healing springs were a famous social attraction. In a 1780 guide-book entitled "Letters of a Swiss Gentleman on Wilhelmsbad by Hanau", Baron Adolph von Knigge (1752–1796), who had spent long visits at the spa, described it in detail, not only as it was, but as it would have become in Wilhelm's never actually realized plans.

A prominent attraction in the park, and an eye-catcher from the promenade, is the oldest permanently installed merry-go-round in the world still in working order. Built in 1780 in the form of a temple, it served, along with the playground below, to maintain the humour as well as the health of the spa's 18th century guests.

In this park the visitor searches in vain for a great house or palace: the hereditary prince lived, true to his very personal style, in an artificial ruin he had had built as a castle keep – one

Promenade with former spa buildings

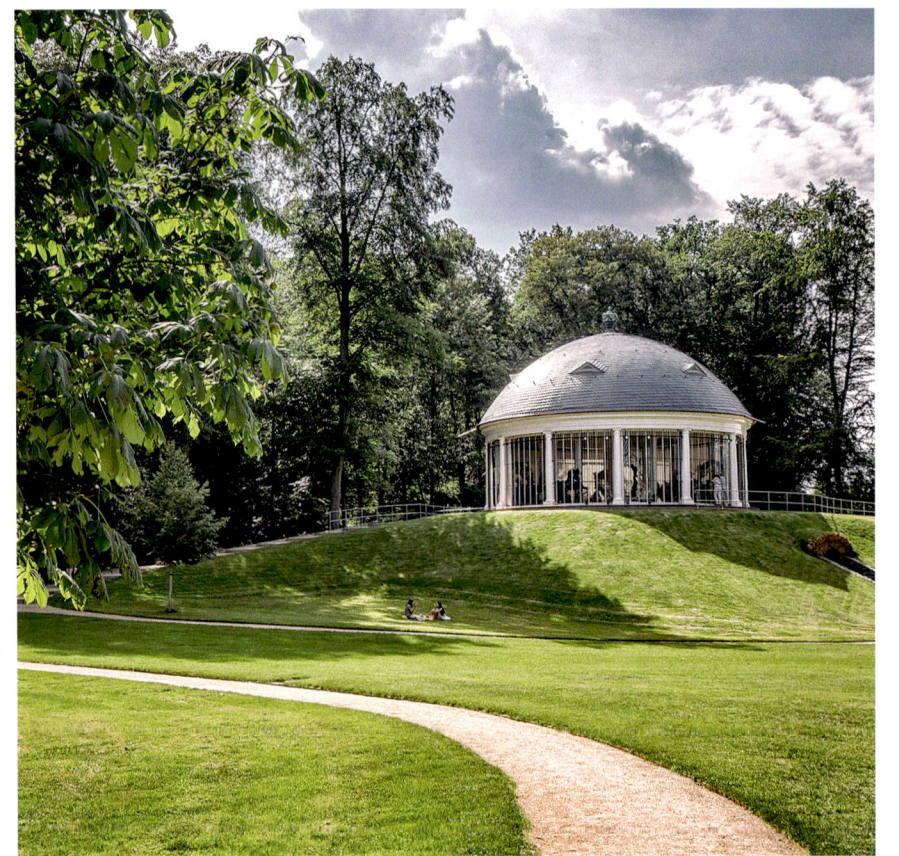

of Germany's earliest examples of the resurgence of medieval building forms. Its noble interior, however, is uncompromisingly Early Neoclassical. Wilhelm liked to withdraw from the courtly round in Hanau and mix with the spa guests from across the globe. "One observes here a prince who, when he builds, plants or improves, is wholly prince, but who, when he seeks company or the solace of nature, reverts within the private man, dwelling tranquilly among the guests at the spring, attending their table, and even their games and dances."

Formal reception room in the castle

The world's oldest still functioning merry-go-round

The castle – externally an artificial ruin, internally the tasteful residence of the founder of the park

100

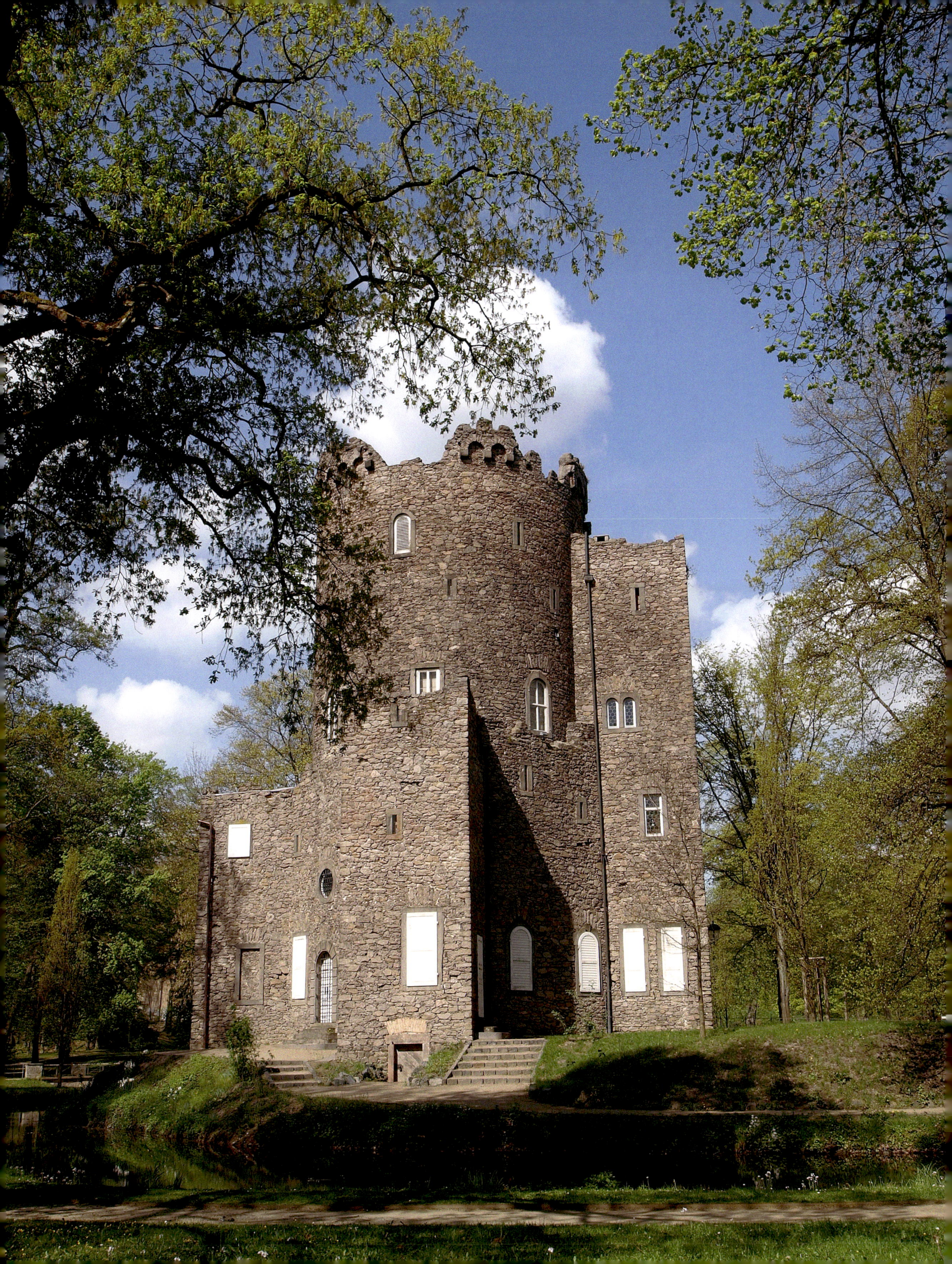

Hartenfels Castle, Torgau
Renaissance masterpiece and political centre of the Reformation

Emperor Charles V, who in April 1547 had been victorious in the Battle of Mühlberg near Torgau on the Elbe, called Hartenfels Castle a "truly imperial castle". Almost 400 years later, in April 1945, American and Soviet forces met not far from here, sealing the end of the Second World War. Again and again over the centuries, Torgau Castle, situated some 50 kilometres distant from both Leipzig and Wittenberg, has witnessed events of outstanding historical importance.

Already in the 11th century an irregular pentagonal complex was erected on an outcrop of hard porphyry rock overlooking the Elbe – hence the name Hartenfels (hard rock). Then, between 1532 and 1547, Elector Johann Friedrich I (the Magnanimous) of Saxony, leader of the Schmalkaldic League, adversary of the Habsburg emperor and ruler of Martin Luther's homeland, transformed the original castle under the influence of the Renaissance into a unique architectural statement of Protestantism. In fact, Hartenfels Castle became the political centre of the Reformation. The Great Wendelstein (literally "twisting stone"), built (1533–37) on novel static principles as a semi-freestanding spiral staircase without a solid core, is, then, much more than a mere staircase tower: It is an emphatic symbol of electoral power. The chapel, inaugurated in 1544 by Martin Luther himself, and directly connected with the Prince's domestic apartments, became the prototype of many future Protestant places of worship. Today it remains a vital centre of Lutheran faith and is open to visitors.

With the defeat of Johann Friedrich in the Schmalkaldic War, the Saxon electorate passed to the Albertine branch of the House of Wettin, who established their main residence in Dresden. Torgau was, however, retained as an important secondary seat. In the course of the Napoleonic Wars Hartenfels Castle became an integral part of the Saxon defences and later a Prussian barracks. Today it is home to the North Saxon regional administration and a venue for important supra-regional exhibitions.

The exhibition "Traces of Injustice" tells the story of Torgau as a place of imprisonment during the 20th century. Two further exhibitions recount the history of the castle in vivid detail: "Torgau – Town of the Renaissance and Reformation", with exhibits from the holdings of the State Art Collections in Dresden, and (in the electoral apartments) "Steadfast, Pious and a Heavy Drinker – Johann Friedrich I, the last Ernestine Elector". In summer, three brown bears can be seen in the Bear Pit (part of the old moat) where they testify to a more than 500 year-old tradition of bear-keeping at Hartenfels Castle

Hartenfels Castle
seen from across the Elbe

The Great Wendelstein is decorated with 16 coats of arms of the great-great-grandparents of Elector Johann Friedrich I.

P. 104: The chapel in Hartenfels Castle

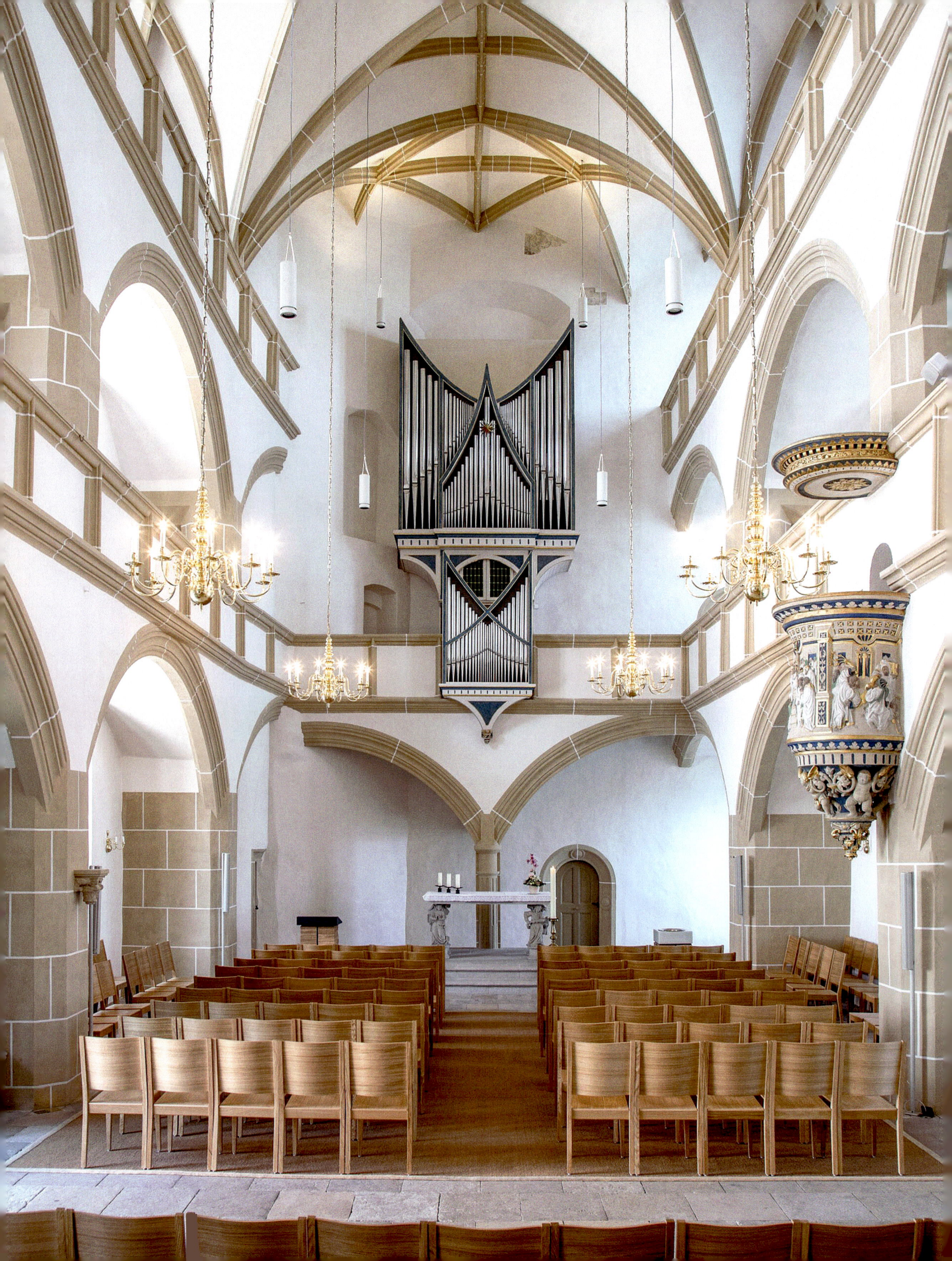

Heidecksburg Palace, Rudolstadt

Rococo *en gros* and *en miniature*

High over Rudolstadt towers a mighty castle furnished with exquisite rooms and rare artworks: Heidecksburg Palace, a striking unity of architecture and collections, is the fruit of centuries of princely living.

One of Thuringia's prime examples of the Baroque schloss, Heidecksburg was from 1571–1918 the residence of the Counts of Schwarzburg-Rudolstadt, a dynasty raised in 1710 to the rank of *Reichsfürsten* (imperial princes). In 1735 part of the castle was destroyed by fire, a circumstance that enabled the then ruler, Prince Friedrich Anton, to rebuild the west wing to meet his growing need for accommodation appropriate to his newly elevated status. To execute the work, the Prince commissioned the chief master builder of the State of Saxony, Johann Christoph Knöffel from Dresden. He was succeeded by Gottfried Heinrich Krohne, whose legacy is evident above all in the interiors, with their dizzily curving south German Rococo forms.

Two storeys high, the ballroom in the west wing is one of Germany's finest ceremonial spaces. Its walls, in varying shades of marbled stucco, are pure Rococo. The rounded corners, inward curving ends, and wave-like line of the musicians' gallery along one side, make for a room entirely without right angles. Two round-arched niches at the eastern end hold sideboards. The arms of Schwarzburg-Rudolstadt and Saxe-Weimar at each end of the room are flanked by figures of the cardinal virtues, while the large ceiling fresco is peopled by the Olympian gods. Next to the ballroom and giving on to the marble gallery are two apartments, each with an anteroom, a salon and a corner retreat. The south wing contains rooms in the style of various epochs from Early Baroque through Classicism to the early 20th century.

Apart from its noble reception rooms and apartments, the treasures of Heidecksburg Palace include a porcelain gallery, an exhibition on Schwarzburg history, the "Tiefer Brunnen" (deep well), and an art collection with

Lower terrace with castle garden and Schallhaus

105

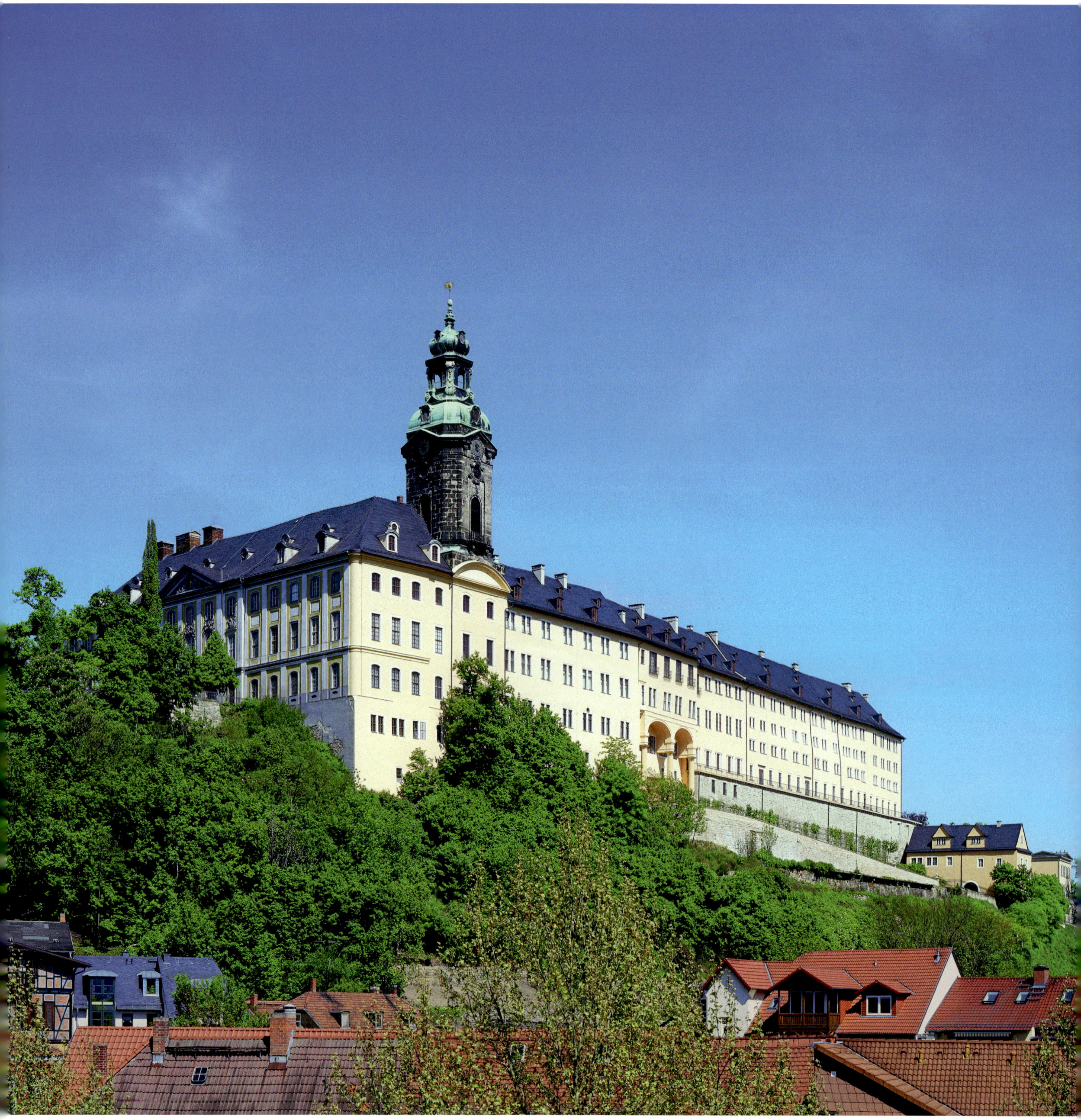

important works by Caspar David Friedrich and Otto Mueller. Of particular interest to visitors is the "Rococo en miniature" exhibition, a Rococo world set in the fantasy Kingdoms of Dyonia and Pelaria.

The middle terrace of the castle garden contains the riding hall (1600), whose façade holds the remains of some powerful Early Baroque wall paintings. The lower terrace was laid out in the second half of the 18th century as a Baroque schloss garden, but already converted at the end of that century into a sentimental-Romantic landscaped garden. At its centre stands a singular rarity, the "Schallhaus" (literally "sounding house"), a concert pavilion with a domed roof designed for special acoustic effects by the musicians.

Heidecksburg Palace in Rudolstadt

Ballroom

Heidelberg Castle
Truly romantic – the world-famous ruins

Heidelberg's most famous view: the castle overlooking the old bridge

Heidelberg Castle is one of Baden-Württemberg's busiest tourist destinations. Soaked in tradition, the world's most famous ruined castle has been the goal of many a Romantic quest. It is at once a place of superlatives and one that repays attention to detail. Not only as a charming ruin languishing in the shade of ancient trees, nor simply for the Romantic view from the garden terraces, but also as an example of a fine Renaissance palace, Heidelberg Castle retains its fascination for the visitor. It is almost impossible not to be drawn by the magic of its mighty walls.

From the Middle Ages onwards, the lords of the Palatinate extended their castle in Heidelberg. For centuries they had sought higher things – for example the monarch's crown – and their residence should make it clear to all that their vision was on the power centres of Europe. The French court, the palaces of the Holy Roman Emperor in Vienna and Prague – when it came to building, these were the measure of their ambitions. The court of Heidelberg reached its zenith in the early 17th century. It was then that the "Hortus Palatinus", the Palatine garden whose renown spread throughout Europe, was laid down on the castle terraces.

But the 17th century was an unsettled time, and towards the end of that century Heidelberg castle fell victim to the War of the Palatine Succession between France and (among other parties) the Electoral Palatinate. The sack of Heidelberg hit the castle at a time when its masters had in any case long cherished other goals than the construction of defensive strongholds in steep river valleys. For their new Baroque residences they sought flat terrain, where extensive buildings and great gardens could spread unhindered. Within their territories their choice fell on the plain of the Rhine, and the palace at Mannheim was built. Heidelberg Castle was left a ruin, and when in the 18th century the ruin was hit by lightning, the castle seemed doomed to perdition.

Yet new life came on the scene. The Romantic poets and painters discovered the beauty of the ruins and celebrated the desolation and decay that so fascinated their age. The thrill of lost grandeur embodied for them the transitory nature of human life. So it was that the ruined castle of Heidelberg became a top destination, a must for every traveller embarked on a European tour at the very inception of tourism.

The zeitgeist may have changed, but the sense of beauty has remained. Many more than a million visitors climb the Schlossberg every year to enjoy the firmly secured and thoughtfully presented walls of the one-time Elector Palatine's residence. Nor are these just tourists from distant lands bent on a dip into German Romanticism. A third of the tourists are from the region. No one, it seems, can withstand the charm of the history-laden castle in the green valley of the Neckar.

Remains of the western fortress: prison tower, gatehouse tower and stone bridge

Elaborately vaulted corridor ceiling on the second floor of the castle museum in the Friedrichsbau

Façade facing the city, with Gläserner Saalbau, (hall-of-mirrors building), Friedrichsbau and Fassbau (barrel building) with Grosser Altan (great terrace)

Valley of the Neckar with Heidelberg Castle and gardens

Royal Gardens of Herrenhausen, Hanover
The Splendour of Garden Art

They rank among Europe's finest park ensembles: for more than 300 years Hanover's splendid triad of Herrenhausen Gardens has represented horticultural art and culture at the highest level. The historic palace, a summer residence of the Guelphs, was destroyed in the Second World War. Rebuilt in 2013 as a conference centre and museum, it once again provides the gardens with a fitting architectonic counterpart.

Herrenhausen Gallery, with its frescoed ballroom, and the historically unique "Hedge Theatre", tell of the former glory and glitter of court life, while the museum – a branch of Hanover's Historical Museum – introduces visitors to the Baroque principality of the Guelphs and the key figures of that epoch, among them Gottfried Wilhelm Leibniz (1646–1716) and Elector Sophie (1630–1714). Varying exhibitions in the west wing present the development of the gardens, along with the great house and other buildings, from their origins to the present day.

With its formal layout and magnificent main terrace, its gushing fountains and cascades, the Great Garden remains virtually unchanged since the Baroque Age. "The garden is my life", wrote Princess Sophie, who from 1679 to 1714 supervised its genesis. A fascinating modern addition is the grotto by the French artist Niki de Saint Phalle, a walk-in artwork of glass mosaic, pebbles and figures that exudes well-being and *joie de vivre*. Radiant throughout the summer with almost 60,000 flowers and 1000 plants in tubs, the Great Garden invites its guests to participate in events ranging from the Herrenhausen "KunstFestSpiele" Festival and the International Fireworks Competition to the "Kleines Fest im Grossen Garten" and Hedge Theatre productions. The evening illuminations also create a wonderful atmosphere.

The botanical Berggarten contains domestic as well as exotic plants, among them one of the world's largest collections of orchids. Flowering magnolias and rhododendrons in spring, prairie shrubs and grasses in late summer, and moorland ponds in winter

Herrenhausen Gallery with Golden Gate in foreground

provide year-round pleasure, while the glasshouses present up to 800 orchids and other plants from across the globe.

The Georgengarten, landscaped in the style of the late 18th and 19th century, was from the beginning intended as a people's park. And it has remained so – a real-life landscape painting replete with lawns, lakes, rare trees and fine perspectives. Beside it, the 1,2 miles (2 kilometre)-long Herrenhäuser Allee, an avenue lined with a double row of lime trees, connected the Prince's summer residence to the city centre. The former mansion of the Count von Wallmoden now houses the Wilhelm Busch Museum for German Caricature and Drawing.

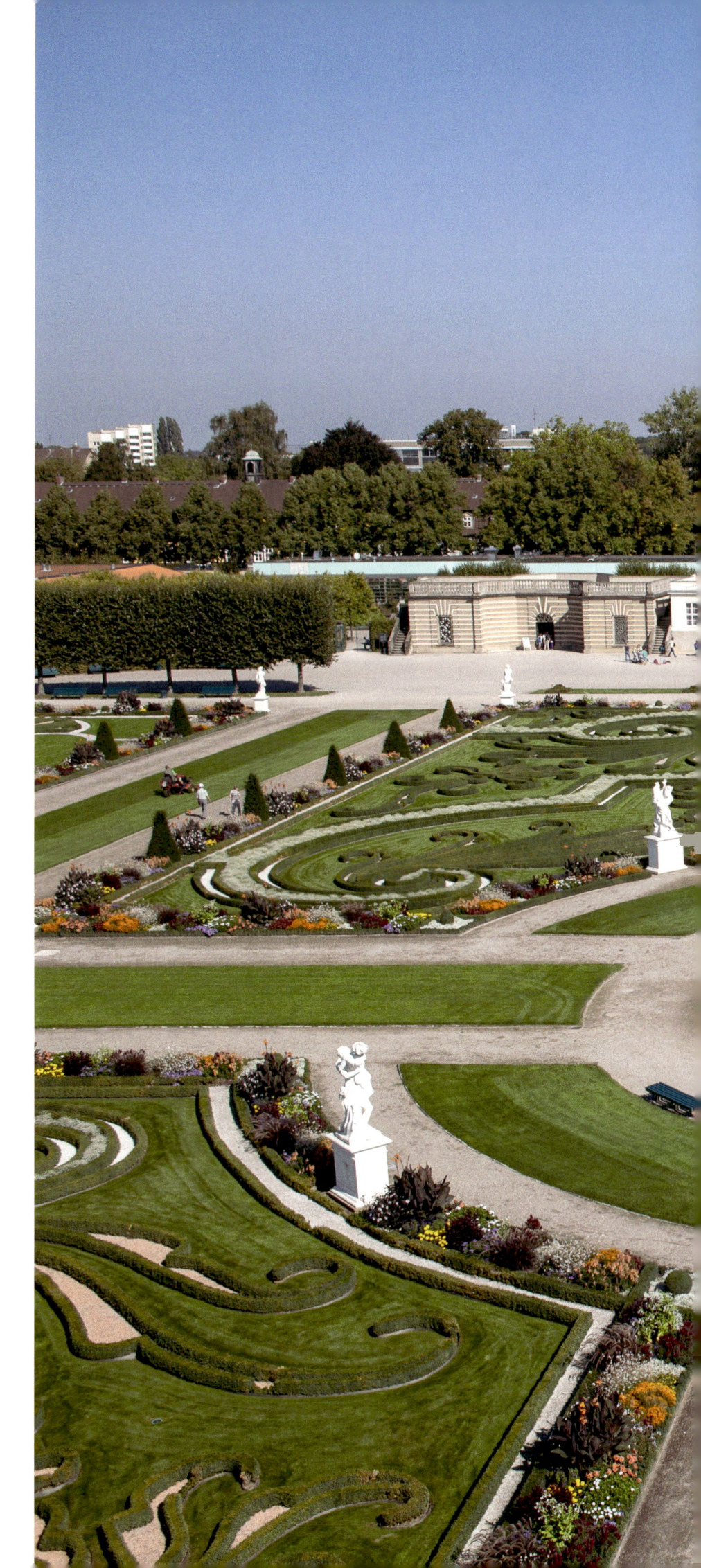

Main Parterre of the Great Garden with Herrenhausen Palace

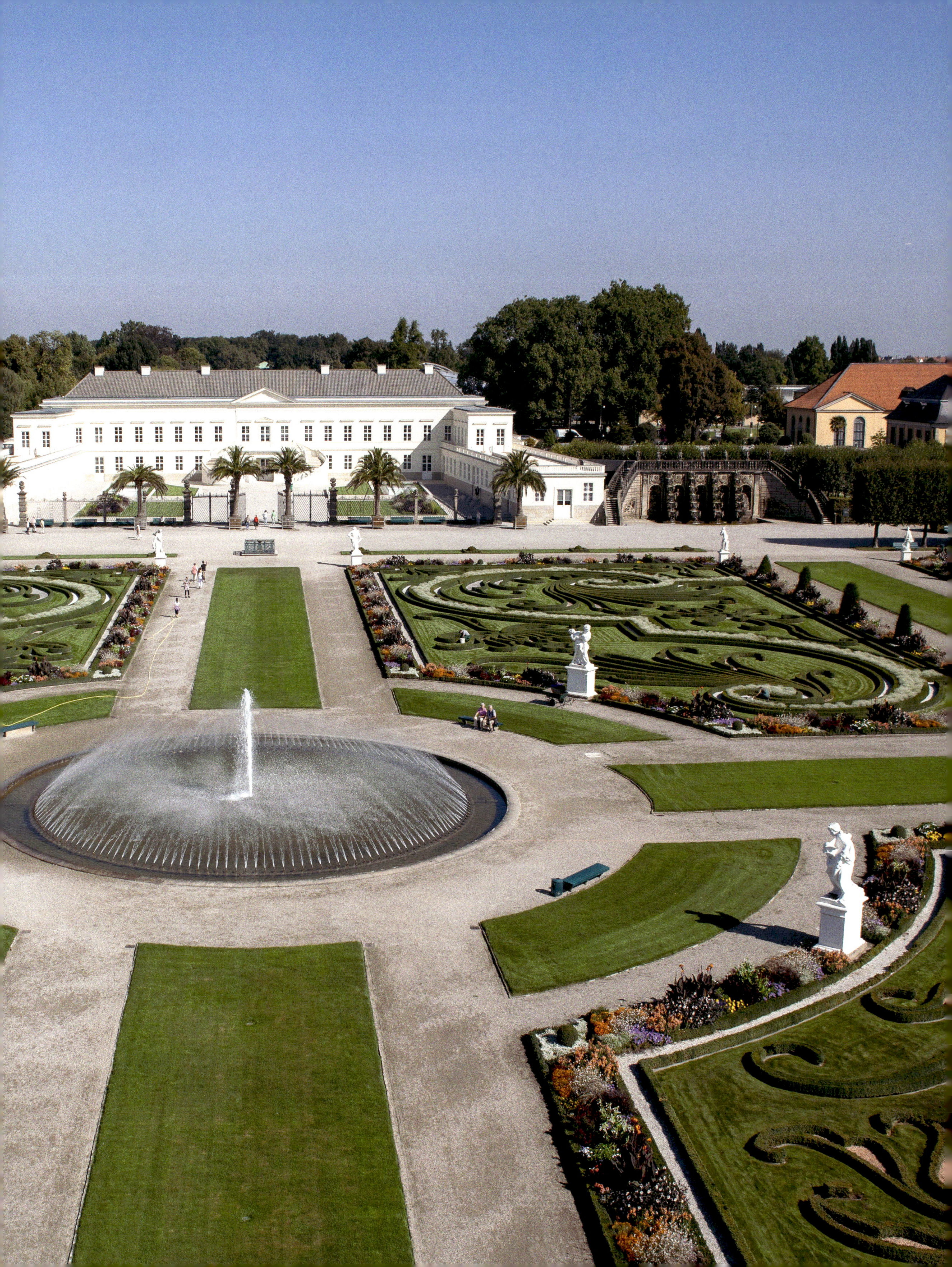

Hohenzollern Castle
History with majestic views

Hohenzollern Castle with its many towers, enthroned majestically on the Zollerberg

Set at the heart of Baden-Württemberg, half way between Stuttgart and Lake Constance, Hohenzollern Castle has been the dynastic home of Swabian counts and princes, Prussian kings, and German emperors.

Standing 855 metres high atop the conical Zollerberg, the stalwart fortress offers unparalleled panoramic views across up to 100 kilometres of open country. Its almost thousand-year history has seen times of both glory and darkness. The House of Hohenzollern is first mentioned in records in 1061, the castle in 1267. Razed in a 15th century war, this original stronghold – built presumably in the first half of the 11th century – remains unknown in appearance, size and furnishings, but it would have been both large and richly endowed with art. Rebuilt soon after its destruction, it was abandoned in the 18th century and fell into disrepair, only to be resurrected in the 19th century by King Frederick Wilhelm IV of Prussia, who elevated his family seat in both size and beauty to levels hitherto unknown. This is the castle we experience today.

Hohenzollern Castle is still in the private hands of the Prussian line and Swabian princely House of Hohenzollern. When the present head of the family, Georg Friedrich Prince of Prussia, is in residence, his standard flies from the flag tower. As a private estate, the castle finances itself without state subsidy, drawing its revenues from events, in-house catering and the museum. Every year Hohenzollern Mountain attracts more than 300,000 visitors from every country in the world, turning the castle courtyard into a veritable Babel of languages.

Informative and entertaining sightseeing tours through the interior are peppered with anecdotes from the life of majesties and highnesses of the royal line, making the account of long-past times entertaining and diverting.

As well as the magnificent Counts' Hall and Blue Salon, the Castle Treasury is of special interest, not only for its suits of gleaming armour and the royal crown of Prussia, but also for the famous snuffbox that saved the life of Frederick the Great. Visitors can now also download a specially developed castle app on their smartphones and undertake their own tour through the public rooms.

Numerous events fill the annual calendar, while the castle restaurant offers regional specialities to both daily visitors and special groups. In summer one of the region's most charming beer gardens is open in the castle garden.

Counts' Hall, the castle's banqueting hall, is still used for events.

Pride of the Treasury: the royal crown of Prussia

115

One of the castle's finest rooms: the queen's Blue Salon

The in-house restaurant, open for daily visitors and private celebrations

P. 117:
View of Schloss Hundisburg from the gardens

Hundisburg Palace and Baroque Garden, Althaldensleben Landscape Park

Baroque splendour in the Magdeburg Börde

With its magnificent Baroque garden and extensive landscaped park boasting more than 150 native and foreign tree species, Hundisburg Palace is among the top cultural monuments of the State of Saxony-Anhalt. The size and grandeur of its park and gardens draw visitors at every season, while the house itself offers a variety of cultural attractions, as well as major music events.

The origins of the historical park and gardens at Hundisburg and Althaldensleben can be traced back to the Late Middle Ages, but the Baroque residence we have today was built for Johann Friedrich von Alvensleben between 1693 and 1712 by the Brunswick master builder Hermann Korb. Between 1699

Reconstructed Baroque garden in the Upper Pleasance

and 1719 Korb also laid down the Baroque garden, one of North Germany's prime examples of its kind. Already in 1753 parts of the garden were reshaped in accordance with the new fashion for landscaping in the English style.

In 1810 the merchant Johann Gottlob Nathusius purchased the recently secularized abbey of Althaldensleben, and the following year he added the neighbouring house and Baroque garden of Hundisburg to his possessions. By the end of the 19th century the two properties were united, under his aegis and that of his sons, into a landscaped estate of some 100 hectares (approx. 250 acres). The plantations were extended deep into what had once been farmland, and included an arboretum whose rich variety of species drew (among other sources) on contacts across North Germany from Harbke and Hanover to Halle and Kassel.

Soon after its partial destruction by fire in 1945 efforts were made to have Hundisburg Palace listed as a protected monument. However, decades of neglect and misappropriation passed before wide-scale measures were taken, beginning in 1991, to save and restore the cultural ensemble of house, garden and park.

Today the palace contains a permanent exhibition of sculptures by Heinrich Apel, as well as Friedrich Loock's collection of paintings, and the historical Alvenslebens library. The "Haus des Waldes" (Forest House) information centre is in the reconstructed north tower. As well as these points of interest, Hundisburg Palace offers the visitor a spinnery, a brewery and a restaurant. Event and overnight stay facilities can also be hired.

A high point in the annual events calendar is the Summer Music Academy, when Hundisburg hosts young musicians from across the globe for ten days of top class study and performance. Since 2000 the house, with its Baroque garden and Althaldenleben Landscape Park, has been part of the tourist heritage network "Garden Dreams – Historic Parks in Saxony-Anhalt".

"Bowling green" in the Lower Pleasance

Langenburg Castle
A castle through changing centuries

Crowning a spur of the hills above the River Jagst, Langenburg Castle traces its origins back to the Hohenstaufen era. Since the 13th century it has been the family seat of the princes of Hohenlohe, who are closely related to the British royal house. In the 17th century the original fortress was converted into a noble residence with a magnificent Renaissance inner courtyard and chapel. A devastating fire in 1963 left the castle almost completely burnt out. However, although some treasures were irretrievably lost, the buildings were eventually restored and their contents replaced with painstaking care. Today, Prince Philipp and his wife Princess Saskia ensure that the heritage of Langenburg is preserved for future generations.

Part of the castle is open to the public, providing interesting insights into the domestic culture of the nobility in earlier days. Special costumed tours are offered, in the course of which, for example, the former chambermaid Münze Bertl may be caught retailing gossip from the genteel corridors. The terrace above the Baroque garden and the rose-bowered café opens up to a splendid view across the valley of the Jagst. The orangery in the Baroque garden and the great barn in the stable block, as well as some of the state rooms in the castle itself, are available for social events, congresses and meetings. They provide a fairytale ambience for family gatherings.

The former stables now contain the German Automobile Museum. Designed with devout attention to detail, the exhibition of vehicles from different epochs in these historic rooms is a joy not only to the motoring enthusiast. The annual "Castle & Cars" event brings racing fans together from near and far. The mixed grid of vintage cars and old-timers, classical sports cars and new hypercars, coupled with the unique atmosphere of Langenburg Castle is an invitation to mingle in pit-talk

Evening light at Langenburg Castle

The Renaissance courtyard has a unique acoustic.

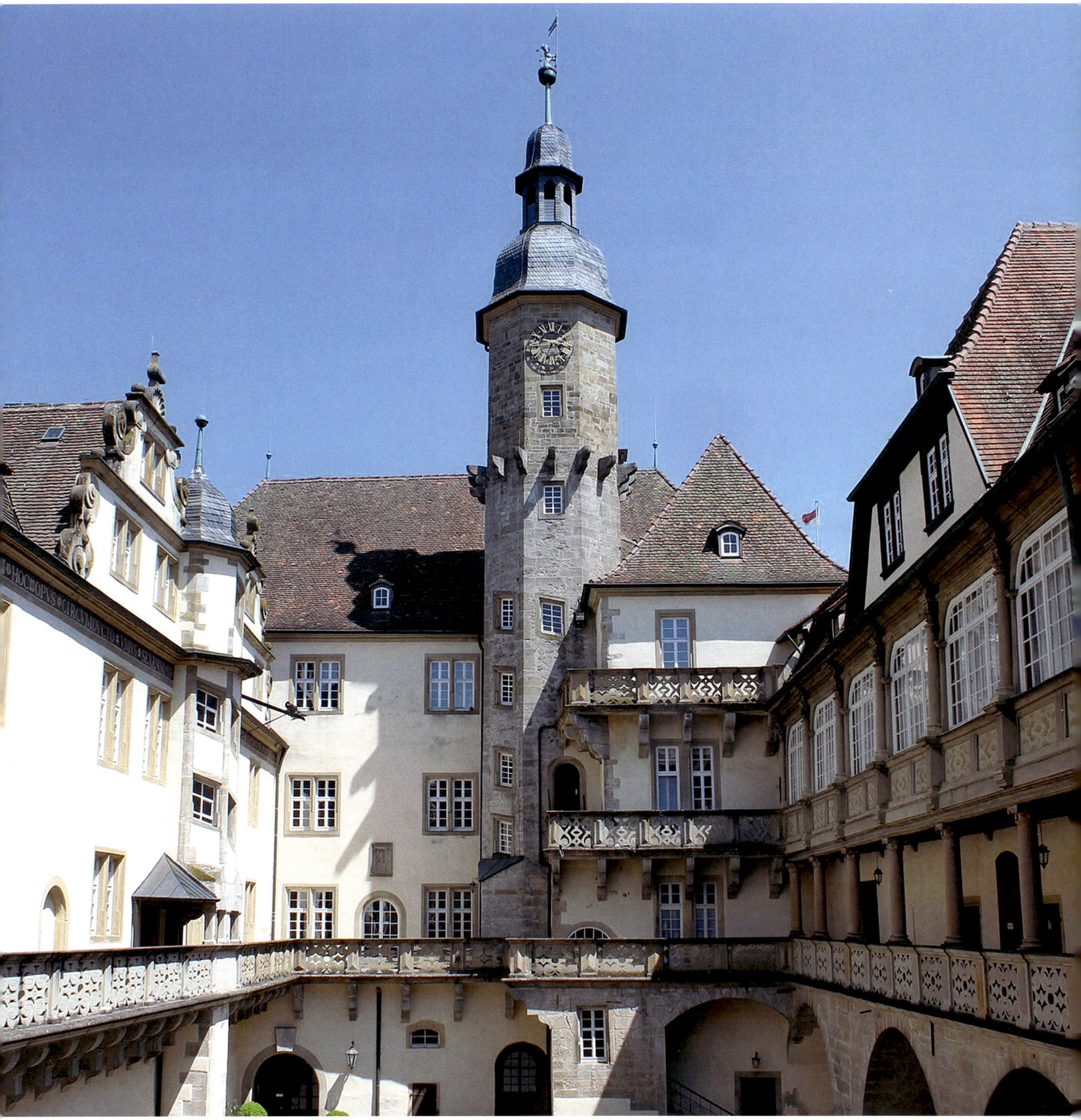

and to experience the heroes of motor racing in the flesh.

Comfortable apartments with historic charm above the automobile museum and in the former coach house are available for holiday rentals. Even an overnight stay in these listed (landmarked) buildings will be unforgettable. The Hohenlohe Area is a fantastic region for (e-)biking and hiking.

A stroll in the park with its ancient oaks and beeches is rewarding at all seasons, and the gardens on the southern slopes – a major project of the Swabian Alb Association – are a paradise for nature lovers.

On the first weekend in September, Langenburg Castle becomes a Mecca for garden fanciers. The entire complex is alive, with more than 150 exclusive firms offering individual ideas for styling garden, house and home. A comprehensive programme of fringe events and regional gastronomic specialities makes South-Germany's biggest private garden show a feast for the senses.

A mystic view of Langenburg Castle and the Hohenlohe plain

Stucco ceiling in Four Seasons Hall

Lichtenstein Castle
Württemberg's fairytale castle

Standing proudly and somewhat stubbornly at the edge of a cliff, 817 metres above sea level, in the middle of the Swabian alps, Lichtenstein Castle is the ideal image of a medieval stronghold. Perfectly situated in the forests of the Echaztal, it embodies the quintessential romantic fantasy.

A medieval fortress, the castle's predecessor, is just a short walk from the present-day castle. Destroyed twice in the 14th century, it was abandoned by the owners, who looked for a new location – one which would be theoretically impenetrable. And they decided upon the aforementioned cliff. But this new fortress was left exposed to the ravages of time and nature, and when Elector Friedrich I of Württemberg, later king of Württemberg, wanted to build a hunting lodge in its place, he found only ruins. This hunting lodge would probably still be there to this day if the famous Swabian poet, Wilhelm Hauff, hadn't let an old description of the fortress influence his masterpiece *Lichtenstein*, which was published in 1826. The novel became a bestseller, and Hauff's reputation reached legendary status after his death at the age of 25. Ten years later, Count Wilhelm of Württemberg, later Duke of Urach, became interested in the hunting lodge, which he bought in 1838. He immediately tore it down and laid the foundation stone for his new summer residence, the present-day castle, in 1840. It was inaugurated in 1842.

With this neo-Gothic building, the Count and his architect, Carl Alexander von Heideloff, realized the ideal of a medieval romantic castle, inspired by the description of the old fortress in Hauff's novel. The castle can thus be seen as a monument to both Hauff and the novel *Lichtenstein*. The medallions inlaid into the walls in the Hall of Knights evoke memories of old Swabian

Lichtenstein Castle: the "Fairytale Castle of Württemberg"

123

124

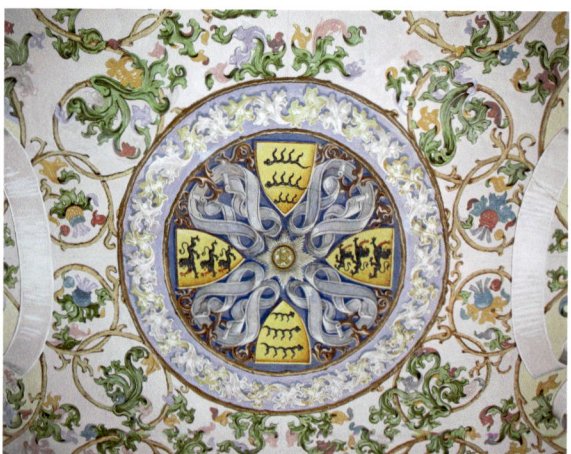

knights, some of whom also make appearances in the novel. A bust of the poet was even erected near the castle while it was being built.

Lichtenstein Castle is still owned by the ducal Urach family, who preserve the spectacular grounds and buildings, making them available to the public with open tours of the castle. But the castle isn't just a monument to Wilhelm, Count of Württemberg's romantic ideas, nor to those of his time. It is now also a beloved backdrop and filming location used for fairytale weddings and festivities. Just a couple of years ago, small replicas of Lichtenstein Castle stood in front gardens throughout Germany, and today it's a very popular motif on social media worldwide.

The Swabian Alb with its typical hilly landscape

Toast in the Hunter's Room

Elaborate ceiling paintings in the King's Room

Knight's Hall, the largest room in the castle with a hidden music room

Catholic castle chapel

125

Lorsch Abbey

From medieval spiritual centre to site of knowledge and learning

In 1991 Lorsch Abbey, together with its original site at nearby Altenmünster, were adopted onto the UNESCO list of World Cultural and Natural Heritage sites. Approaching the abbey site from the east, one is initially faced with a high, seemingly impenetrable wall. Behind this, contrary to expectations, are none of the buildings usually associated with an abbey – church, cloisters, refec-

Gatehouse or King's Hall – its function is still unclear

Newly laid-out abbey precincts

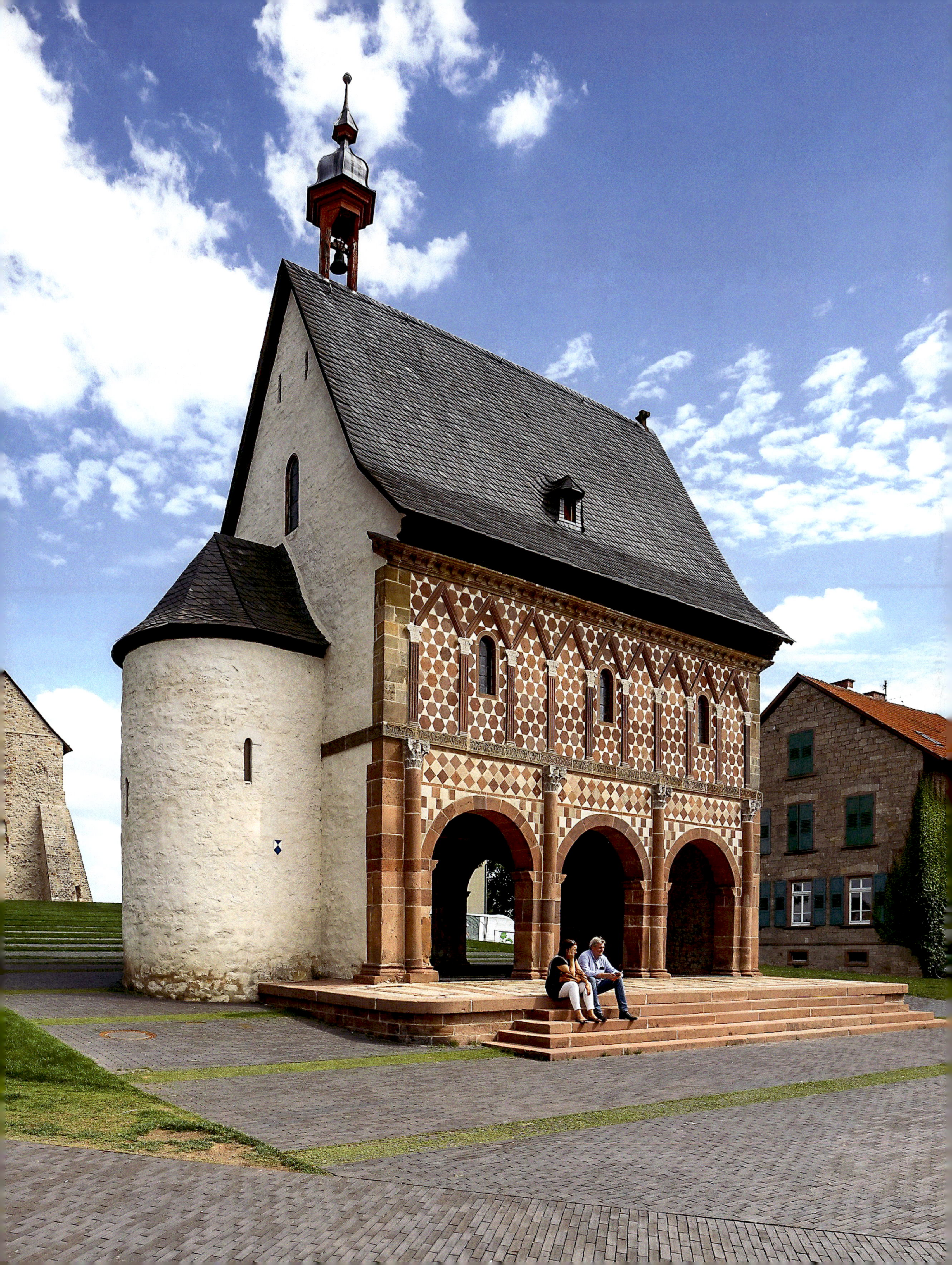

tory etc. – but a magical area of green lawns dotted with the few still extant remnants of the Benedictine abbey, dissolved in 1557. Since the reshaping of the site in 2014 – a much awarded project – the positions of the once impressive buildings of the Carolingian abbey have been marked out on the ground, making the complex of monastery, workshops and service buildings once again, albeit differently, visible.

Founded as a proprietary church and monastery in 764, Lorsch stood continually at the focal point of historical and political events. A clever move in a legal quarrel led to the Benedictine abbey being put under the direct control of Charlemagne, who declared it a royal and imperial abbey in 772. In 1052 Pope Leo IX consecrated the burial place of Ludwig the German and his descendants in the abbey grounds. As well as the usual monastic obligations to pray for the secular rulers and pay due tithes, Lorsch Abbey maintained a famous scriptorium. Here, manuscripts were produced and copied with great skill, and the abbey, with its great library, soon became the leading centre of scriptorial culture on the right bank of the Rhine. The *Lorsch Pharmacopoeia*, since 2013 listed in the UNESCO Memory of the World; the *Lorsch Codex*, a comprehensive charter with the first documentary record of some 4000 places; and the richly illuminated *Codex Aureus or Lorsch Gospels* with its finely worked ivory cover – these are only three of the many important and influential manuscripts from Lorsch Abbey.

Apart from the imposing wall around the enclosure, the remains of the abbey consist of a fragment of the former Church of St. Nazarius and the famous early medieval Gatehouse or King's Hall, whose function and significance, with its coloured masonry and unusual decoration, remains something of a mystery. The Zehntscheune (Tithe Barn), opened as an exhibition hall in 2015, is interesting not only for the archaeological finds displayed there – primarily decorated sculpture – but also for its innovative presentational technique. This takes visitors on a spotlight journey of discovery through the abbey's history. Behind the long barn is a herbarium with herbs and other plants used in medieval medicine.

Landscape framed by arches of the ruined church

Ludwigsburg Residential Palace
One of the largest Baroque palaces in Germany

The approach is grandiose – in its sheer size Ludwigsburg Palace is already impressive. However, its actual dimensions only become apparent when, coming from the Baroque city centre, one crosses the first courtyard. The broad rectangle of the Ehrenhof (courtyard of honour) stretches before one, and a little time is needed to take in the variety of Baroque buildings on each side of the vast space – almost as big as a football field. The former residence of the Dukes of Württemberg has more than 400 rooms, ranging from Early Baroque ceremonial apartments from the era of Eberhard Ludwig, who founded the palace, through fine Rococo interiors, to a unique series of Classicistic rooms from the time of the first Württembergian monarchy. The palace also boasts two churches, a theatre and several museums.

The story began 300 years ago with an ambitious duke who desired a setting that would reflect his self-image as an absolutist ruler. In the event, his initial idea of a hunting lodge was revised so often, and so many wings and subsidiary buildings were added, that it took almost 30 years to complete the palace. Duke Eberhard Ludwig then set about constructing a town to match his residence, a town bearing his own name – Ludwigsburg.

In the mid-18th century another duke, Carl Eugen catapulted provincial Württemberg into the centre of European courtly life – or so the much-travelled adventurer Giacomo Casanova tells us. A lover of the arts, the Duke built a theatre and drew players from across Europe to his court, plunging his duchy into financial disaster but bequeathing to us the oldest still functioning stage machinery in the world. After 250 years that is something of a miracle.

The Napoleonic era changed the face of Europe, and did so to Württemberg's advantage. The duchy substantially extended its territories and the Duke was crowned king. To reflect their new rank, King Friedrich I and Queen Charlotte Mathilde had several apartments in the south wing of the schloss amalgamated and fitted out in the best Classicistic style. These rooms have been preserved in detail down to the present day.

Eagle with royal crown on the inner courtyard fountain – a homage to the Order of the Golden Eagle

Southern gardens with the magnificent garden façade of the new corps de logis

A tour of the magnificent interior can be complemented by a visit to one or more of the palace museums, which display holdings both from the Württemberg State Museum and from the Staatsgalerie Stuttgart. A rarity in the German museum landscape is the Fashion Museum; and the vast holdings of the Ceramics Museum include the world's largest collection of porcelain from the Ludwigsburg manufactory. The Baroque gallery exhibits Italian and German masters of the 17th and 18th centuries. All in all, Ludwigsburg Palace presents the entire cosmos of the courtly world.

Former dining room in the old corps de logis with two Brussels tapestries

Second anteroom in the apartment of Duke Carl Eugen with richly decorated Rococo panelling

A glance into the private apartments of Duke Carl Eugen in the new corps de logis

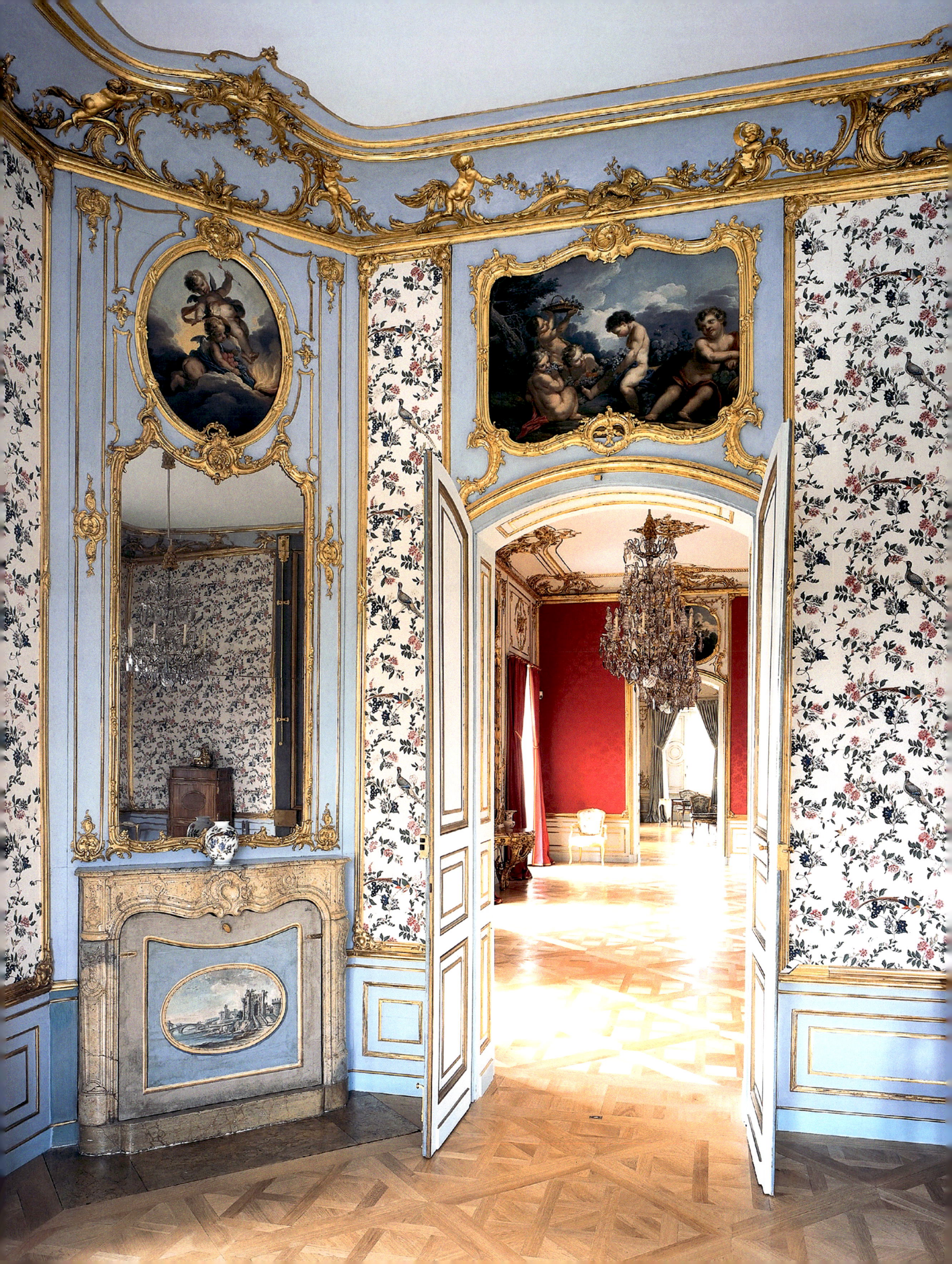

Ludwigshöhe Castle
"A villa in the Italian style"

Ludwigshöhe Castle holds a dominant position overlooking the vineyards and the picturesque small town of Edenkoben in the Palatinate. Set prominently on the hill beneath the ruins of Rietburg Castle, it originally had three buildings, the King's and Cavaliers' Buildings and the Royal Stables. Today only the King's Building remains intact.

The Wittelsbach King Ludwig I of Bavaria is thought to have taken the decision to build a summer residence near Edenkoben in 1843 while travelling through the Palatinate, a region which since 1214 had been part of his domain. He had long wanted "a villa in the Italian style", where he could spend the summer months in the warmest part of his kingdom.

Ludwig commissioned his court architect, Friedrich von Gärtner, to draw up plans, and the foundation stone was duly laid in 1846. But von Gärtner died in 1847 and execution of the plans fell to his successor, Leo von Klenze. After a brief interruption in 1848 – the year of revolutions across Europe – work was resumed and completed in 1852. However, in 1848 an affair with the dancer Lola Montez had led to Ludwig's abdication in favour of his son, Maximilian II Joseph. Nevertheless, in the 20 years until his death in 1868, Ludwig visited his "Italian villa" every other year to celebrate his birthday on August 25.

With its flat roofs and loggias, Ludwigshöhe Castle exactly reflected the King's wishes. Both in its architecture and in the decoration of its ceilings, walls and floors, the references to antiquity are unmistakable – although the impressive Pompeian wall paintings in

View from the south-west

the dining room were a later addition under the regency of Luitpold of Bavaria. The apartments of the king and queen are exquisitely furnished. However, not all the furniture is original; certain items were also transferred to Ludwigshöhe from other Bavarian noble houses in the 1950s under Crown Prince Rupprecht. Most of the paintings in the villa are also acquisitions from recent decades that illustrate the life and times of Ludwig I and the Wittelsbachs.

Since 1980 the work of Max Slevogt has been firmly established at Ludwigshöhe Castle, where it is presented to the public in varying exhibitions. The historical cellar vaults also feature an exhibition of the Hinder-Reimers collection of 20th century ceramics. The elegant ground floor dining room is today used for cultural events, especially for concerts organized by the Villa Musica state foundation.

Above: Main kitchens

Right: Staircase

P. 134 above: Reception room

P. 134 below: Max Slevogt Gallery

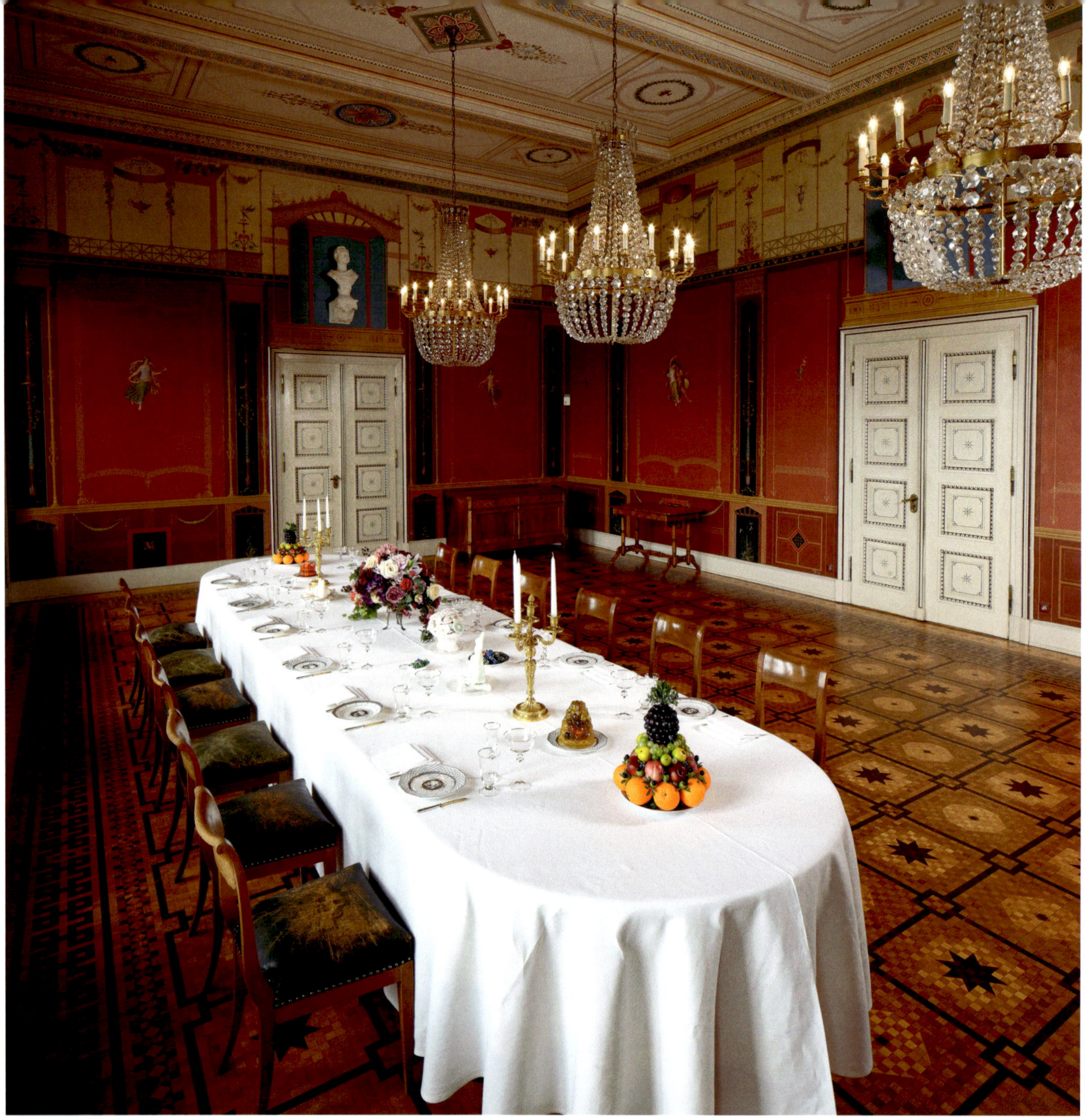

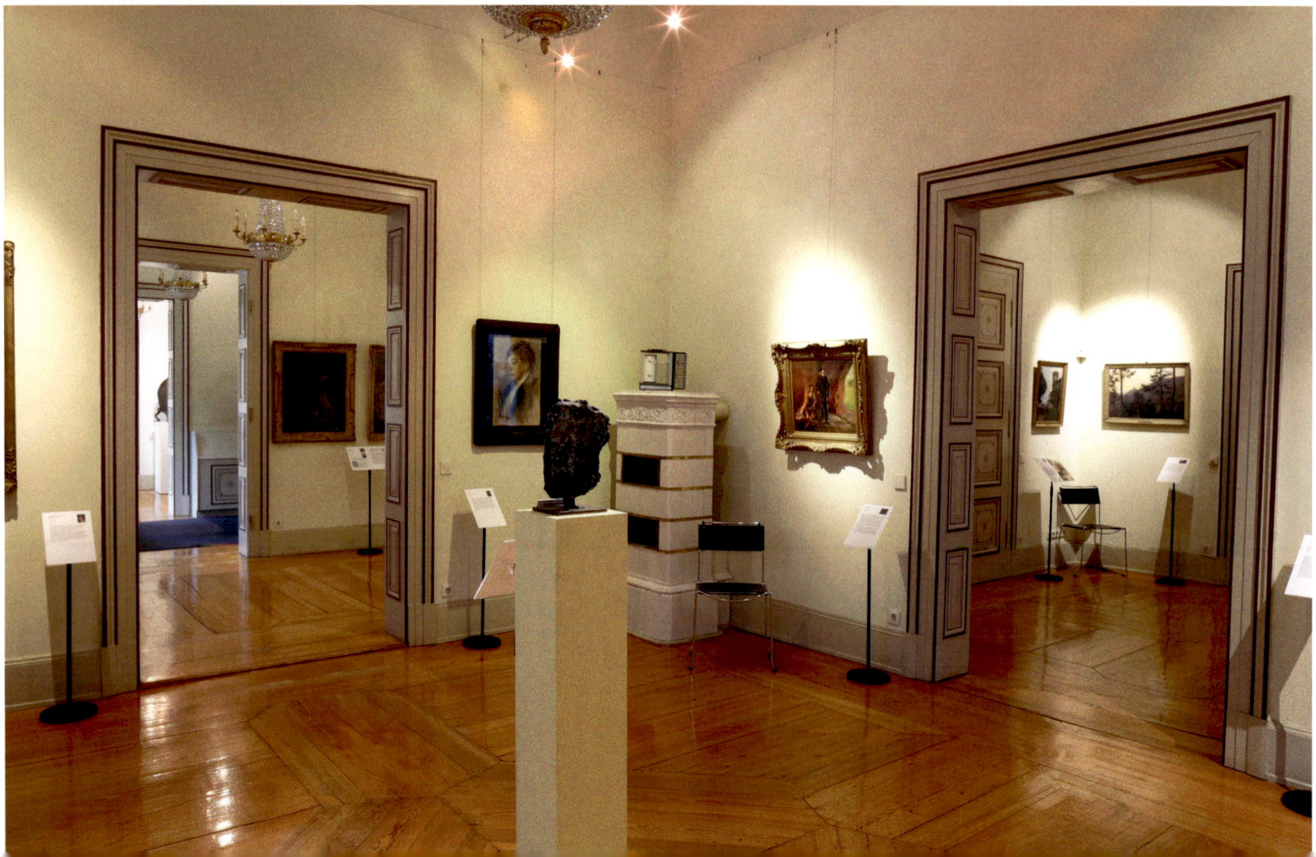

Ludwigslust Palace
Sandstone, gold and papier mâché

For more than 200 years Ludwigslust has exercised a powerful attraction on its visitors. The Irish travel writer Thomas Nugent wrote in 1766: "I must admit, this place has greatly exceeded all my expectations". It all began with a small hunting lodge, built in 1735 in what at the time was still called Klenow. The modest gem was extended several times over the following decades, and Duke Christian II Ludwig named it "Ludwigs-Lust" (Ludwig's Pleasance). In due course his son and successor, Friedrich, withdrew here from his official residence in Schwerin and continued the work his father had begun. Duke Friedrich created a wonderland, extending the gardens and building a new town, complete with its own court church, around the schloss. Finally, between 1772 and 1776 he replaced the existing residence with an entirely new building designed by the leading French architect Jean Laurent Le Geay.

As a result, Ludwigslust Palace today is a uniquely impressive Late-Absolutist ensemble. The ducal residence is embedded within strictly ordered sightlines. To the front these take in the church and town across multiple cascades of water, and to the back they embrace the palace gardens against a backdrop of carefully styled nature. The fascinating interplay of these elements invites the visitor, after investigating the treasures of the house, to take a stroll in the extensive park. Landscaped in the English fashion, this still reveals its underlying Baroque structure as an aesthetic synthesis of nature, horticultural art and flowing water.

After five years of unstinting labour, eighteen rooms of the east wing have been newly designed to display artworks of every category. The focal point of the palace is the Golden Hall, where monumental Corinthian columns, richly ornamented mirrors, priceless crystal candelabras, and a magnificently restored parquet floor demonstrate the social and political claims of the ducal family and take the visitor back to bygone days of lavish balls and concerts. The picture gallery is especially impressive: After removal of later additions, the room, resplendent in its former glory, makes a fitting background for numerous works

Avenues, canals and special water-features adorn the park.

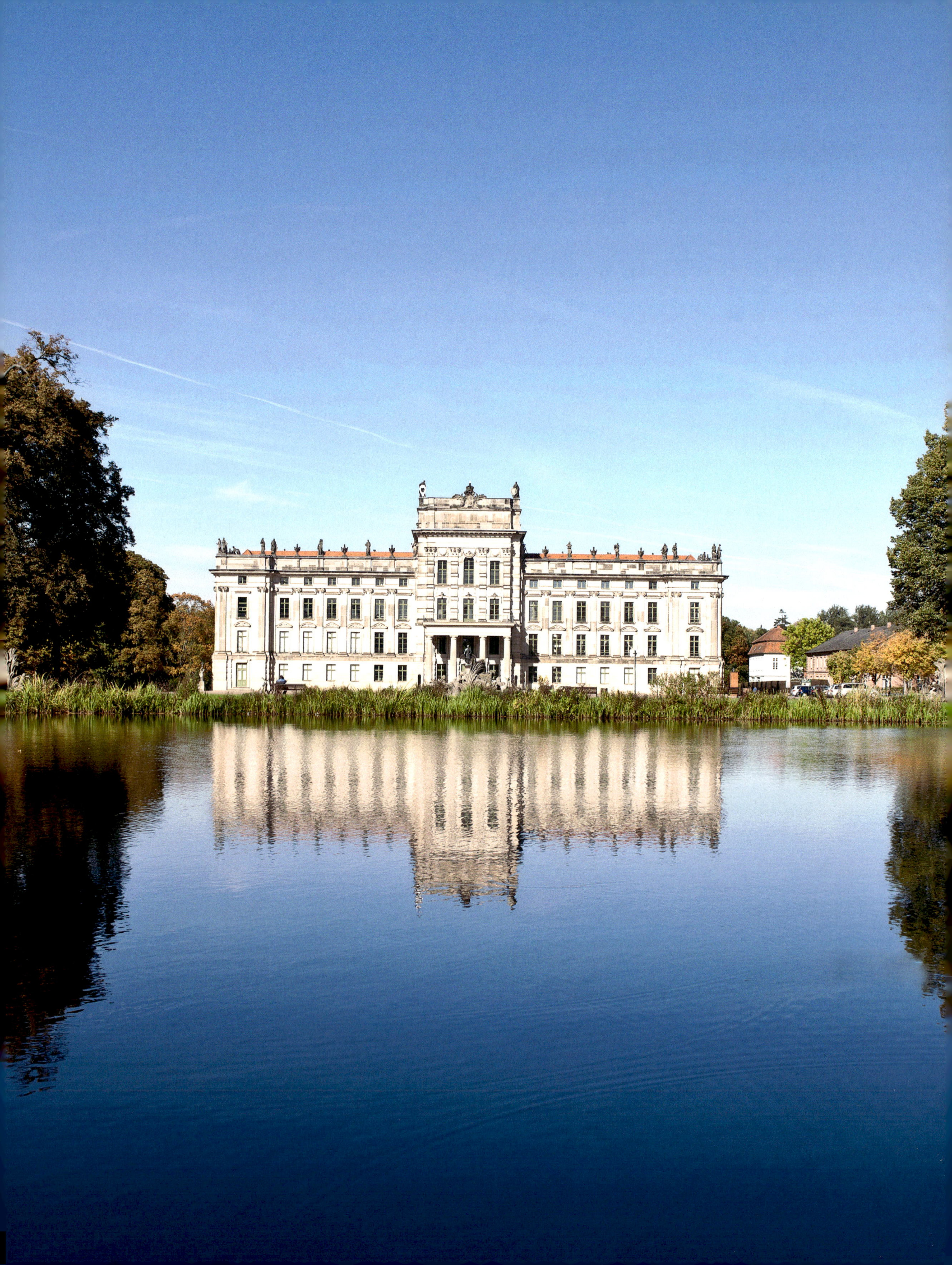

by Frans Snyders, Bernardo Bellotto and Johann Dietrich Findorff, among others. Most of the guest apartments on the second floor had three rooms, of which the largest served as a living room. With their pale turquoise damask wall coverings, white wood panelling set off with papier mâché gold decorations, and fine marquetry flooring, they allow the works of the Ludwigslust court painters and of the French hunting-scene specialist Jean-Baptiste Oudry to be experienced with a new intensity. Further items of interest include busts by Jean-Antoine Houdon, valuable furniture and ivory, and the ducal collection of clocks and watches.

Ludwigslust is one of North Germany's biggest Late Baroque palaces.

Centrepiece of the palace – the magnificent Golden Hall

Guest rooms contain well-known works by Jean-Baptiste Oudry from the State Museum of Schwerin.

137

Mainau Island

Baroque splendour, botanical treasures

Among the highlights of a visit to Mainau Island, as well as its park and gardens, is the Baroque complex of palace, courtyard and church. The ensemble has been the very heart of the island for more than 250 years. Mainau Palace is itself not just a living witness of Baroque splendour, but is nowadays also used as a venue for exhibitions, events and conferences. Apart from these functions, it serves as the residence of the comital family and as a manufactory of fashionable millinery created by the atelier of Countess Diana Bernadotte.

For a total of 534 years (1272–1806), Mainau belonged to the Teutonic Order, and the island's image was mainly characterised by viticulture and the cultivation of land, vegetables and fruits rather than ornamental plants. In the mid-18th century, the Order commissioned the master builder Johann Caspar Bagnato with the erection of a monument to its presence on the island: first a church in the Baroque style, consecrated in 1739, and subsequently Mainau Palace, completed in 1746 as a residence of representative grandeur with three wings and a stately forecourt. The splendid coats of arms dominating the central façade towards both lakefront and courtyard still remind today's visitors of the power of its builders. The palace's centrepiece is the White Hall in the central wing, a room whose walls and ceiling are decorated completely in white and gold. In 1883, the Teutonic Order's former audience chamber received its present shape. In 2003, Mainau Island was in its entirety placed under protection as a historical monument, and a part of the island – including Mainau Palace and the Palace Church St. Marien – was registered in the book of monuments "as a cultural landmark of special significance".

Considered as the founder of Mainau Park with its botanical treasures, Grand Duke Friedrich I of Baden purchased the island in 1853. Not only did he and his wife Luise establish Mainau Island as their summer residence, but they started to redevelop the place by, for instance, having rare and exotic conifers and deciduous trees planted from all over the world. Essential elements of the present-day park, like the arboretum or the Italian Rose Garden – once a flower garden in the Italian style – date back to that period, as do the first winter con-

The Fountain Arena offers a unique panoramic view of Lake Constance and its landscape.

servatories for exotic plants. The Duke's great-grandson, Count Lennart Bernadotte, born a Swedish prince, made it his life's work to develop Mainau into a Flower Island. From 1932 onward, he gradually shaped the island in harmony with nature and opened its doors to tourists. Today, Countess Bettina and Count Björn Bernadotte, two of his children, are the managing directors of Mainau Island, which welcomes about 1.2 million visitors to Lake Constance every year.

Mainau Palace with the Palace Church St. Marien

Grand Duke Friedrich I of Baden had the Italian Rose Garden built in the 1860s.

P. 140: The Italian Floral Water Cascade was modelled on Italian Renaissance gardens.

The White Hall is the centrepiece of Mainau Palace.

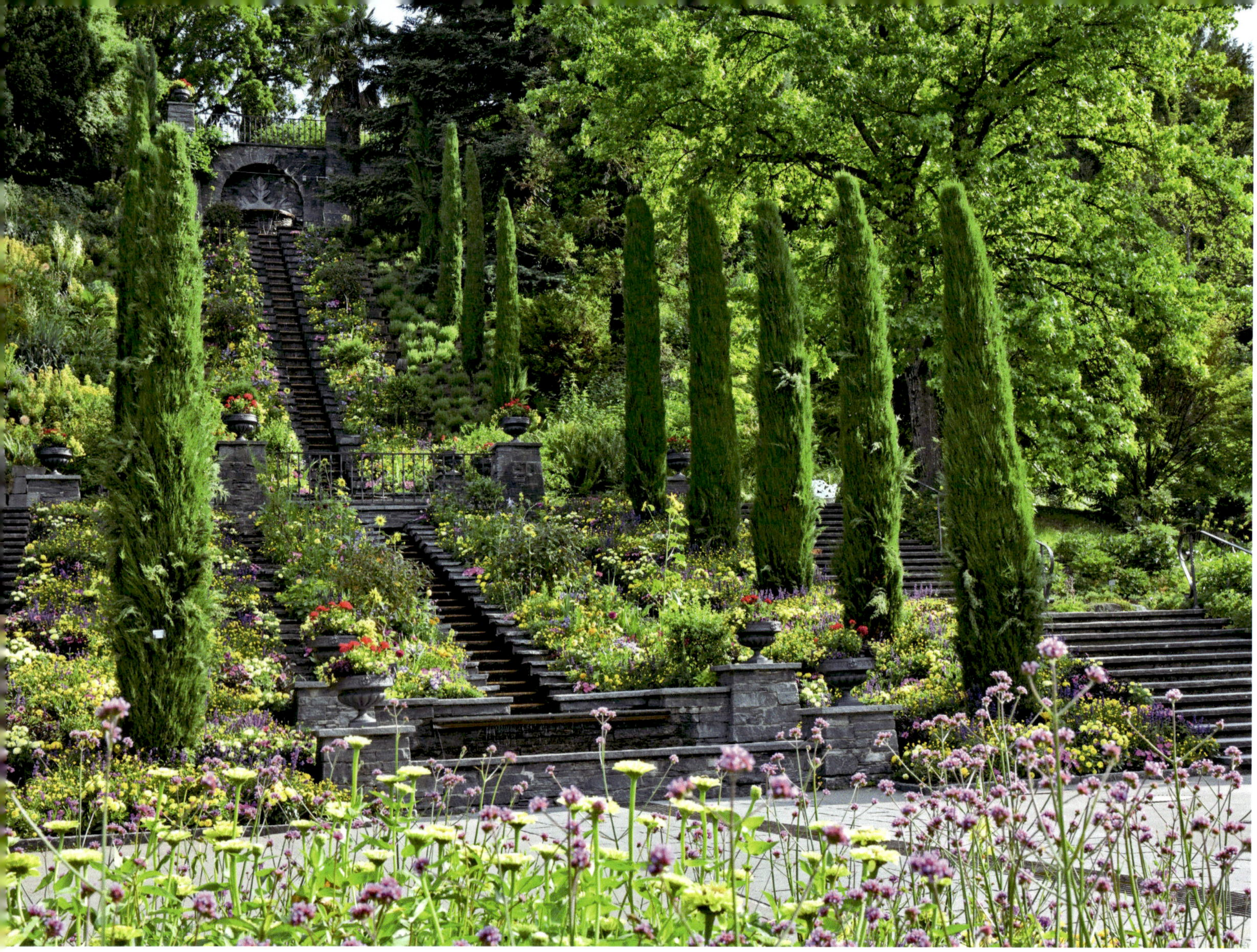

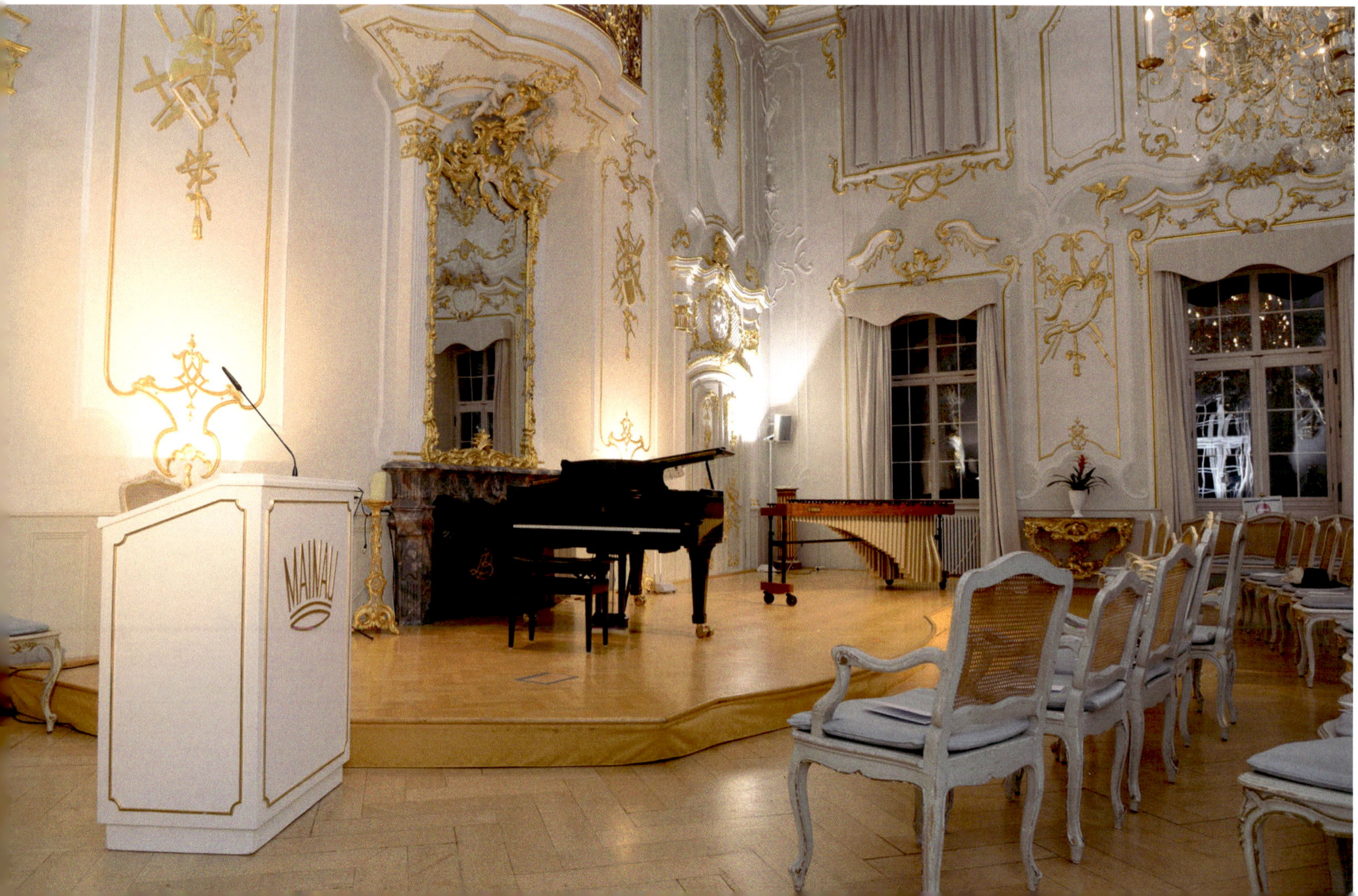
MAINAU

Marienburg Castle
Seat of the Royal House of Guelph

Visible from a considerable distance, Marienburg Castle, North Germany's only royal castle, crowns the south-western slopes of the Marienberg, a prominent hill to the south of Hanover and north-west of Hildesheim. The summer residence of the Guelphs, Europe's oldest noble line, the castle was built between 1858 and 1867 by King Georg V, the last monarch of the Kingdom of Hanover. The romantic castle with its charming variety of towers, roofs and façades and its richly appointed interior has been authentically preserved. It ranks as one of Germany's prime neo-Gothic monuments.

On her 40th birthday, in 1857, King Georg V (1819–1878) made his wife, Queen Marie (1818–1907), a present of Schulenburg Hill – thereafter to be called Marienberg – with the promise of a castle to be built there to her own specifications as the family's summer residence. The site chosen by the king was not only idyllic, it was close to both the ancient dynastic castle of the Guelphs at Calenberg and the monarch's formal residence in Hanover. The king entrusted construction of the castle to the master builder Conrad Wilhelm Hase, but at the queen's wish the task was later assumed by a pupil of Hase's, the architect Edwin Oppler.

In 1866 war broke out between the kingdoms of Hanover and Prussia. Severe military losses forced Georg to capitulate, and when the war ended he went into exile with his son, Crown Prince Ernst August, to Austria. As a gesture of resistance, Queen Marie and her daughters Friederike and Mary remained in Hanover. But only a year later the queen was given notice that she was to receive a formal visit from the Prussian court. To avoid this humiliation, she and her daughters followed her husband into exile on July 23, 1867. Thereafter, Marienburg Castle remained uninhabited for almost 80 years until 1945. Then, after the end of the Second World War, a grandson of Marie and Georg V, Duke Ernst August of Brunswick-Lüneburg, moved into the house with his wife Viktoria Luise, daughter of Kaiser Wilhelm II, for twelve years.

Today Marienburg Castle, with its countless towers and pinnacles and its glorious apartments, is an attrac-

A treasured birthday present from the last Hanoverian king to his wife, Queen Marie

141

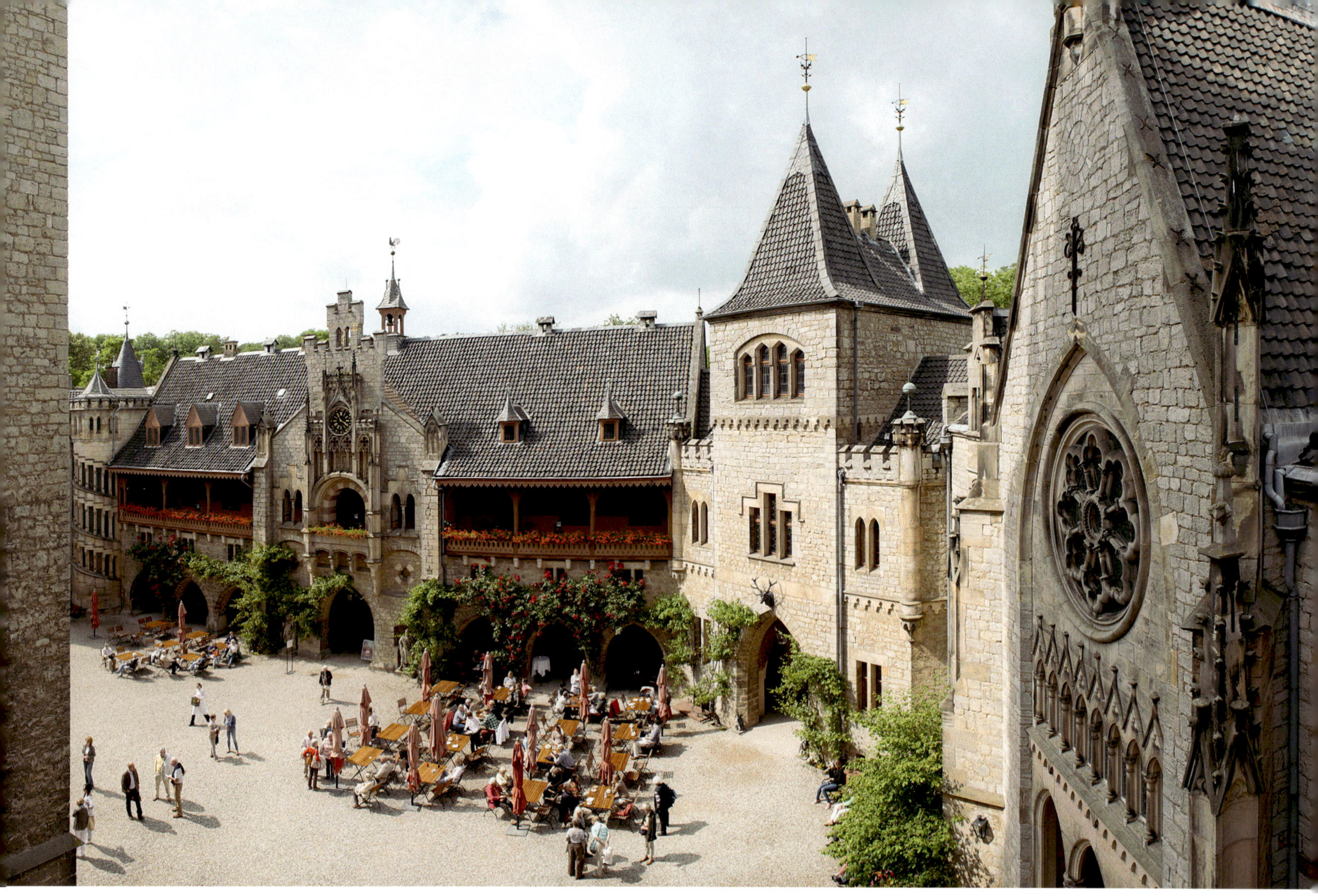

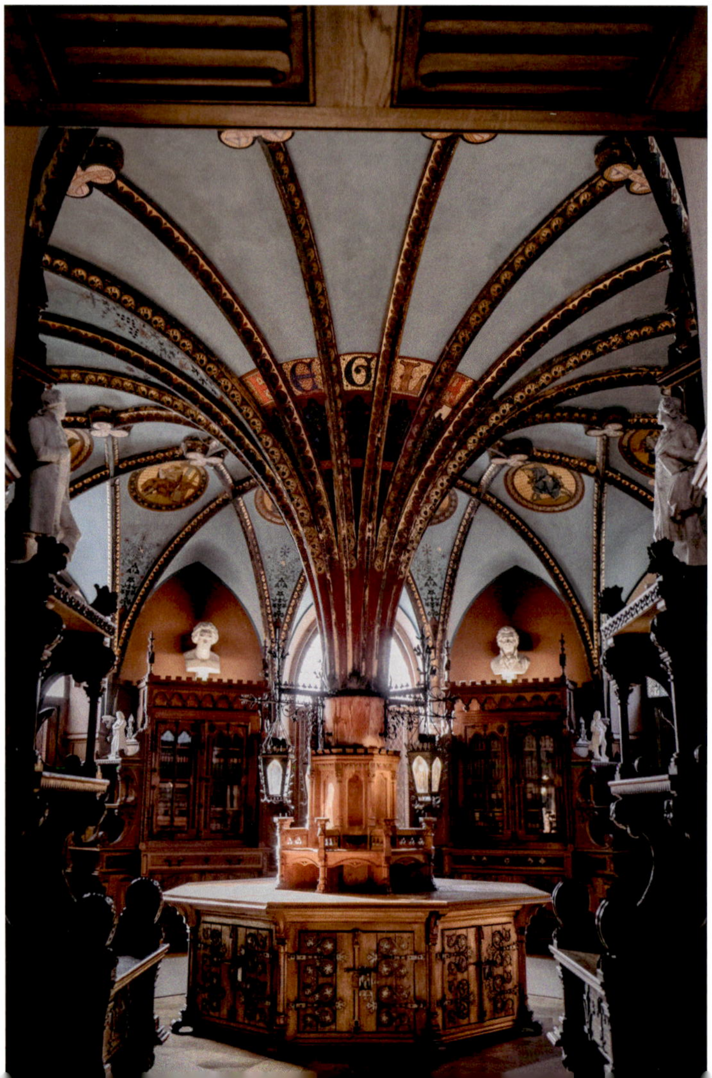

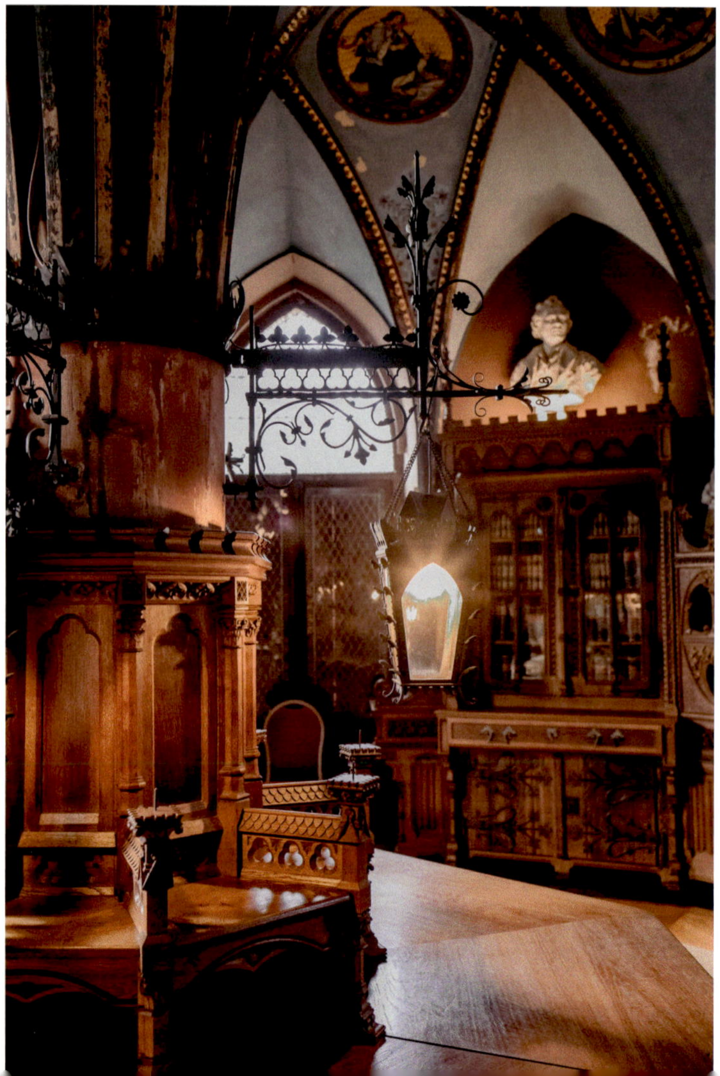

tive destination for visitors from every corner of the globe and a unique setting for events. With its virtually intact interior furnishings, it enjoys an outstanding place in the German castle landscape.

The inner courtyard – a backdrop full of atmosphere, not only for open-air events

Lavishly adorned with painted medallions and gold leaf, the vaulted ceiling of the castle library branches out like an umbrella.

With its copper pans and vessels, the castle kitchen has remained unchanged since its last use in 1867.

The interior furnishings from the time of the royal couple have been preserved virtually intact.

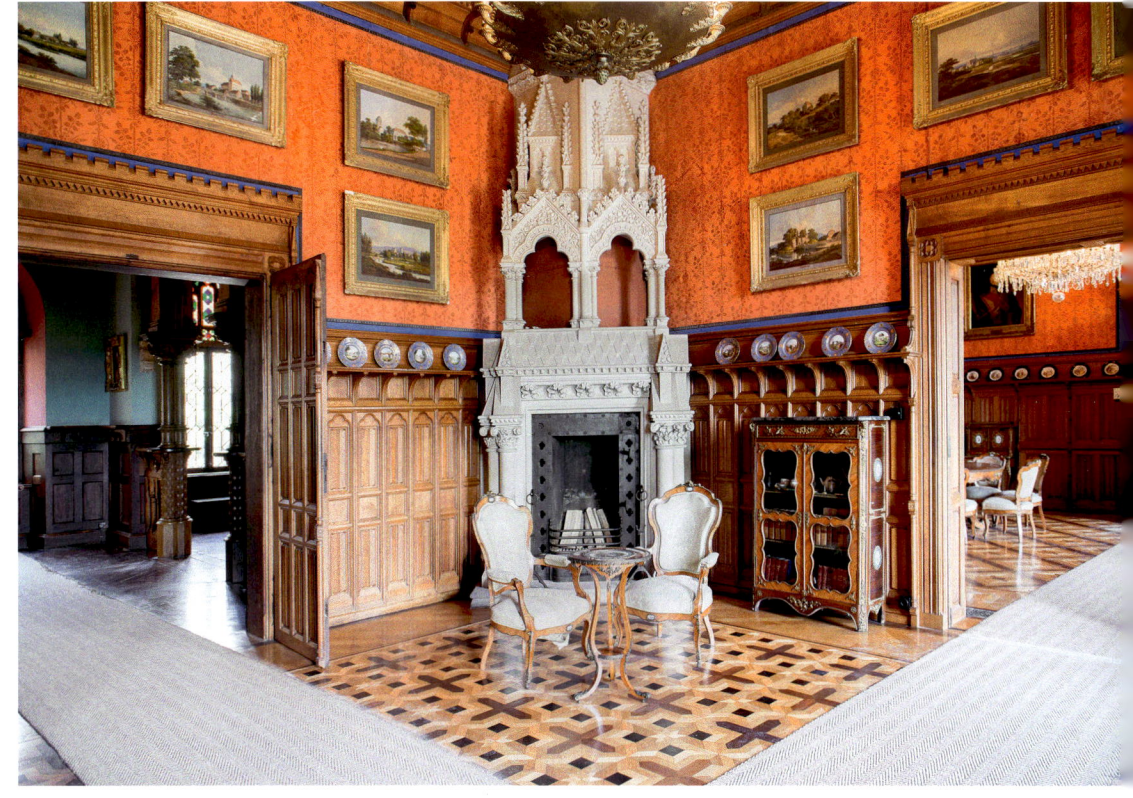

Marksburg

Home of the German Castles Association

The Upper Middle Rhine Valley between Rüdesheim and Koblenz, adopted by UNESCO as a "world heritage site", boasts more castles along its course than almost any other European region. Many, once desolate ruins, were rebuilt or restored in the Romantic age. Marksburg is the only medieval hilltop castle on the Rhine that was never destroyed, and as such a monument of national significance.

Its dominant position on a steep outcrop of rock above the romantic little town of Braubach, near Koblenz, and its excellent state of preservation, make Marksburg – which is open all year round – the most visited castle on the Rhine. It exemplifies the development from high medieval defensive fort to Early Modern bastioned stronghold, and its furnishings, too, graphically illustrate life in a late medieval castle.

The heart of the castle complex was erected in the first half of the 13th century by the Counts of Eppstein; then in 1283 the Counts of Katzenelnbogen acquired the property. In 1479 it passed by inheritance to the Landgraves of Hesse, who, not wanting to live there themselves, took steps to transform the medieval castle into a contemporary fortress. From 1803 Marksburg served the Duchy of Nassau as a prison, until in 1866 it was taken over by Prussia. In 1900 it was purchased by the German Castles Association, which had been founded the previous year.

Evolving over the course of centuries, the castle precincts, with their buildings, towers, and double curtain wall, are grouped around the summit of the rock. Entering the castle, the visitor passes through four gates and crosses a number of baileys before reaching the castle core with its Romanesque Great Hall (1239) and Gothic residential quarters (1435). Here the keep rises almost 40 metres above the central courtyard, which also contains the polygonal chapel tower (1371) and an early 18th century timber-frame building. This central part

Marksburg, the only true hilltop castle in the Valley of the Loreley, stands 90 metres above the Rhine.

Philippsburg Palace, built at the foot of the castle rock as a later complement to Marksburg, has belonged to the German Castles Association since 1997.

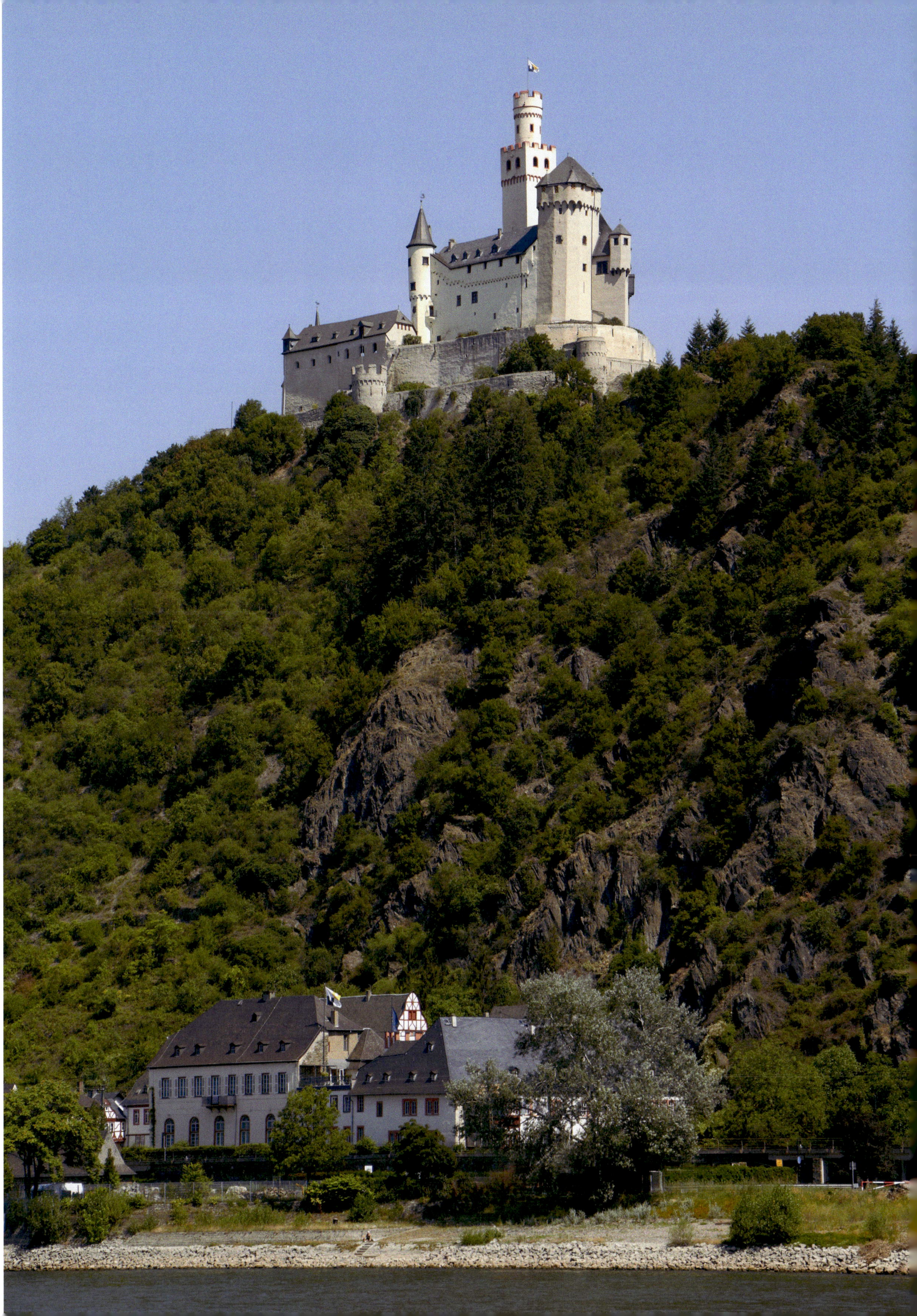

of the castle is surrounded by a system of defensive walls and corridors, half-towers and bastions.

As well as its authentically equipped rooms – including kitchens, ladies' bower, knights' hall, chapel, wine cellar, and smithy – Marksburg possesses a unique collection of 14 warrior figures illustrating the development of armour from the Bronze Age to the Early Modern period. Also of interest is the medieval botanical garden in the bailey, with its 150 medicinal, magical and culinary herbs, and the cannon battery, from which a magnificent view opens onto the Rhine Valley 90 metres below.

This impressive castle has now been owned for more than a century by the German Castles Association, Germany's oldest private supra-regional body dedicated to the conservation of monuments. The associations offices are in the Romanesque Great Hall.

On the banks of the Rhine at the foot of the castle rock stands Philippsburg Palace, a Renaissance palace built c. 1570 as dowager residence of the Landgraves of Hesse. Today it is home to the European Castles Institute, part of the German Castles Association.

Left: The castle chapel, with its elaborate star vaulting and reconstructed frescoes (1903), is situated in the Chapel Tower (1371).

Top: Window nook in the Ladie's Bower of the Gothic residence (1435).

A Marksburg highlight is the collection of 14 historical warrior figures (1880).

146

Maulbronn Monastery

UNESCO World Heritage Site with a vibrant atmosphere

Set amidst the woods and vineyards of Stromberg-Heuchelberg Nature Park, Maulbronn Monastery, a masterly achievement of medieval Cistercian monasticism has, along with valuable traces of monastic agriculture, been preserved almost intact to the present day – reason enough for UNESCO to adopt the entire complex as early as 1993 onto its list of World Cultural Heritage Sites.

The former monastery contains some wonderful art treasures. One of these, created around 1220 in the earliest phase of Gothic building, is the narthex (porch) of the church. Known as the "Paradise", it has given this name to the unknown master who designed it. But other aspects of the monastery also justifiably excite admiration: the cloisters with the famous triple-basin fountain, the monks' refectory (dining hall) with its fine rib-vaulted ceiling and, of course, the awesome monastery church itself, whose doors date back 800 years to the time of its construction – the oldest datable doors in Germany.

It all began with a legend, according to which the noble founder of the monastery sent out a mule laden with a sack of money. The monastery was to be built where the mule stopped; and it stopped by a spring of water. Old documents actually call the place Mulenbrunnen (mule fount), although this is more likely a variant for Mühlenbrunnen (mill fount). At all events it is an indication of the presence of the water needed by the monks for their life and labour – an essential prerequisite for a Cistercian settlement. The Cistercian order was particularly renowned for its sophisticated use of water. Maulbronn has retained a great deal of the system of lakes, ponds and canals laid down by the medieval monks. Even today this defines the surroundings of the former monastery .

Another still living monastic tradition is the cultivation of vines and wine-making: the old monastery vineyards are visible from the courtyard. Eilfinger Hill, for example, already worked by the Cistercian monks, provides one of the region's best known wines. For today's visitors to Maulbronn, this particular tradition may also afford some moments of enjoyment.

Today the ancient walls of Maulbronn Monastery have housed pupils of the abbey school longer than they ever

Cloister garden with Brunnenhaus (fountain house) and west wing of cloisters

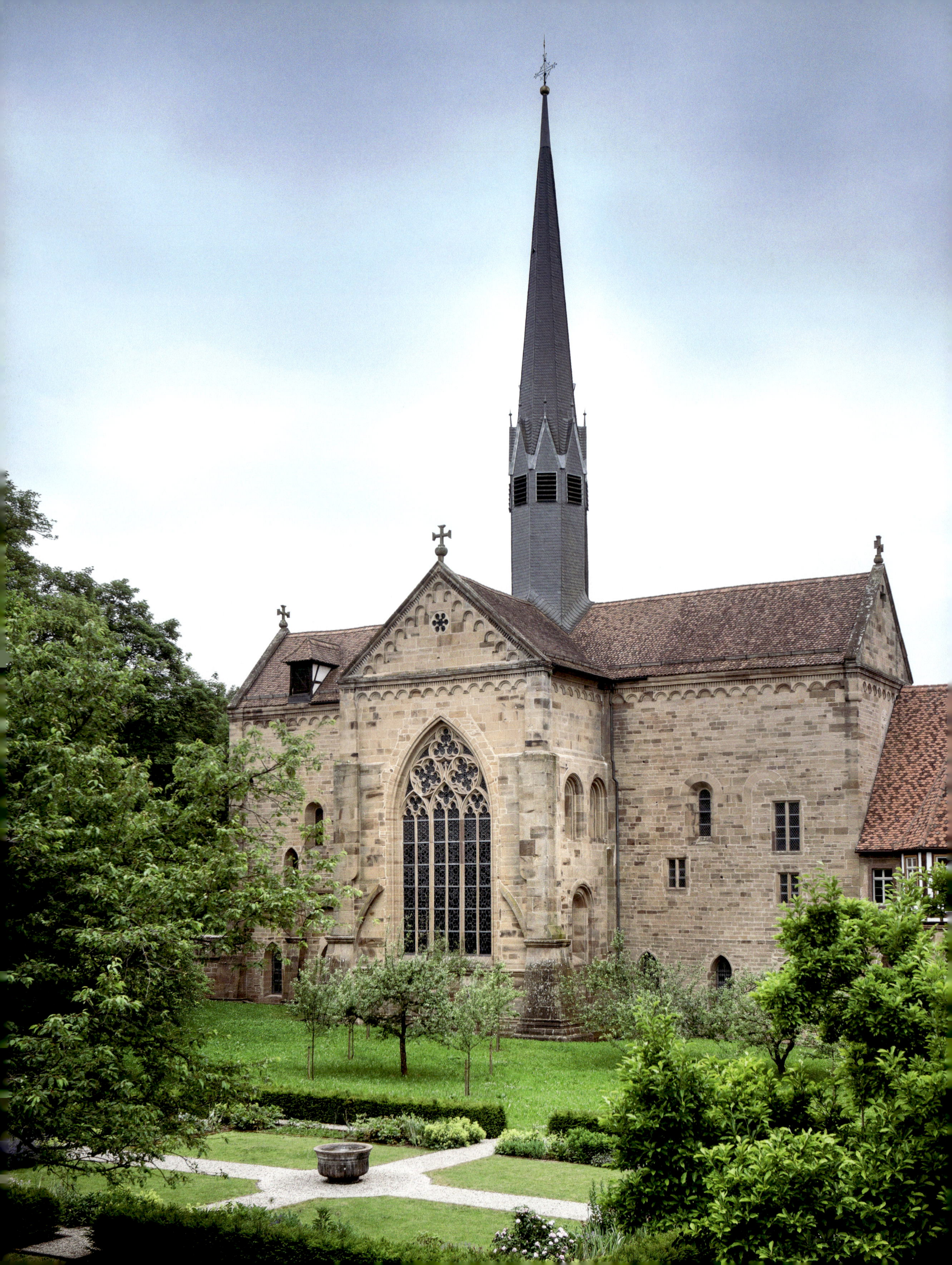

did Cistercian monks. The school was opened soon after the Reformation, and since 1969 girls have also been admitted. For 450 years it has existed as a pioneering Protestant boarding (high) school, accepting talented students without regard to their origins. Its most famous alumnus is undoubtedly Hermann Hesse, who depicted his unhappy schooldays in his novel *Unterm Rad (Beneath the Wheel)*. That his work is read as a standard text in Japanese schools may explain the remarkably high proportion of Japanese tourists who find their way to rural Maulbronn.

Monastery church with monks' choir and garden of the "Ephorus" (school principal)

Monumental nave of the monastery church with choir screen

North and west cloisters with High Gothic window tracery

A Cultural Landscape of Manorial Estates and Houses

Mecklenburg-Western Pomerania

The land east of the River Elbe is a region of large agricultural estates. Here, beginning with the eastward colonization of the 12th century, a cultural landscape unique in Europe has developed. Mecklenburg-Western Pomerania has more than 2000 castles, manor houses and parks, half of them listed as protected monuments. Nowhere else in Europe are there so many of these estates; nowhere is the almost thousand-year heritage of their villages so marked as in this region.

The nobles serving Duke Henry III (the Lion) of Saxony mingled through intermarriage with the native Slav nobility to create the rooted Mecklenburgian aristocracy. The same names frequently recur as enfeoffed by the grand dukes who later ruled the region: The von Oertzens, von Maltzahns, von Bülows, von Plessens, von Hahns, von Bassewitzes and von Blüchers came in this way to own vast tracts of land. And with the growing wealth of the Early Modern period (post-16th century) the houses on these estates between the Peene and Elbe grew in size and splendour. The Thirty Years' War boosted the noble estates still further, and by the late 18th century they were the defining element in the Mecklenburgian landscape.

Change as opportunity

The first caesura for the landed aristocracy came with their dispossession at the end of the Second World War in 1945. Under the GDR regime most of the great houses were used as schools, community centres or administrative offices of the local LPG (Agricultural Production Cooperative); others were left derelict, and the land of the former estates was in any case separated from the old manor houses; in some cases a modern apartment block was set directly in front of the house. With the political turnaround of German reuni-

Built c. 1880, Alt Sammit Manor lies amid the woods of Mecklenburg's lakeland.

Set on the crown of a hill, the former seat of the Count von Schlitz is surrounded by a landscaped park with a chapel and obelisks.

Typical of the region, an avenue of trees leads to the manor-house at Stolpe an der Peene, which once belonged to the families von Bülow and Maltzahn.

Built in the Tudor style, Vogelsang Manor serves today as a splendid backdrop for events and weddings.

151

fication in 1989–90 a new era opened. Many private investors and enthusiasts for listed heritage buildings cooperated to restore these properties, and today several hundred manor houses are once more privately owned and used, or serve cultural or tourist purposes.

Idyllic vacations in historic buildings

Far from the turmoil of everyday life – and equally far from the one-time "Junkers" or landed gentry – the rural spaces of Mecklenburg-Western Pomerania, with their characteristic manorial villages, offer gems of individual hospitality. These are places that have been converted with passion and creativity into very special hotels, holiday apartments, or cultural centres. In each of these houses one feels the history, not only of past centuries, but also of more recent upheavals and the visions they have stimulated. With such a wide range of accommodations and settings, potential guests can choose between luxury and modern simplicity, or can tour – on foot, by bicycle, or by car – from one former estate to another. They can look forward to relaxing, at the end of a journey through legendary landscapes, in a beautiful old manor house.

A lime-tree avenue leads directly from the neo-Classical manor house in Gross Schwansee to the Baltic.

View of the tower of Kaarz Manor House against the background of the park

Ludorf Manor House on the Müritz, built in the style of the Danish "clinker-brick Renaissannce", is one of the oldest in the region.

Mirow Palace

A Baroque and Rococo jewel

Set on a picturesque islet in Mecklenburg's lakeland, Mirow Palace was built c. 1709 as the dowager seat of Duchess Christiane Aemilie Anthonie of Mecklenburg-Strelitz. From outside, the mansion appears modestly idyllic, but it cherishes memories of eccentric dukes and powerful duchesses, and of princesses who left to become queens. The Prussian King Frederick the Great liked to refer to his Strelitz neighbours rather disrespectfully as the "Miroquois". However, the youngest of them, Princess Charlotte, spent her last night in Mirow on August 17, 1761; on the following day she left home to become queen of Britain. Mirow Palace is the sole witness to her origins and the birth of the Strelitz dynasty.

The manifold importance of Mirow for the history of art is only evident from inside the mansion. At the heart of the building, the High Baroque state room by the Italian stucco master Giovanni Battista Clerici has been preserved in all its glory. Unexpected in these interiors are elements of so-called Frederician Rococo. Frederick's entry into the Seven Years' War in 1756 brought with it an almost complete cessation of his building activities, and the artists and craftsmen he had hitherto employed

Mirow Palace – set on a picturesque islet in Mecklenburg's lakeland

153

now sought contracts outside Prussia. This quirk of history accounts for a new phase of interior decoration in Mirow between 1756 and 1761, when Duchess Elisabeth Albertine had her apartments reappointed with original Frederician fittings of the highest quality. Mirow Palace takes its place in that respect in one of 18th century Europe's most famous design phenomena. Another interesting aspect of the house's décor is its hand-embroidered or flower-strewn wall coverings.

The peace of the park is a delightful complement to any visit. Here one strolls pleasurably along twisting paths and Baroque avenues, by the lakeside or on Lovers' Island. The idyllic natural environment joins its impact with the traces of the past. Mansion and park form a single whole enriched with two further architectonic gems: the Renaissance Gatehouse and the Church of the Order of St. John, which contains the burial vault of the Ducal House of Strelitz. The Baroque Cavaliers' House opposite the palace contains a visitors' centre and café. Further gastronomic facilities are also available, as are boat moorings and trips on the lake.

Lovers' Island radiates idyllic peace.

Fresh and modern, the exhibition relates the history of the palace and its visitors.

Mirococo – Mirow's Palace interiors show all the splendour of the Baroque and Rococo.

WITWE UND BAUHERRIN   WITWE UND REGENTIN

DIE BAUHERRIN
THE PATRON

DIE REGENTIN
THE REGENT

Moritzburg Castle

A fairy-tale castle and its treasures

Only twenty minutes by car from the centre of Dresden, Moritzburg Castle and its small counterpart, the Moritzburg Little Pheasant Castle, lie amidst a dream landscape of lakes and forests in one of the city's most popular recreational areas.

Moritzburg Castle in winter – the season when it mounts its popular exhibition on the fairytale film "Three Wishes for Cinderella", partly filmed here.

In 1542 Duke Maurice of Saxony had a Renaissance-style hunting lodge built on a granite hillock in the Friede Forest, an area rich in game and venison. The lodge, later named after its founder, soon became the centre of Saxon hunting society.

However, Elector Augustus the Strong had other plans for Moritzburg, and 1723 saw the start of major rebuilding works that would convert the Renaissance lodge into a Baroque palace dedicated to hunting and pleasure. Here the Elector planned to hold his untrammelled celebrations, with opulent banquets and hunting feasts. His dream was to erect a "temple to Diana" surrounded by enclosures of exotic animals – lions, cheetahs and wisents (European bison) – and lakes on which sea battles would be re-enacted before him. He commissioned the architect Matthaeus Daniel Poeppelmann to realize his vision, and the best craftsmen and artists of Saxony worked to embellish the seven stately halls and more than 200 rooms of the Castle.

Around 1800, a great grandson of the Elector determined to set the Castle in a more fitting and harmonious landscape. He built the Moritzburg Little Pheasent Castle with its nearby harbour and lighthouse with pier on Lower Great Lake Baernsdorf. From 1933 until the dispossession of the House of Wettin in 1945, Moritzburg was the residence of Prince Ernest Henry of Saxony. He and his sons buried some of the palace treasures in the castle, but – with a few exceptions – these were found and confiscated by advancing Soviet forces. However, in 1996 several crates of bejewelled goldsmiths' work were discovered by hobby archaeologists and ascribed to the "Wettin treasure".

Valuable porcelain, furniture and paintings still impressively testify to the domestic and dining culture of the 18th century court. Large format painted and ornamented leather tapestries make the reception rooms of the Castle a veritable picture book of ancient myth, and one of Europe's most copious collections of hunting trophies recalls the passion for the chase shared by Wettin rulers and their guests. As well as the recently reopened Porcelain Quarter, a further high-point of any visit is the legendary Feather Room with the splendid bed of Augustus the Strong, a masterpiece adorned with tapestries of almost two million coloured feathers.

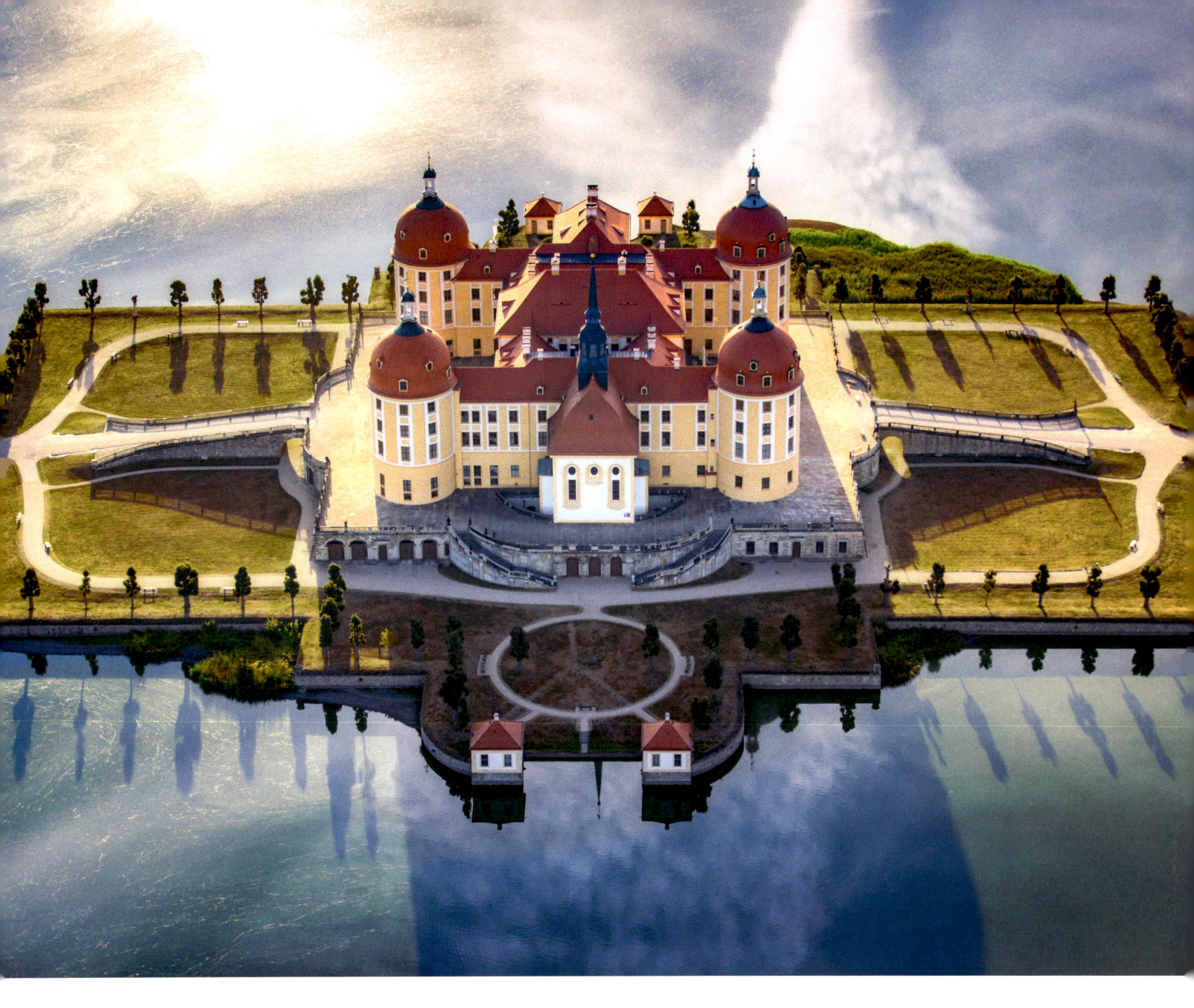

It is, however, above all in winter that Moritzburg Castle draws the crowds, with its exhibition entitled "Three Wishes for Cinderella", where visitors can rediscover the magic of one of the world's loveliest fairytale movies in the setting where it was filmed.

Set idyllically on an artificial island, Moritzburg Castle served not only as a hunting lodge but also for extravagant feasting.

P. 158 top: The Banqueting Hall, its table set with Meissen porcelain, presents a unique vision of the courtly ambience of Schloss Moritzburg society.

P. 158 bottom: The Hall of Monstrosities, with its collection of abnormal antlers, so calles monstrosities, and a view into the Stone Hall

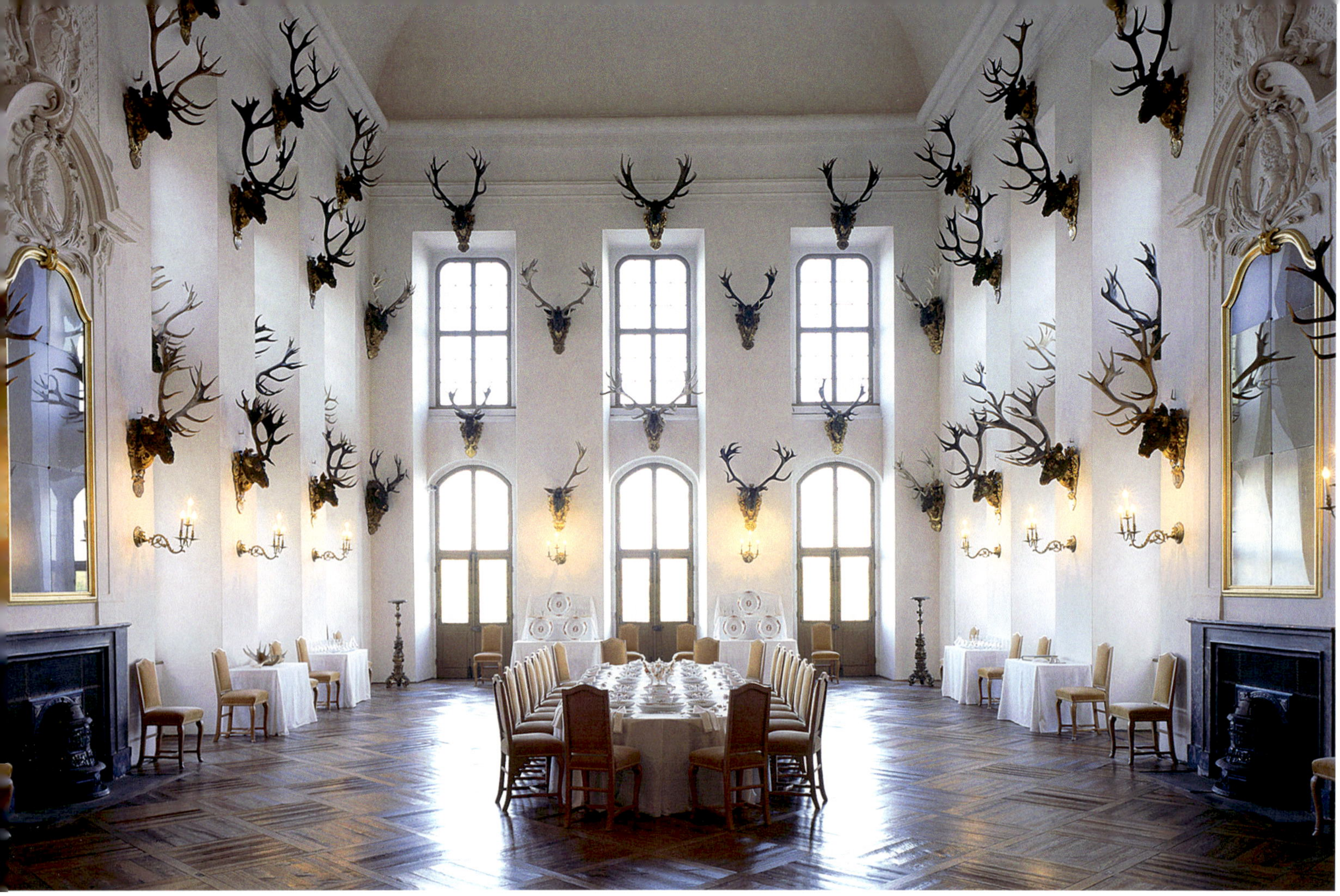

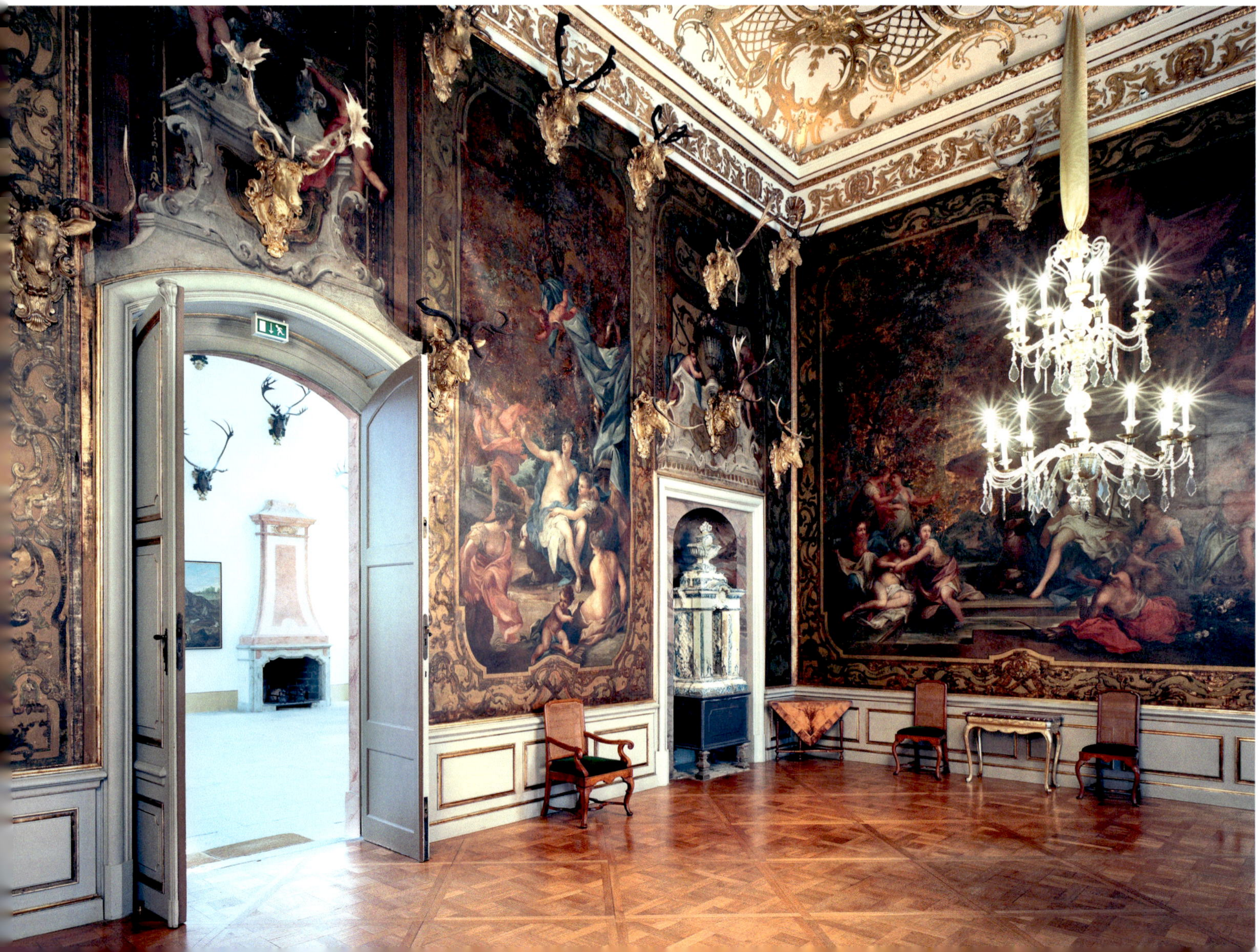

Oettingen Castle

A noble residence in an enchanting town

On the northern edge of Ries Geopark, at the heart of the small timber-frame town of Oettingen, lies a fine 17th century Baroque castle. Its richly decorated interiors reflect the standing of its princely house and form a fitting background to the Residence Concerts whose fame reaches well beyond the region of Oettingen.

First mentioned in deeds of 1141, the House of Oettingen is one of Bavaria's oldest still extant noble families. The important European role of the counts – and later princes – of that line grew above all through the marriages arranged for her daughters by Princess Christine Louise zu Oettingen-Oettingen (1671–1747): Her daughter Elisabeth Christine married Emperor Charles VI, father of Empress Maria Theresa of Austria; a second daughter, Charlotte Christine Sophie, married Alexei, the son of Peter the Great and heir to the Russian throne; one of her granddaughters married King Frederick II (the Great) of Prussia, and another King Frederick V of Denmark.

The family inheritance split on several occasions, giving rise to different lines and different stately homes. Schloss Oettingen, residence of the Oettingen-Spielberg line and still in their possession, was built between 1679 and 1687. The master builder Mathias Weiss from Kassel was in charge of the project; the magnificent stucco work was created by Mathias Schmuzer from Wessobrunn – the ceiling stucco in the light-flooded state room is an outstanding example of Early South German Baroque. Every year between May and October the architecture and acoustics of this room delight musicians and audiences from all over the world.

The castle and its special exhibition are only open to visitors on guided tours. These take in the former domestic apartments of the Prince and his family, with exquisite furniture, magnificent faience stoves, and portraits of leading figures of their age. Groups are treated to a glass of champagne, after which they are shown round the residential and state rooms, including the great ballroom and the Prince's richly ornamented private study. In summer months a nocturnal tour with festal illumination is offered. The "Hofgeschichten" exhibition – the term covers

The castle is a fine example of Baroque architecture.

both the history of, and stories about, the castle – covers multiple facets of the 900-year life of the princely house and family: their connections with the world's great dynasties, their religious affiliation and education at court, worldly matters such as hunting and forestry, and a great deal more. Special tours introduce younger visitors to the history of the castle and House of Oettingen.

Oettingen Castle: a perfect unity with the town

The Ballroom is a fine venue for the Residence Concerts, a series famous well beyond the region.

The Red and Golden Salons

160

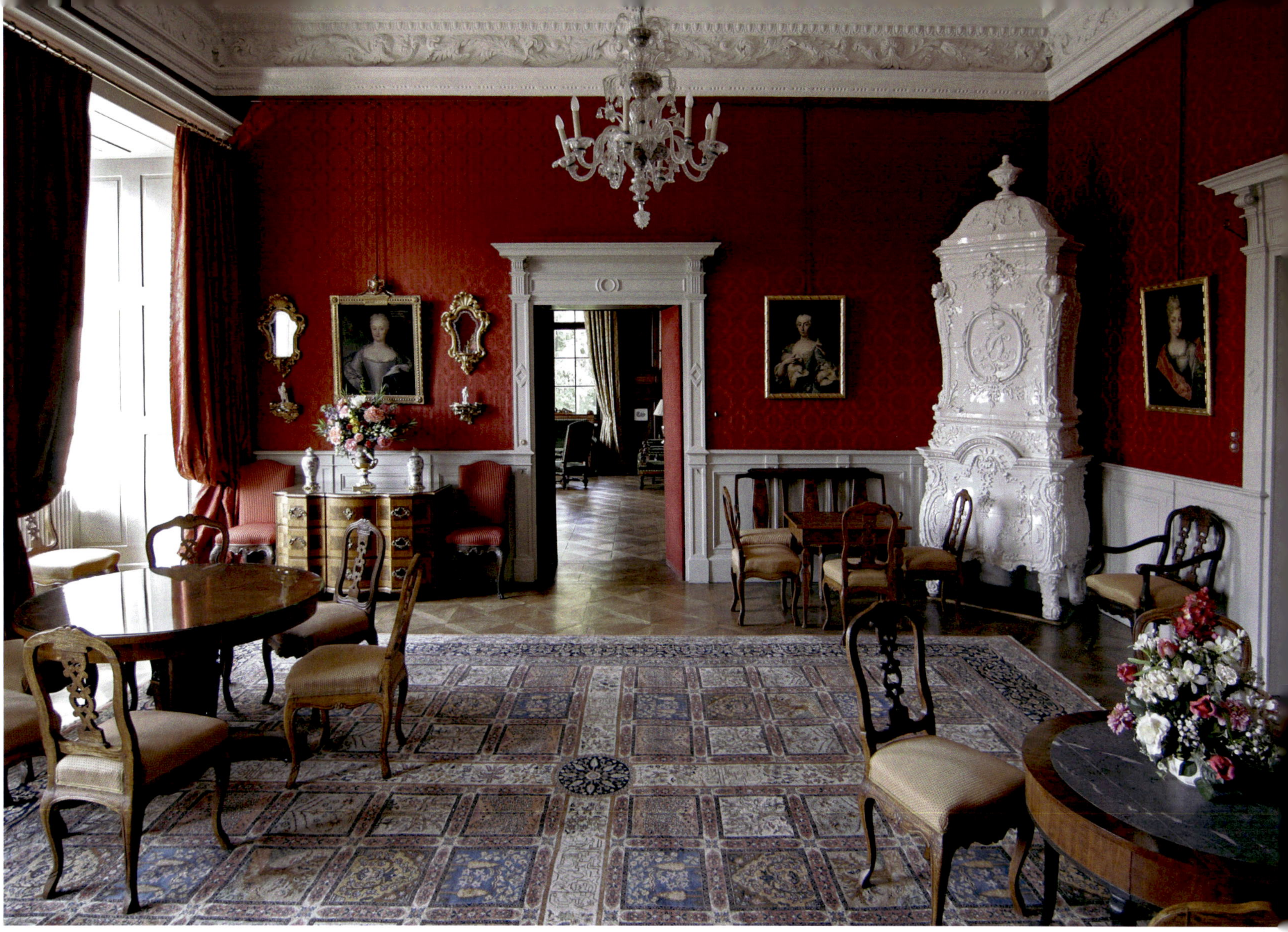

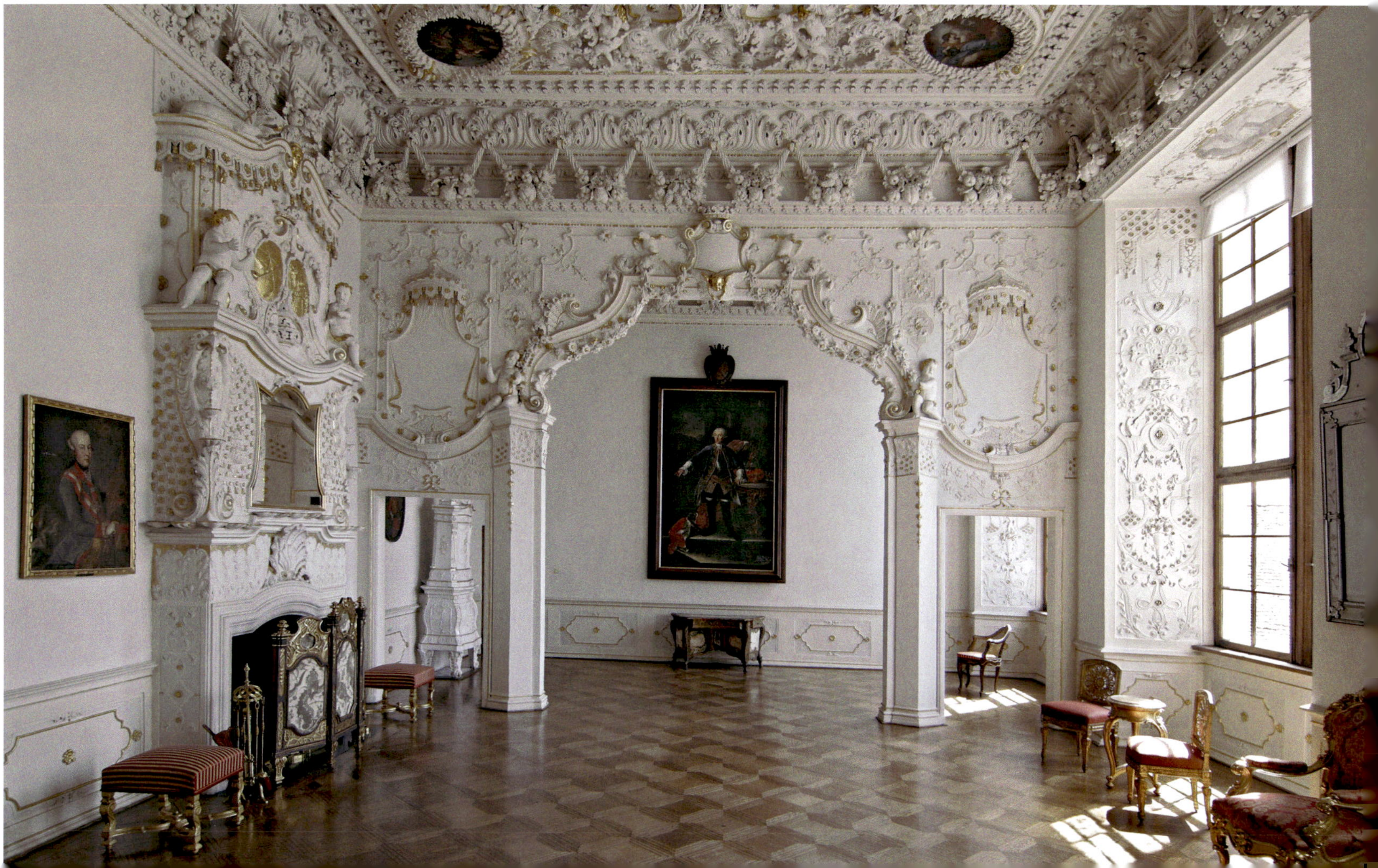

Pappenheim Castle

Gateway to the Altmühl Valley

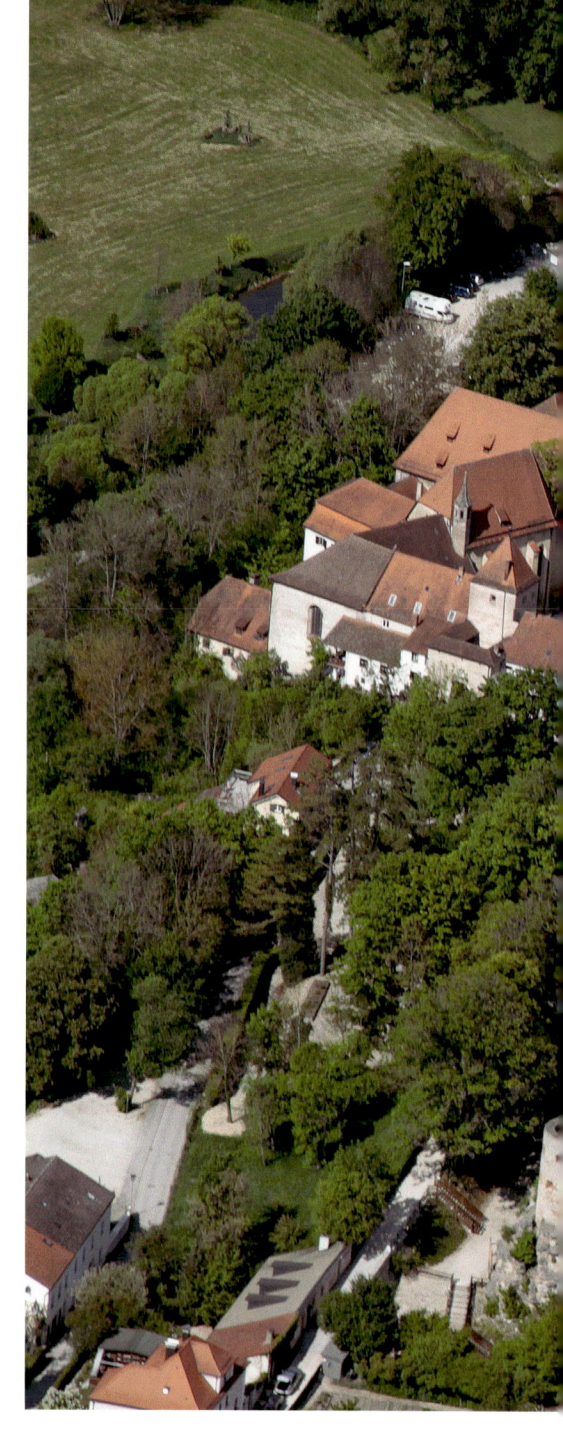

Nestling idyllically in a bend of the River Altmühl at the heart of Altmühl Valley Nature Park, south of the Franconian lakeland, is the historic town of Pappenheim. Its medieval alleys are dominated by the castle, former seat of the hereditary imperial Marshals and later Counts of Pappenheim. From here one has a panoramic view over the Altmühl Valley.

The classical residence of a medieval ruling family, Pappenheim Castle is a typical hilltop fortress with two wards. A triple curtain wall protects the main buildings, which comprise the keep, Great Hall and chapel, as well as the gatehouse and outer bailey. The main castle and barbican are today connected with a strong stone bridge.

In the course of the 13th century, Kalteneck Castle (as Pappenheim Castle was called throughout almost the entire Middle Ages) saw a great deal of fighting, with many resultant changes to its buildings in successive phases over the following two centuries. The town and castle were taken and sacked by Swedish regiments in the Thirty Years' War, and in 1703 the castle was again plundered, this time by French troops, in the War of the Spanish Succession. Partly destroyed by artillery fire, the buildings were subsequently left derelict.

Today the castle and its precincts have been largely and lovingly restored. With its Natural History and Hunting

Castle Chapel with stellar vault

Aerial view of Pappenheim Castle and the Old Town

Ancestral Hall

Castle Register Office – a perfect place for weddings

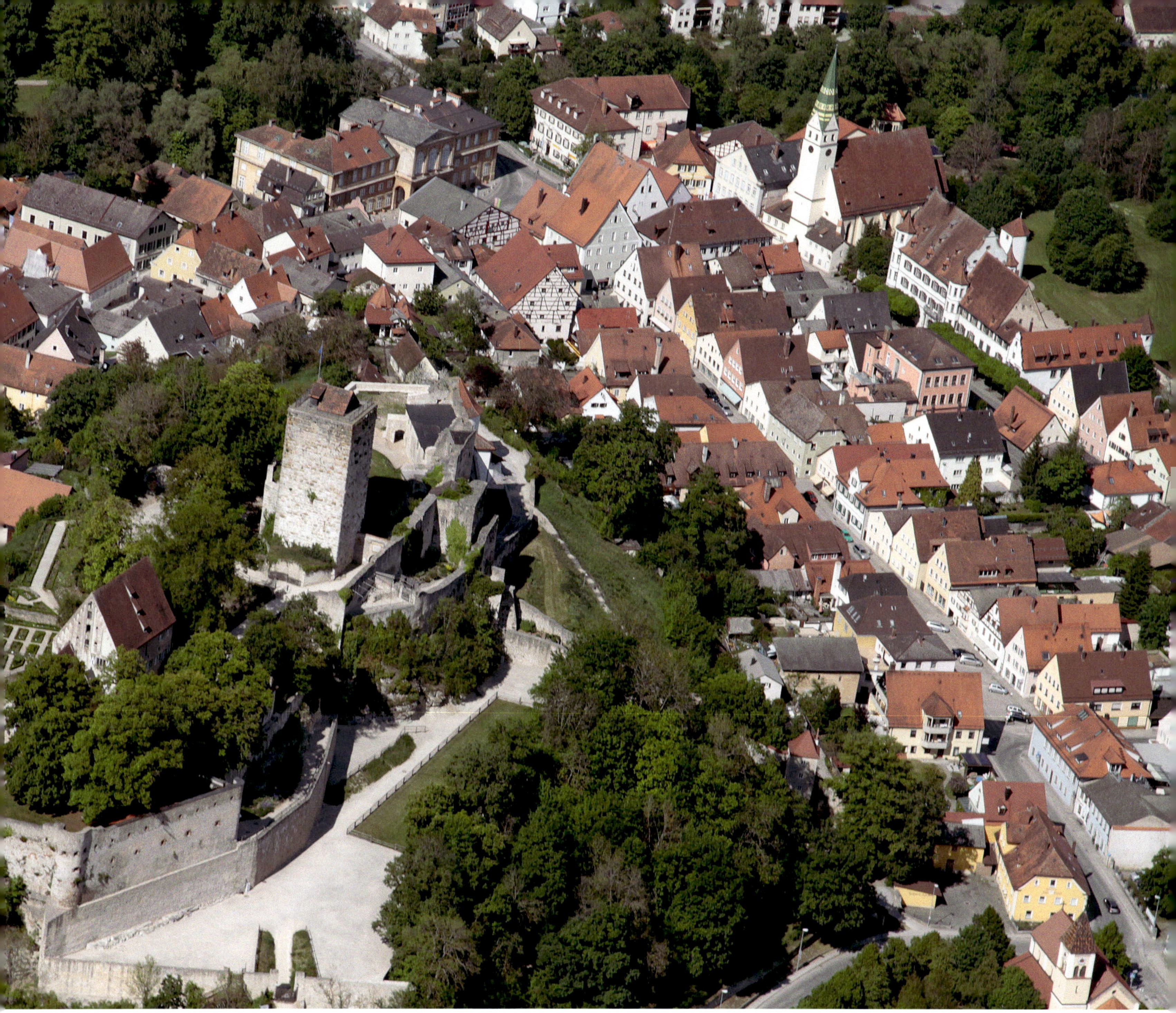

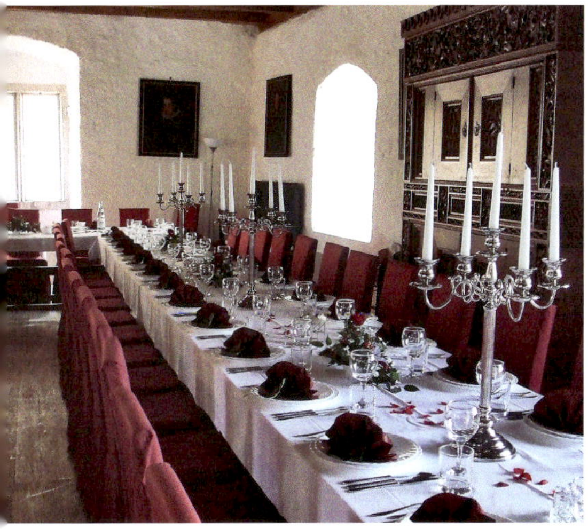

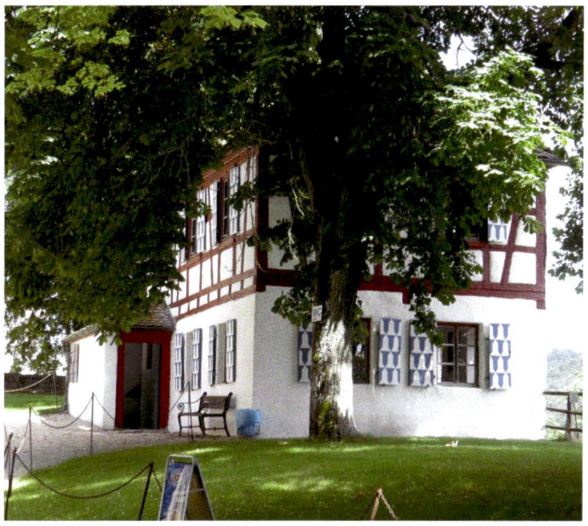

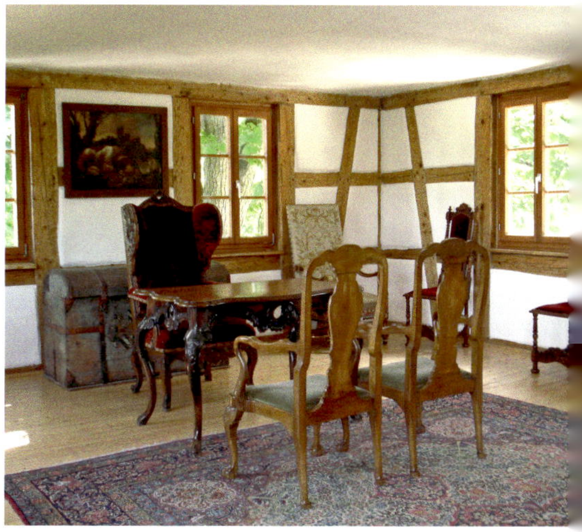

Museum and its Historical Museum Pappenheim Castle offers a wealth of interesting aspects to the visitor. Its romantic environment also makes it a popular place for weddings and celebrations. The Ancestral Hall and Heraldic Hall, as well as the chapel – which accommodates both Lutheran and Catholic rite – civil registry and outdoor areas are available for this purpose.

Situated in the former Marstall (stable block) coach-house, the Natural History and Hunting Museum has exhibitions of the fauna and flora of the Altmühl Valley and Jura Hills, and of the history of hunting. Included are examples of all the animals covered by game law, as well as all the birds, mammals and fishes of the region, and arboreal fungi, mosses and principal woods.

The Historical Museum in the Preissinger House (former armoury) relates on 32 illustrated panels in three sections, with many hitherto unpublished images, the history of the imperial marshals – a hereditary rank of considerable importance in the Middle Ages – as well as that of the castle, town and county of Pappenheim. A special section of the exhibition is devoted to Field Marshal Gottfried Heinrich zu Pappenheim, celebrated in Schiller's *Wallenstein*, when the general says of the cuirassiers appearing before him "That's how I know my Pappenheimers".

Heraldic Hall

Castle beerhouse

Natural Environment and Hunting Museum

164

Pillnitz Palace & Park
A *maison de plaisance* with botanical rarities

Just outside the gates of the Saxon state capital of Dresden, Augustus the Strong, King of Poland and Elector of Saxony, commissioned Matthaeus Daniel Poeppelmann to build a matching pair of palaces: a water palace on the Elbe and a second on the hill behind. Pillnitz Palace (1720–1724) duly became the foundation stone of Europe's largest and most significant Chinoise ensemble.

Augustus the Strong had given the old knightly estate of Pillnitz to his mistress, Countess von Cosel. Here he would celebrate his Baroque festivities, with skittles, swings and seesaws, merry-go-rounds and helter-skelters erected in the park, and the high-born company dressed up as peasants or vineyard workers. Events of this sort were on the one hand a demonstration of power, on the other an occasion of untrammelled amusement for the court and its illustrious guests.

Under Frederick Augustus I, the Righteous the Baroque complex became, from 1768 onward, the summer residence of the Saxon monarchy. Influenced by the style of the English landscaped garden, the elector's cultural and scientific interests found expression in the English and Chinese gardens and their respective pavilions. In 1859 a Palm House was erected for the royal botanical collection, soon followed by an orangery.

Today the New Palace contains the Palace Museum, while the Riverside Palace and Hillside Palace house the Museum of Decorative Arts. The park provides the people of Dresden, as well as tourists from across the globe, with the city's most charming recreational oasis. Famous for its botanical riches, it boasts a more than 250-year-old camellia as well as some 400 plants in tubs and some magnificent old trees. The palm house contains plants from as far afield as South Africa and Australia.

The priceless camellia– the biggest and oldest north of the Alps – is for many visitors a particular attraction. Legend has it that in 1779 a Swedish botanist brought four camellia plants back from his travels in Japan for the Royal Botanical Gardens in Kew (near London). One plant is said to have remained there, while the other three went to Hanover, Schoenbrunn (Vienna) and Pillnitz. If that were so, the Pillnitz

Pillnitz Palace & Park – garden pleasance with Hillside Palace and New Palace

plant would be the only survivor. Recent genetic research disproves the legend, but unfortunately without being able to determine the exact origin of the plant. One thing, however, is certain: the massive bush – now 8.94 metres tall and with a crown almost 12 metres in diameter – was set in its present position in 1801 by the court gardener Terscheck. From mid-February until April it bears tens of thousands of bell-shaped carmine blossoms. Cuttings of the legendary plant are sold at this time of year, and visitors can in this way take a small but very special piece of Pillnitz Palace home with them.

Pillnitz Palace & Park – Riverside Palace with Monumental staircase to the Elbe. The Palace houses the Museum of Decorative Arts.

The Pillnitz camellia is one of the oldest and largest in Europe. Its exact origin has not yet been clarified. In winter it is protected by a movable glasshouse.

Some of the specially cultivated standard lilacs in the Lilac Courtyard are more than 100 years old.

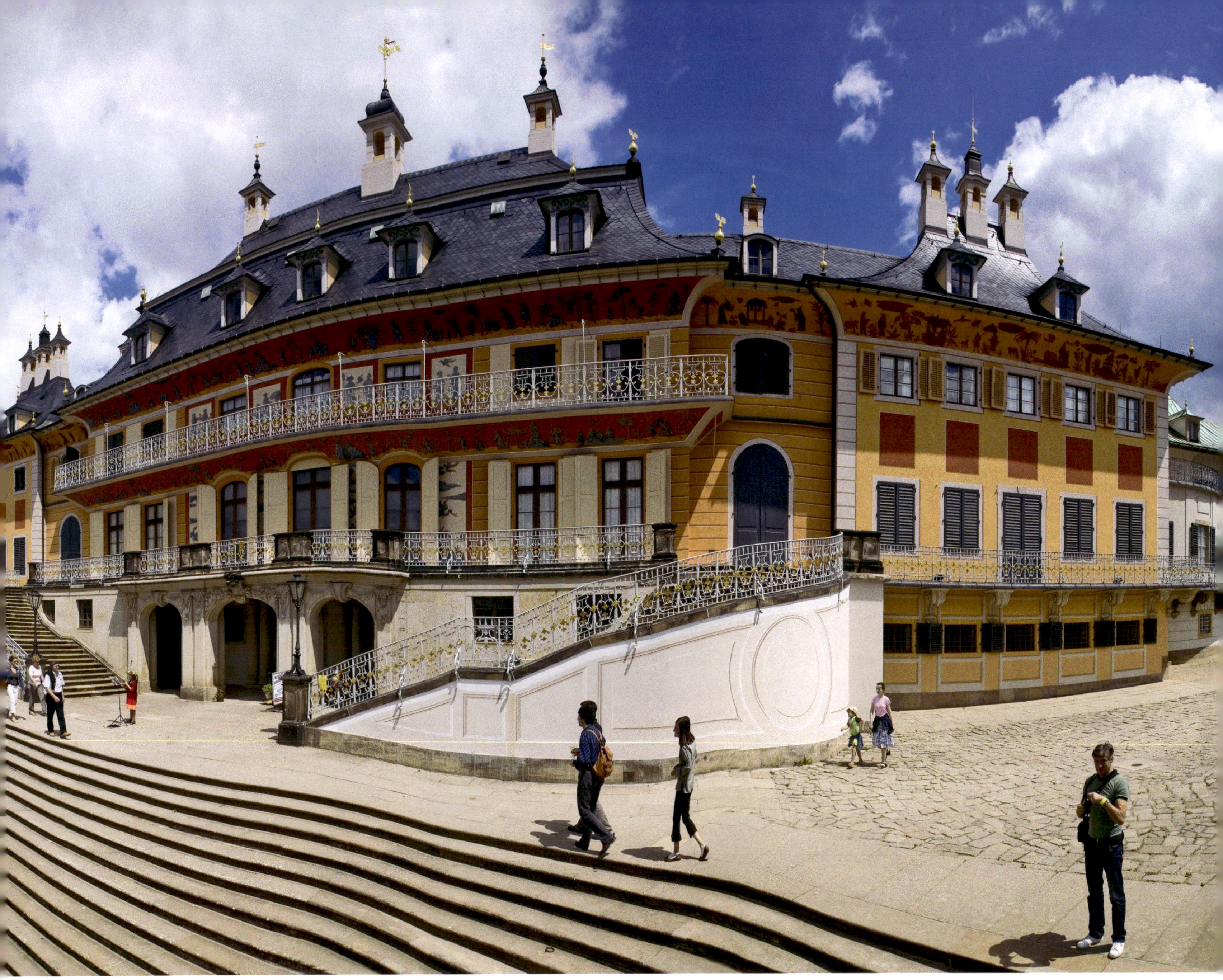
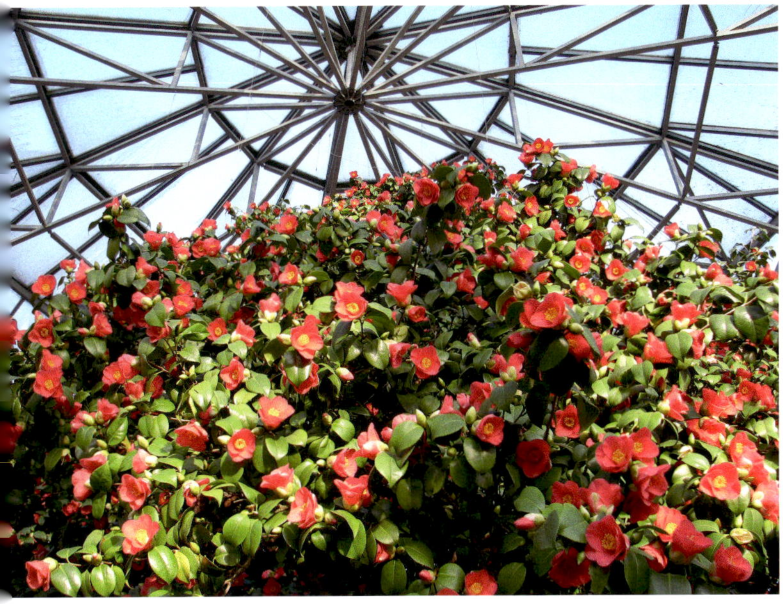
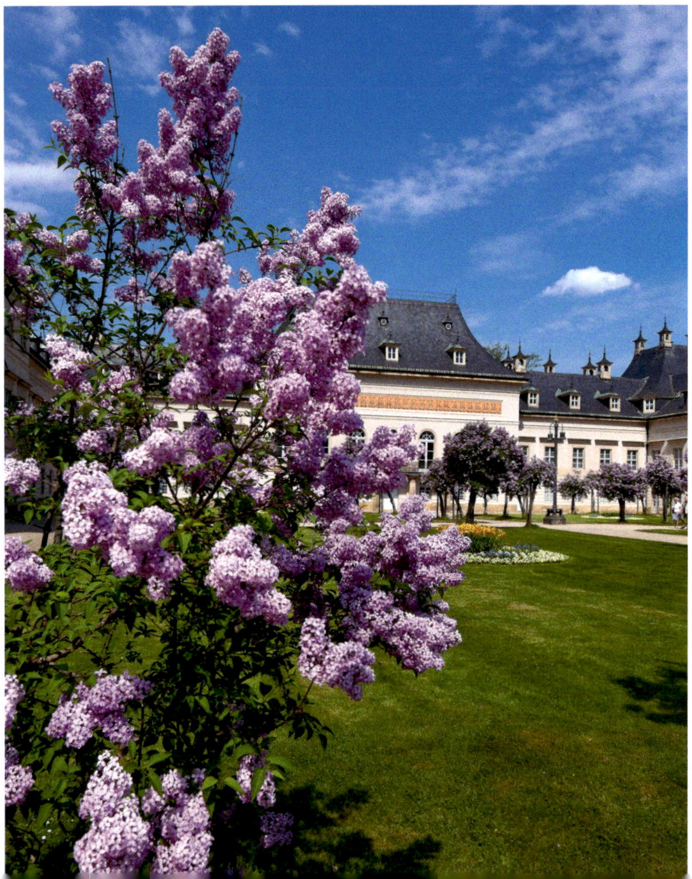

Rochlitz Castle

Fat, one-eyed, revolutionary!

Proud, mysterious and slightly uncanny, Rochlitz Castle stands guard over the town whose name it bears. Its walls tell of a thousand years of history – of emperors, kings and princes, and of those who served and cared for them. Fascinating presentations and hands-on events take the visitor on a trip back in time that promises an exciting immersion in history.

Rochlitz Castle on the Zwickauer Mulde River – with its thousand-year history one of Saxony's oldest castles and the one with the most colourful history

Alongside Meissen' Albrechtsburg Castle, Rochlitz Castle is one of the most important seats of the House of Wettin. Its rooms speak eloquently of the varying fortunes of history, from phases of intense use as an imperial castle, princely residence and administrative centre, through relegation to the rank of prison and site of banishment, to resurrection as an academy for princes, a hunting lodge, or a dowager's residence – and, between all this, prolonged periods of neglect and dereliction.

Twenty years of intensive refurbishment have given the noble inmates of this glorious castle a new and vital presence. A state-of-the-art interactive multi-media exhibition brings the history of Rochlitz Castle palpably close. From imposing residential apartments and state rooms to the vast castle kitchen there is much to marvel at – a memorable experience for the whole family!

A unique feature of the exhibition, and a sensational find during the work of restoration, is a sequence of graffiti scratched into the plaster walls of the castle hall more than 500 years ago, probably by the brothers Ernest and Albert of Saxony and/or Ernest's son, Frederick (later "the Wise") – countless scenes of everyday and military life, ornaments and texts, houses and towers. Restorers discovered this "medieval comic" beneath a layer of 16th century plasterwork. One cannot but wonder at its magic, especially as it is possible to leave one's own graffito on these same walls for posterity.

Another figure at Rochlitz Castle that should not be passed over is Elisabeth of Rochlitz, one of the most influential women of the Reformation period, who lived and worked here between 1537 and 1547. Against the will of her powerful father-in-law, Duke George of Saxony, she introduced Lutheranism throughout her territories, negotiating on equal terms with the Protestant princes Margrave Philip of Hesse (her brother) and Elector John Frederick of Saxony (her cousin). As the only woman in the Schmalkaldic League and a tireless mediator, she became a driving force in the propagation of Luther's reforms by the ruling houses of Saxony. Her (largely preserved) secret correspondence provides an image of this strong woman, generally ignored by history, and the exhibition allows many insights into the events of her life and the role of women in the Reformation.

Top: Rochlitz Castle is also an important Reformation site: Elisabeth of Rochlitz lived here and introduced the Reformation against the will of the Elector.

A modern exhibition presents the thousand-year architectural history of the castle.

P. 170 above: The medieval "Black Kitchen" is preserved, fully functioning, in its original state. Medieval cookery courses are offered for those interested in trying out original recipes.

P. 170 below: Looking into the Red Room with its Renaissance-period painted cassette ceiling

170

Salem Monastery and Palace

One of the most majestic Cistercian monasteries in Southern Germany

A vast palace ensemble in the pastel colours of the Baroque Age, coupled with a majestic minster church with a mighty roof and Gothic windows – the many centuries of Salem history are apparent at the very first glance. Set amid meadows and gentle green hills, on clear days with an intimation of the Alps rising beyond the great mirror of Lake Constance, the former Cistercian monastery of Salem enjoys a paradisal charm.

The monks who, from 1134 onward, lived and worked at Salem Monastery had their share in the creation of this paradise. The Cistercian order was renowned for its profound knowledge and ceaseless labour in agriculture and husbandry. One can still see in the landscape today where the so-called "white monks" – or more particularly the lay brothers of the order – were active. In Salem, too, the typical "Paradise garden" left by the Cistercians is evident in the fertile combination of fields, vineyards and orchards interspersed with ponds for the supply of fish and water.

The impression left by the former monastery of Salem is of a far-flung but essentially rural complex. In its heyday it was both rich and powerful – as an imperial monastery subject only to the Holy Roman Emperor it ruled over extensive lands. In the 18th century it was at the height of its worldly power; indeed the abbot general of the Cistercian order resided here from 1790 to 1802. Then, in 1803, came the secularization of all church property, and Salem passed to the Grand Dukes of Baden. It was they who turned the abbot's residence into a palace.

At the centre of the monastery complex was the Gothic church. Around it stood the monastery and prelature (abbot's residence), as well as administrative, horticultural and agricultural buildings. A catastrophic fire in 1697 spared only the church; for the rest of the monastery it became an occasion for widespread and unstinting reconstruction.

The monumental impact of the imperial Abbey stems from this time. The regular, High Baroque proportions of the 180 meter long prelature façade are the work of the well-known master builder Franz Beer from the Vorarlberg. The interior owes its wealth of ornament to the great masters of the age, first and foremost the sculptor Franz Joseph Feuchtmayer. At its heart is the Kaisersaal, which occupies one-and-a-half storeys at the centre of the east wing and is adorned with magnificent stucco figures by Feuchtmayer on the walls and ceiling.

The present-day Hofgarten (court garden) was laid down on the site of the old monastery garden.

The medieval minster, which miraculously survived the fire, also received a facelift at this time. Under Abbot Anselm II the sculptors Johann Georg Dirr and Johann Georg Wieland created one of the most outstanding – and to this day best preserved – examples of early south German Classicism.

Prelature and minster – Baroque and Gothic next to each other

Nave of Salem Minster with early Classicistic artworks

Salem winery with wine press from 1706

The Kaisersaal (Imperial Hall) – ceremonial showpiece of the monastery

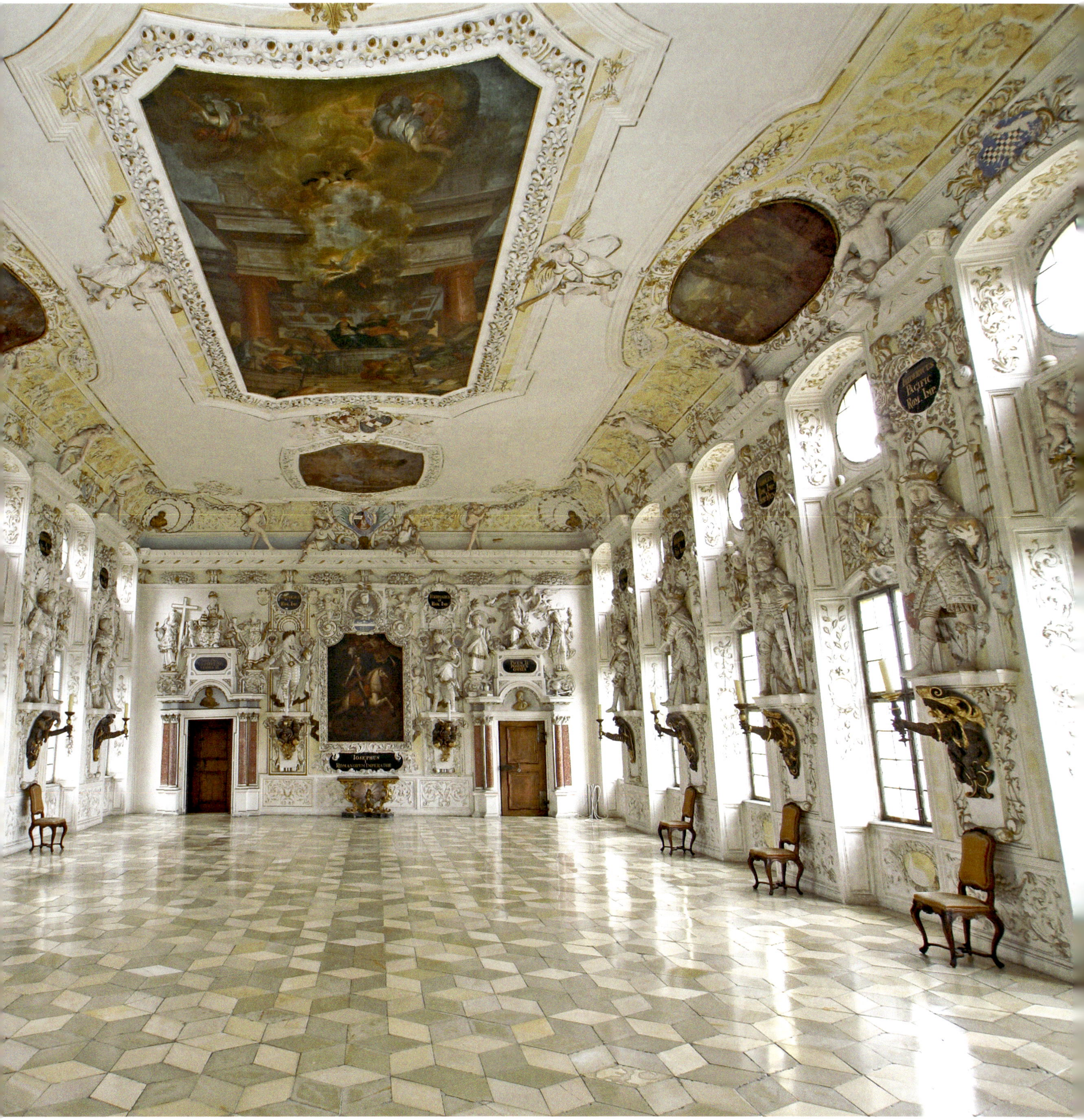

The Europa-Rosarium, Sangerhausen

The world's biggest collection of roses

Sangerhausen, a more than 1000 year-old town between the southern Harz Mountains and Kyffhäuser Hills is home to the Europa-Rosarium (European Rose Gardens). With more than 8600 cultivars, 500 wild rose species and some 850 climbing roses from various countries and epochs, this is the largest collection of roses worldwide, assembled by rose-growers and rose-lovers with a dedication that has lasted more than a century. Among its rarities are the Green Rose, the Black Rose, and the so-called barbed-wire rose. Historical and endangered rose species are another speciality, and in this respect the Europa-Rosarium functions as both a gene bank and a living museum that provides a full historical account of the development and diversification of the rose.

Initiated by the Sangerhäuser Verschönerungsverein, the Rosarium

The Jubilee Garden presents a selection of 20th century roses

Radiant blossoms in the Pillar Garden

Jubilee Garden with Hohe Linde mine tip in the background

174

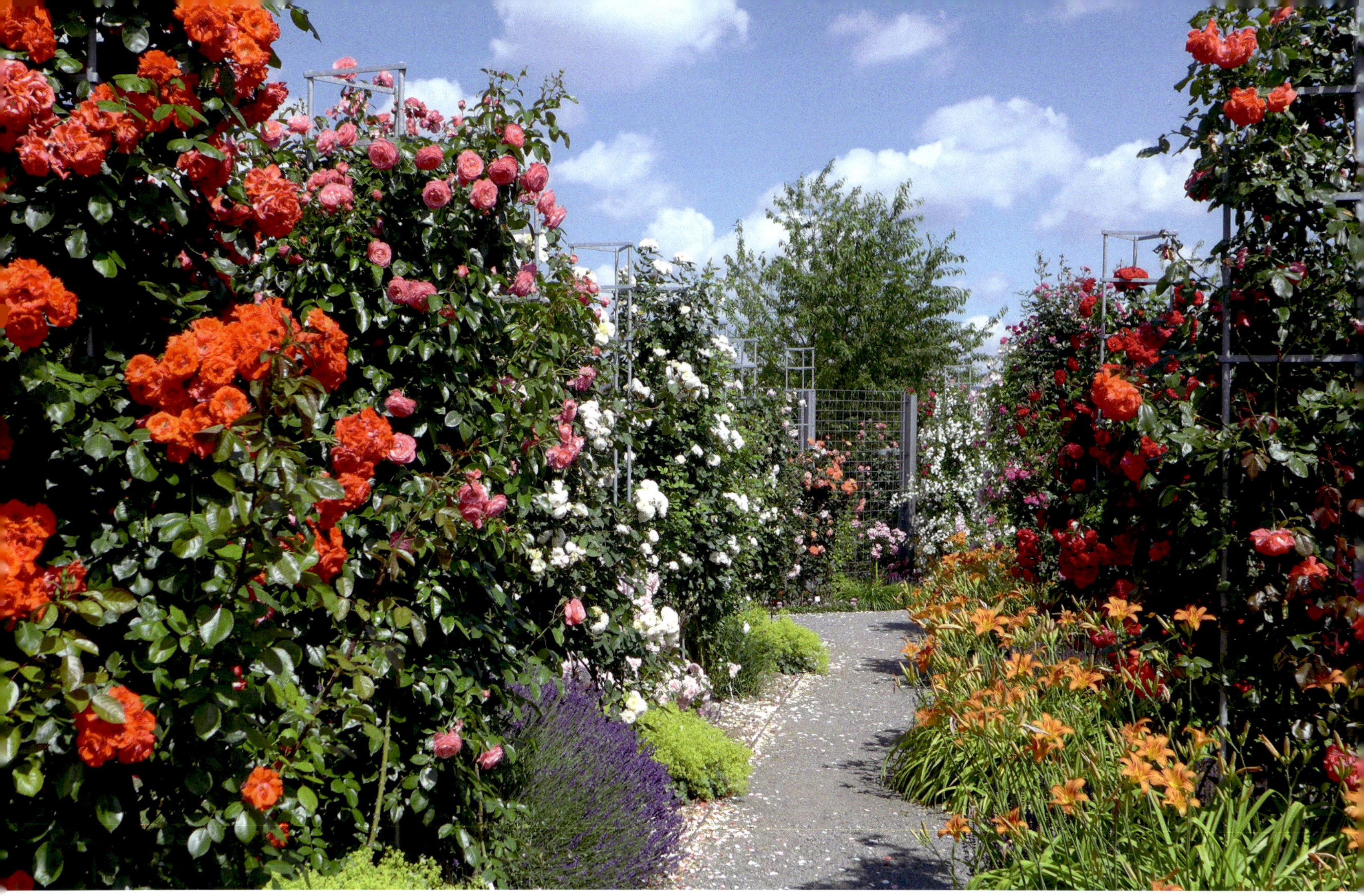

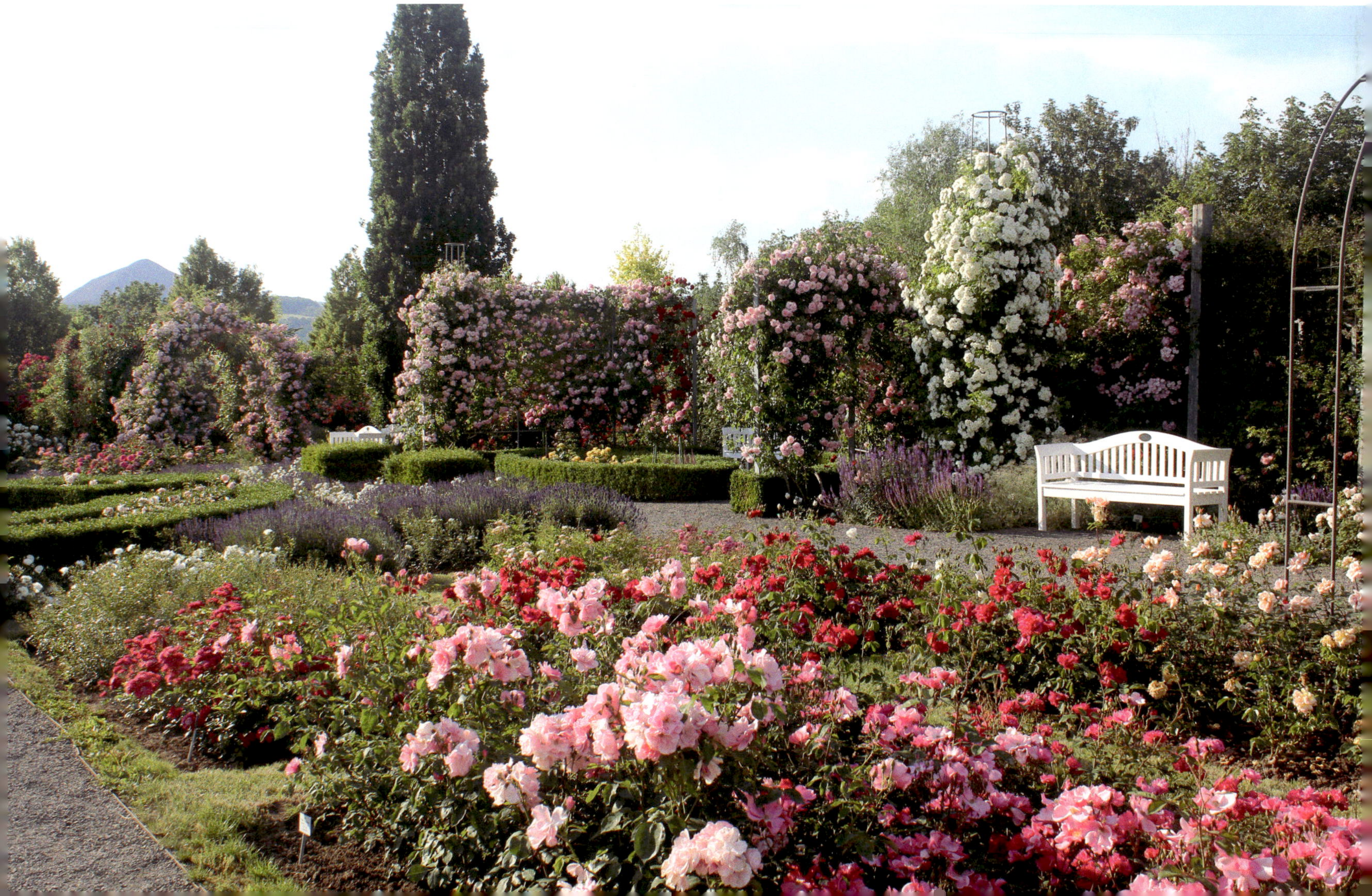

Sangerhausen opened on the occasion of the Society of German Rose Lovers' Congress in 1903. Over the years the premises have grown in size and now cover an area of 13 hectares (c. 32.5 acres).

The park is notable above all for its diversity. In spring, some 20,000 early flowering plants bring the first colour to the park, and this is followed by an impressive display of rhododendrons; finally when the peak season begins, from early summer until late autumn, the many and varied show and theme gardens come into their own and the whole of the park turns into a sea of roses. Some 300 rare trees and shrubs – among them the giant sequoia, yellow sandalwood, and Kentucky coffee tree – form an attractive backdrop for the roses. The highest point of the Europa-Rosarium – the Alpinum – and the semi-wild "Wolf's abyss" offer stunning views of the park, and beyond it of the Mansfeld countryside. Another feature is the many artworks, with constant new additions, that embellish the gardens. The Rose Café, with its in-house patisserie, and the multifunctional play and adventure world opened in 2016, add to the attraction of the Europa-Rosarium for families.

Beginning in mid-June, the traditional Mining and Rose Festival Weeks end every year with the Day of the Miners in mid-July. A further highlight at the onset of the second blossoming period is the Night of a Thousand Lights on the second weekend in August. The Sangerhausen Rose School and individual consultations provide advice on the cultivation and care of roses.

The Rosarium Sangerhausen was awarded the title "Europa-Rosarium" in 1993, when the town was also officially designated Rose Town by the the Society of German Rose Lovers. Since 2000 the Europa-Rosarium has been included in the cultural heritage and tourist network "Garden Dreams – Historic Parks in Saxony-Anhalt".

The Leonardo da Vinci rose in full bloom

Sayn – Castle and Schloss
"A veritable fairytale castle"

On his first visit to Sayn, in 1851, King Friedrich Wilhelm IV of Prussia confessed to being "dazzled, full of wonder and absolutely enchanted"; six years later his brother, the later Kaiser Wilhelm I, confided his admiration to the guest book in the phrase "a veritable fairytale castle."

High on a rocky spur by Bendorf stands the ancient castle of the counts of Sayn, while at the foot of the spur his ministers built a corresponding fortified dwelling. When, in 1848, Prince Ludwig zu Sayn-Wittgenstein-Sayn returned with his wife, Princess Leonilla, from Russia, he had this latter – still medieval – building transformed by the Louvre architect Alphonse Girard into a comfortable residence. Neo-Gothic architectonic elements include cast iron from the local Sayn smeltery and a steam engine, introduced to pump water up to a tank next to the old castle in order to feed the fountains in the schloss park. Valuable paintings, busts and furniture from the extensive collections of the princely couple still adorn the rooms of the schloss, despite its variegated history.

Requisitioned by occupying troops in the aftermath of the First World War, the schloss later served to house homeless people, then as a kindergarten, finally as a needlecraft school. Towards the end of the Second World War a massive explosion from a bridge demolition by retreating German troops damaged the buildings so badly that they were given up to ruin. Only in 1995 could Prince Alexander and Princess Gabriela, aided by the State of Rhineland-Palatinate, begin rebuilding and revitalizing this nationally significant monument.

Visitors today experience a symbiosis of the historical and modern. The new museum, opened in 2020, presents the history of the Sayn dynasty, now in its 28th generation. Here one meets personalities as various as Princess Leonilla, *grande dame* of the 18th century, and the much admired pho-

The Red Salon is notable for its large paintings by Franz X. Winterhalter and Horace Vernet.

Above the schloss looms the ancient dynastic castle of the House of Sayn – a fascinating ensemble

The Blue Hall of the New Museum – an exhibition of 19th century dining culture

tographer Princess Marianne, whose work covers eight decades of social life. Finally one learns of Princess Gabriela's commitment to nature, above all in the neighbouring Butterfly Gardens.

Festal celebrations, conference meetings and the schloss restaurant regularly infuse the noble halls and salons with new life. Wedding couples love the polychrome décor of the neo-Gothic chapel, whose altar houses the precious arm reliquary of St. Elizabeth of Hungary. Facilities for civil weddings are available in the Gobelin Hall.

The ancient castle on the rocky peak above the schloss can be reached on foot. Destroyed in the Thirty Years' War, it was partly restored in the 1980s, when it became a popular destination for excursions. The keep, as well as the decorative floor of the two-storey medieval chapel, testify to the significance of the extensive 12th century complex under the mighty counts of Sayn.

Sayn Palace Gardens

Delight of princes and butterflies

In the mid-19th century Prince Louis zu Sayn-Wittgenstein-Sayn created an impressive artistic synthesis fully in step with his time: Sayn Palace was restructured as a neo-Gothic residence, and the ruins of his ancestral castle, set atop a hilly ridge between Sayn and Brex, were integrated into a park laid out in High Romantic style.

Landscaped in the English manner, the gardens were the work of Carl Friedrich Thelemann, designer of the botanical gardens in St. Petersburg, and of the Frankfurt garden architect Heinrich Siesmayer, whose memoirs contain the following details: "The total cost of this c. 30 *Morgen* (c. 20 acre) park with its hillside gardens amounted to no less than 60,000 Taler; some 150 men and 20–25 horses were employed in its making. The prince and his high-born guests, among them the famous Prince Pückler-Muskau, were delighted with the results, which caused quite a stir with the public and earned me as a landscape gardener considerable merit."

Around 20 acres in extent, Sayn palace gardens today draw their particular charm from the lake and an artificial grotto, from the Lady Chapel with its cast iron Way of the Cross, and from the ruins of a Baroque pavilion. Princess Gabriela and Prince Alexander have added further rare trees, launched a park care programme and engaged contemporary artists to renew bridge walls and railings – work that enhances the estate and paves the way to the future. A high priority remains the reinstallation of the open staircase that formerly linked the lower garden via the terrace to the castle hill with its ruins and pathways, opening the palace to the park and surrounding landscape.

Created by Princess Gabriela, Sayn Palace Butterfly Garden is today the major attraction of the park. Here, visitors

The Butterfly Garden's nature trail informs visitors about supporting biodiversity.

Schloss Sayn links the English garden with the castle hill and its romantic ruins.

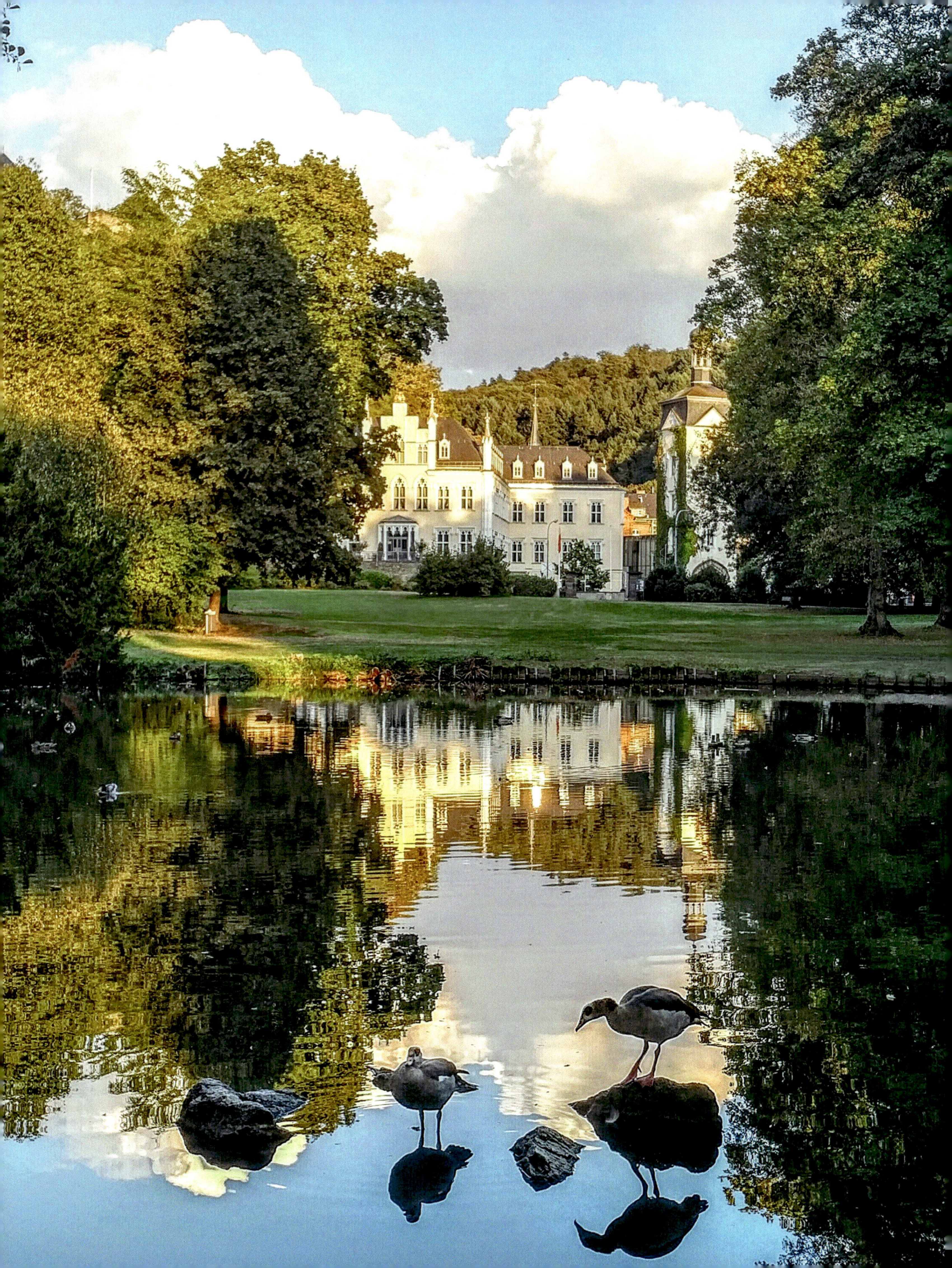

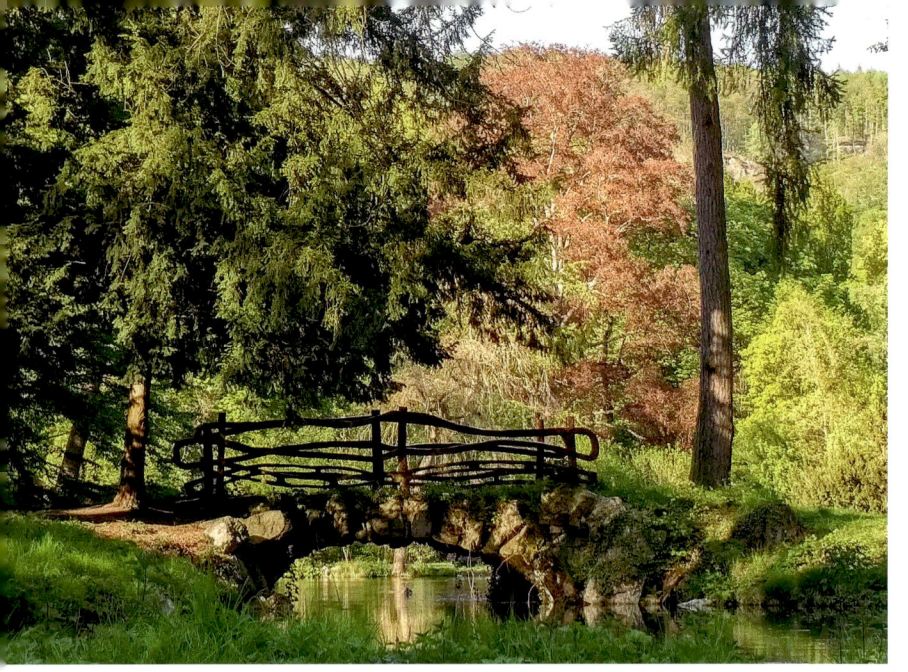

stroll past babbling waterfalls through groves of hibiscus, banana, and other southern plants, the habitat of blue quail, tropical finches, and green iguana, while at every step the 'jewels of the air' flutter past. An educational nature trail provides new insights into this rich environment, while art exhibitions are offered in a pavilion. Apart from the neo-Gothic palace itself, Sayn Cultural Park offers such attractions as the nearby Romanesque abbey and a tree-top climbing course, all framed by the World Heritage Site of Roman Limes. Close by, another cultural treasure, Sayn Foundry Hall, has recently been saved from ruin and reinstated as a potential concert and exhibition venue. Built in 1830, this magnificent basilica of filigree ironwork is an industrial monument of international significance.

Top: Bridges designed by contemporary artists span the streams and ponds of the Schloss Park

Bottom left: The tropical Butterfly Garden – a living fairytale of 1001 butterflies

Bottom right: Sayn Foundry Hall – an industrial monument of international significance

Schwerin Palace

Fairytale castle at the pulse of the state

Schwerin Palace has been the seat of power in the North German state since the 10th century, when the Obotrite forefathers of the Mecklenburgian ruling house built a fortress here. In the 16th century this was extended by the dukes of Mecklenburg to form an impressive Renaissance residence reflecting their status. Then, in the 17th century, Duke Adolph Friedrich I had the palace remodelled and unified in the style of the Late Renaissance. However, the work remained unfinished, initially for domestic political reasons, but finally because the court relocated in 1763–65 to Ludwigslust.

However, in 1837, under Grand Duke Paul Friedrich, the court returned to Schwerin. His successor Friedrich Franz II, aware of the dawning of a new political order, decided on a radical rebuilding of the palace, not least as a symbol of his innate dynastic superiority to the up and coming bourgeoisie.

At the suggestion of his uncle, Friedrich Wilhelm IV of Prussia, the Grand Duke commissioned his court architect, Georg Adolph Demmler, to extend the existing building into a monumental residence, which, however, retained certain aspects of the Renaissance palace. With the participation of the Schwerin court master builder Hermann Willebrand, the occasional involvement of Gottfried Semper, and the later assumption of responsibility for both planning and realization by the Berlin court architect August Stüler, the palace as we know it today finally came into being between 1843 and 1857. In its mixture of local features with elements of the French Renaissance, it is both in itself a grandiose architectonic statement and an irrefutable embodiment of political power, centralized in the state capital city of Schwerin. After 1918 the palace was used for various purposes; today it houses the state parliament of Mecklenburg-Western Pomerania.

In the Grand Ducal domestic and state apartments the visitor is surrounded with court history. In the Ancestral Gallery the portraits of all the dukes from the 14th to the 18th century underline the long Mecklenburgian dynastic tradition, while the lavishly appointed Throne Hall represents the summit

The Throne Hall – opulent in both artworks and décor

183

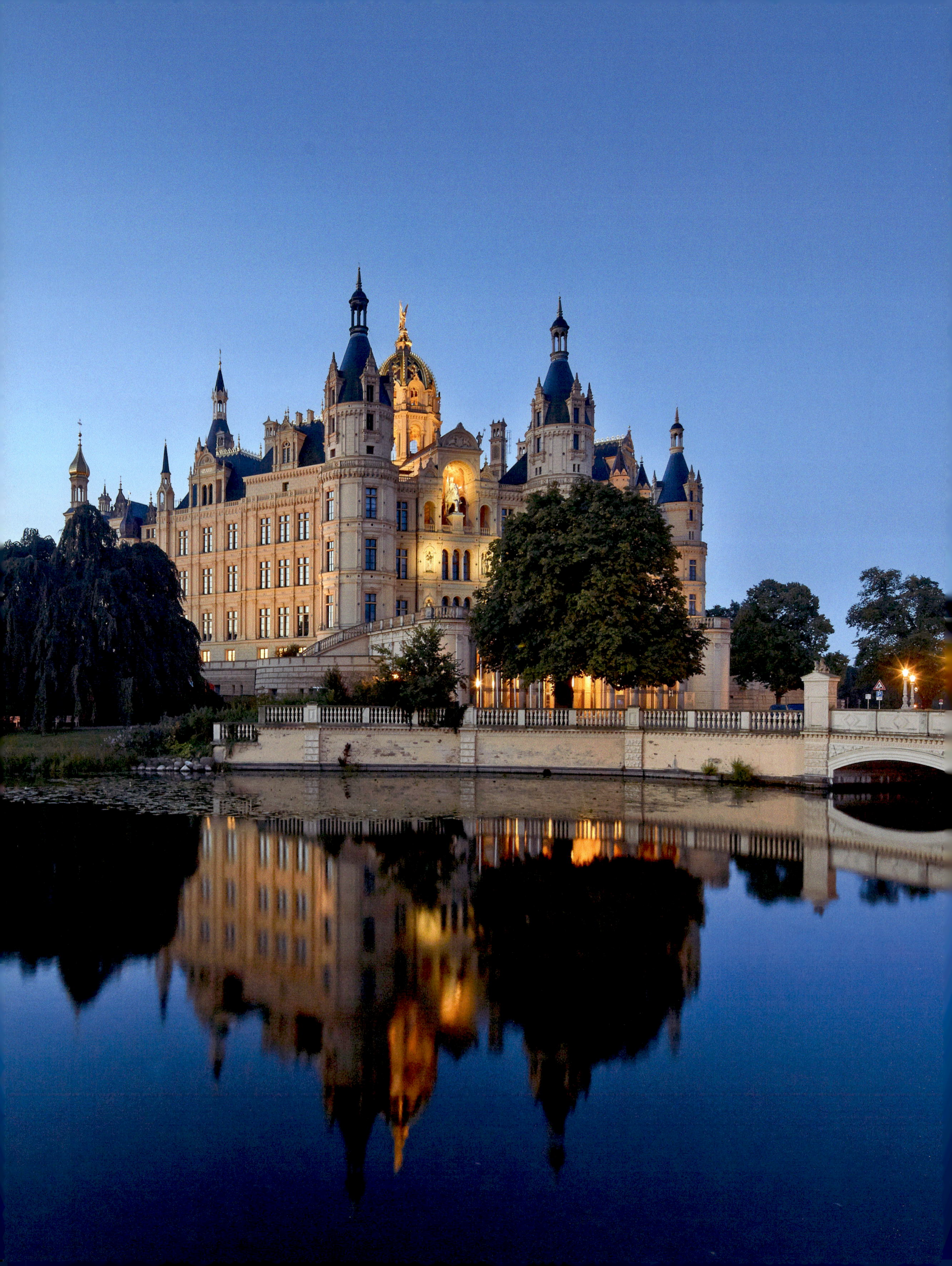

of social splendour, as well as political power. The Dining Room, Tea Room and Flower Room provide a gracious environment for selected artworks from the 17th to 19th centuries.

Schwerin Palace – afloat in a picturesque lakeland

The Ancestral Gallery – more than 1000 years of Mecklenburgian dynastic tradition

Schwetzingen Palace and Gardens

Gardens of extraordinary European renown

A green paradise ruled by the arts: that may well have been the vision of Carl Theodor, 18th century Elector Palatine, out of which the elegantly furnished summer residence in Schwetzingen arose: a palace possessing numerous state rooms, a Rococo theatre, and a grandiose garden – and moreover with a delightful Baroque town on its doorstep.

The foundations for the palace garden were laid by the art-loving Carl Theodor's predecessor. When Elector Carl Philipp moved into his vast, newly built Baroque palace in Mannheim in 1731, he had the small palace in Schwetzingen converted into a charming summer seat and hunting lodge; and a garden was laid down at the same time, albeit on a much smaller scale than the one we know today. An important feature for Carl Philipp was the orangery, where the exotic fruits that graced his gardens – southern delicacies such as oranges, figs and pomegranates – could safely pass the winter months. In warmer weather tub plants of this kind still adorn the Schwetzingen gardens.

Under Elector Carl Theodor the garden of the summer residence was first laid out in French Baroque style. The famous circular parterre was created in 1753 in perfect symmetry, half surrounded by the many-arched Zirkelgebäude (quarter-circle pavilions) and complemented with pergolas, geometrical flower beds and elegant waterworks, as well as corners of hedged seclusion. Carl Theodor had his garden continually extended and, above all, beautified. A prince's garden, after all, should have a wealth of fine sculptures and sophisticated architectural objects. Among these in Schwetzingen is the bath-house in whose privacy the Elector would receive his chosen guests for conversation or music-making. Especially impressive is the rare garden mosque, the only extant example anywhere of an exot-

A purpose-built ruin – the Temple of Mercury in the palace garden

The Garden Mosque is the only extant example of its kind

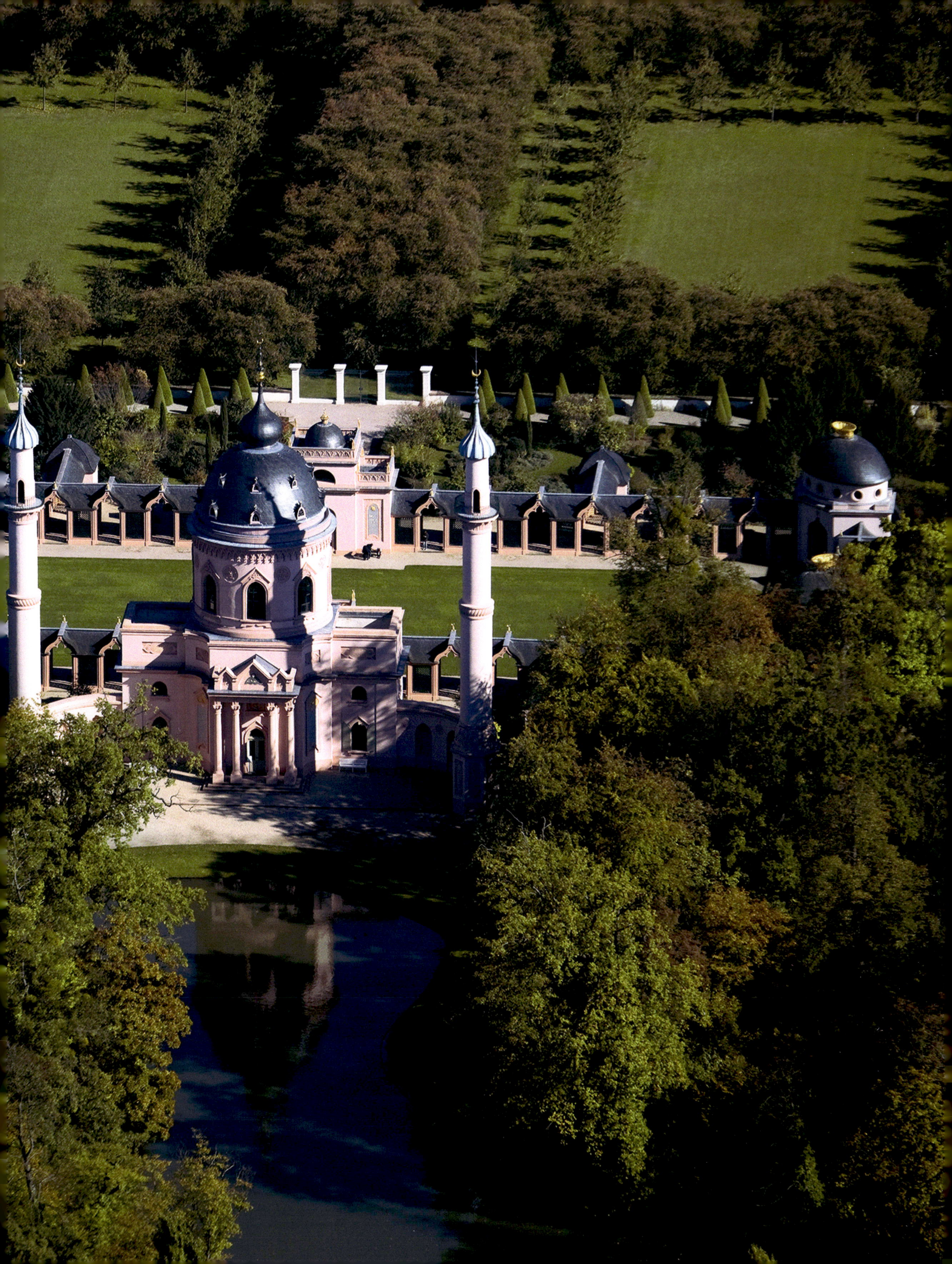

ic 18th century fashion. With temples and artificial ruins, winding paths and streams, broad expanses of water and unusual perspectives the prince claimed his place at the stylistic forefront of the day. He had his new garden designer, Friedrich Ludwig von Sckell, trained in England – the English were the trendsetters in landscaping – and brought the landscaped garden to Schwetzingen as one of the first of its kind in Germany. Sckell's best-known masterpiece, the English Garden in Munich, is a later work.

The palace itself presents freshly renovated Baroque suites from the time of Prince Elector Carl Theodor as well as (on the second floor) outstanding early 19th century Empire period interiors whose walls, papered with finely printed landscapes, are a fragile rarity.

Looking towards the palace from the garden parterre

Hidden corners line the circular parterre

At the Stag Fountain, sculptures illustrate the theme of hunting

Three Saxon Highlights

Triad from the Ore Mountains and Central Saxony

Set in a triangle around Chemnitz, the Three Saxon Highlights – Augustusburg Castle, Scharfenstein Castle, and Lichtenwalde Castle & Park – are among the most interesting cultural monuments in the Ore Mountains and Central Saxony.

The 'crown of the Ore Mountains', Augustusburg Castle (aka. 'bikers' castle') is well known for its collection of motorcycles – one of Europe's largest – as well as for the Elector's carriages and one of Saxony's most valuable Cranach paintings. Its grandeur and treasures place it among Central Europe's finest Renaissance palaces. The very site chosen by Saxony's Elector Augustus for his 'hunting lodge and *maison de plaisance*' (built 1568–1572) is telling: a 516 metre high quartz-porphyry cone above the valley of the Zschopau. The altar painting executed by Lucas Cranach the Younger for the castle chapel between 1568 and 1571 counts among the finest in Saxon history.

Erected c. 1250 during the early settlement period of the Ore Mountains, Scharfenstein Castle radiates a unique aura of myth and magic. As one of Saxony's oldest noble residences, dwelt in continuously for more than 750 years, it combines several different phases of construction: the keep is from the original medieval castle, while the Renaissance entrance portal was added some 400 years later. The castle museum is dedicated especially to the Ore Mountains craft tradition of wooden toy and Christmas decoration carving – a feature that ensures Scharfenstein's popularity as a 'family castle'.

Built between 1722 and 1726 by a minister of Elector Augustus the Strong, Lichtenwalde Castle was raised to perfection by the Baroque park set around it by the minister's son. Reconstructed in line with its historical model, Lichtenwalde Park today offers 335 historical fountains, as well as magnificent pathways and perspectives with hidden pavilions and corners for relaxation. As such it holds its own with Germany's greatest parks. Guided tours of the castle take in the King's Room – which accommodated the Saxon king himself as well as his high-born guests – the red and green salons, the Chinese room, and the chapel, which contains one of the few still extant Donati organs; finally the tea-house in the splendid inner courtyard. Two aspects of special interest are the Treasury Museum, some of whose pieces from distant cultures are several thousand years old, and a collection of German silhouette cuttings – three centuries of charming filigrees.

Welcome to Lichtenwalde Castle & Park – rendezvous of the arts.

Augustusburg Castle ranks today among Central Europe's finest Renaissance palaces.

Top exhibit of the Coach Museum: the magnificent 'Berline' state carriage (1790) from the former royal stables in Dresden

The Cranach altar painting and pulpit: again resplendent, after restoration in 2015, in the full depth of their original colours

Medieval Scharfenstein Castle, where myth and magic create family enchantment

More than 1000 exhibits demonstrate the skill and creativity of the local handicraft tradition.

Ore Mountains handiwork traditions take pride of place in the Toy and Christmas Craft Museum.

Lichtenwalde Castle & Park – a fine Baroque setting for a stroll

The Red Salon and Chinese Room – awesome reception rooms

Sigmaringen Palace

A millennium of political, cultural and family history

As if grown from the rock, Sigmaringen Palace, Germany's second biggest castle built within urban limits, stands high above the Danube. For almost 500 years it has been in the unbroken possession of the Hohenzollerns, one of Europe's oldest and most renowned noble houses. Its c. 450 rooms provide ample testimony to the eventful family history, including art treasures of the 15th and 16th centuries and one of Europe's most comprehensive private collections of weapons, with some 3000 exhibits from seven centuries. Karl Anton von Hohenzollern (1811–1885) was a prince with exceptionally wide cultural and artistic interests, and his collections are today open to visitors. In this respect, too, Sigmaringen Palace is a cultural landmark far beyond the borders of Baden-Württemberg.

Since 1535 the castle has been the traditional seat of the Swabian Hohenzollerns, who in their thousand-year history have served as imperial counsellors, generals and regimental leaders. Today the family is especially dedicated to the promotion of culture, tourism and the economy, as well as to social concerns.

Early Roman and Alemannic settlements are thought to have existed on the cliff above the Danube, but any evidence of these is buried inaccessibly under the castle's medieval ramparts. The first documentary mention of Sigmaringen Palace is in records from the 11th century, but the earliest architectural evidence visible today stems from the 12th century. Two centuries later the castle was extended into its present impressive size. Refurbishment took place on several occasions, notably after damage during the Thirty Years War and after a serious fire at the end of the 19th century. This also explains the stylistic differences visible in the castle – variations that offer an insight into German architectural history. Thus the entrance gate opens onto what appears to be a medieval fortress, but just a few metres further on the visitor stands before a 20th century princely residence.

Not all the castle's 450 rooms can, of course, be opened to the public, but daily guided tours of 15 noble rooms and salons, as well as various special

Towering over all it surveys and yet part of the town – the seat of the Swabian dynasty.

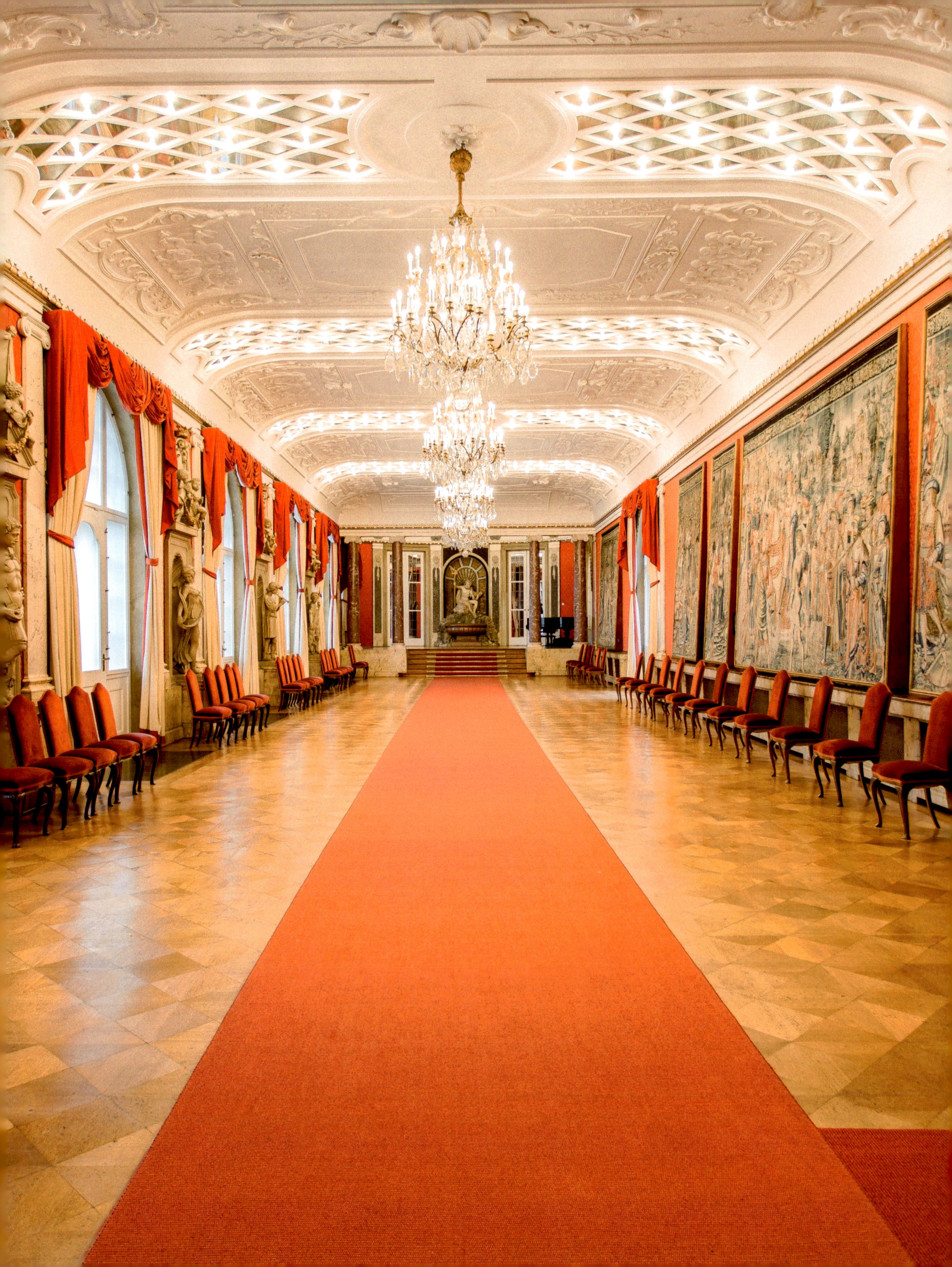

tours, offer fascinating insights into life at this once so mighty court of princes, for many centuries a meeting place of Europe's high nobility. In the armoury, with its many unusual and unique weapons and suits of armour, the visitor can individually explore the history of weaponry from the 14th to the 20th century – also with an audio guide.

Top: Viewed from the Danube, the castle still reveals its origins as a knightly stronghold.

Left: The Portuguese Gallery provides an appropriate setting for concerts and theatrical performances.

Right: The Empire style Green Salon with its impressive marble fireplace

Stolzenfels Castle

Monument of Prussian Rhine-romanticism

Stolzenfels Castle, south of Koblenz, is a prime witness to the historical romanticism that gripped the new masters of the Rhineland in the first half of the 19th century. Together with its park and gardens, and especially its original interior furnishings, it presents visitors today with an artistic synthesis that embodies the politics, beliefs and *zeitgeist* of an entire epoch.

View from the north-east

In 1823 the City of Koblenz – since 1822 capital of the Prussian Rhine Province – presented Crown Prince Friedrich Wilhelm with the ruined castle of Stolzenfels, once a customs post of the Archbishop-Elector of Trier. Refurbishment of the ruins began in 1836 to plans by the famous architect Karl Friedrich Schinkel, and the project was thoroughly expanded when the prince mounted the throne in 1840 as King Friedrich Wilhelm IV of Prussia. The original idea of a picturesque ruin in a landscaped park gave way to that of a royal summer residence – a monument to "Prussian Rhineland". The medieval remnants of Stolzenfels were largely retained and harmonized into a neo-Gothic ensemble in the English manner. This included some entirely new elements like the two Klause outbuildings (servants' quarters and services) and the chapel.

The castle was duly appointed with selected furniture, paintings, stained glass, sculptures, weapons, a collection of glass and ceramics and many other items of applied art specially bought for the purpose or requisitioned from the royal collections. Stolzenfels was to look like the product of unbroken centuries of Prussian rule on the Rhine.

The concept included a 9 hectare (c. 23 acre) park and gardens designed by Peter Joseph Lenné. Conceived as an integral part of the complex, the richly planted gardens – pools of intimacy between interior and exterior – find their highest expression in the Pergola garden. In contrast, the park was designed to speak with the pure voice of nature, its dark watery ravines set off against the broad, light-flooded plain of the Rhine. At the same time, varying sightlines connecting castle, park and landscape were enhanced and clarified.

Stolzenfels Castle was opened personally, with appropriate festivities,

Greater Knights' Hall

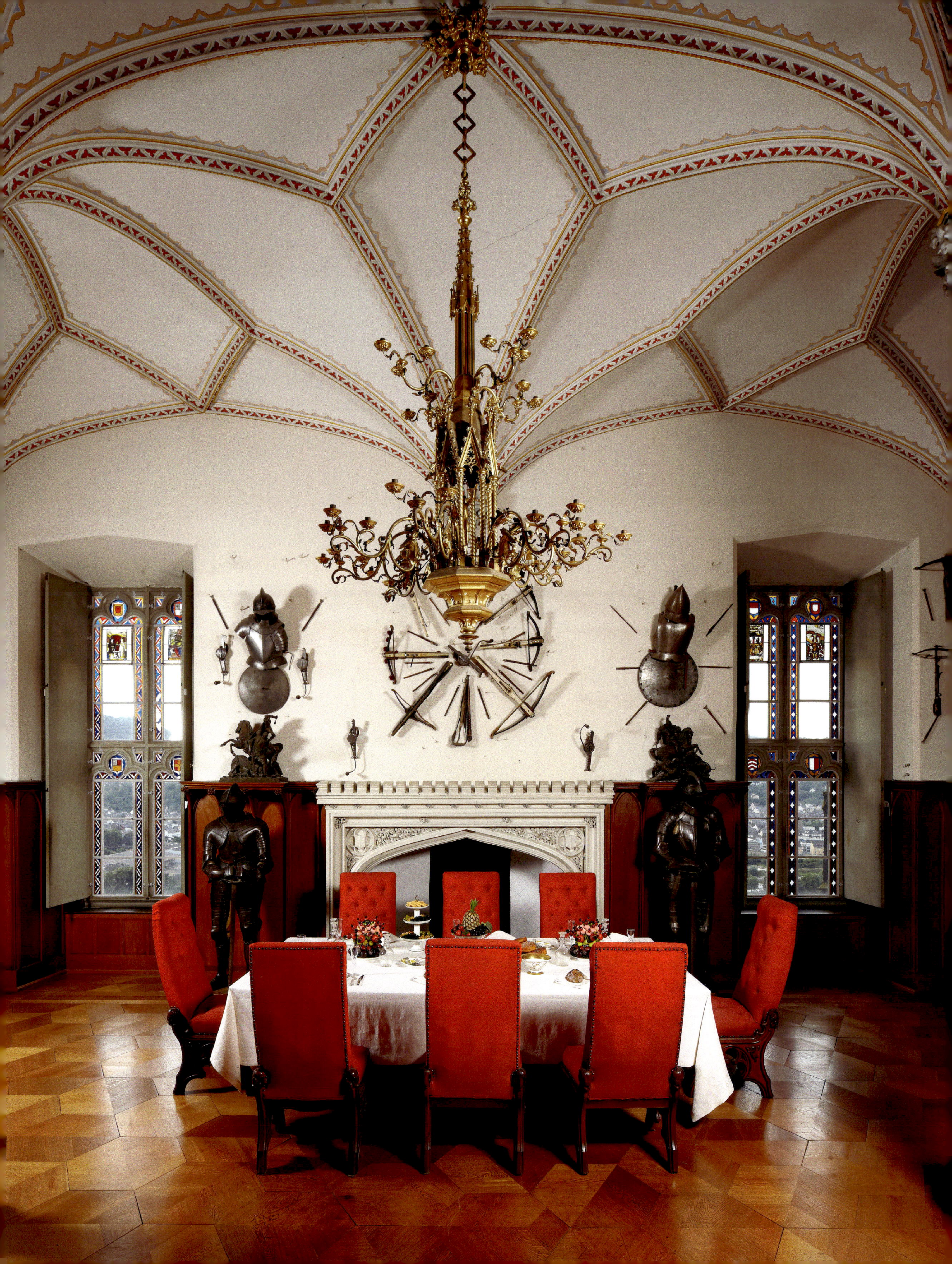

by Friedrich Wilhelm IV in September 1842. Both castle and park were soon afterwards also opened to the public: the King's subjects should form for themselves an image of their new ruler, with his appeal to ancient tradition. Today's visitors can still gain many insights into the romantically tinted understanding of the Prussian monarch's relation to the Rhine. A broad programme of readings, concerts and events has its high-point in the annual Castle Festival, which recalls and re-enacts the legendary royal opening ceremony.

Pergola garden

Chapel

Tiefurt Mansion and Park
Garden landscape of the Muses

A few kilometres east of Weimar in a landscape of wide fields and cottage gardens the 21 hectare (c. 52 acre) landscaped park of Tiefurt Mansion extends on either side of the River Ilm. Gently sloping meadows with picturesque clusters of trees lead from the modest country house down to the river bank. The park has retained its original rural, idyllic character to the present day. Tablets and monuments inscribed "to love and friendship" bear witness to the early Sentimental phase of the landscaped garden.

In the memory of later ages Tiefurt Mansion remains the creative and social centre associated above all with the Dowager Duchess Anna Amalia (1739–1807), who from 1781 until the end of her life spent the summer months here with her family and court, surrounded by poets and artists from Weimar, as well as by important guests from near and far.

The transformation of a former minor property into a ducal summer residence was the result of an unfortunate accident. In 1774 the Weimar City Castle, seat of the dukes of Saxe-Weimar, burned down to its foundations. Seeking suitable accommodation for her younger son Constantin (1758–1793), Anna Amalia's choice fell on Tiefurt Mansion, which had been reappointed only ten years earlier. The young nobleman duly moved there with his tutor Carl Ludwig von Knebel and a few servants in May 1776. With Knebel, Constantin began to reshape the surrounding landscape, creating the first elements of Tiefurt Park between the mansion and the river.

In 1781 the prince embarked on his Grand Tour to England, France and Italy, whereupon Duchess Anna Amalia transferred her summer seat to Tiefurt and continued the landscaping of the park. It was then that the mansion gradually became a temple of the Muses for the Weimar court and their guests. Social life focused on literary readings and performances, and was even accompanied by its own news medium, the *Tiefurt Journal*.

A number of artworks in the mansion derive from Anna Amalia's Italian journey of 1788–1790, while statues and busts by the court sculptor Gottlieb Martin Klauer on the staircase, as well as porcelain from China, Meissen,

Tiefurt Mansion with connecting balcony, from the east

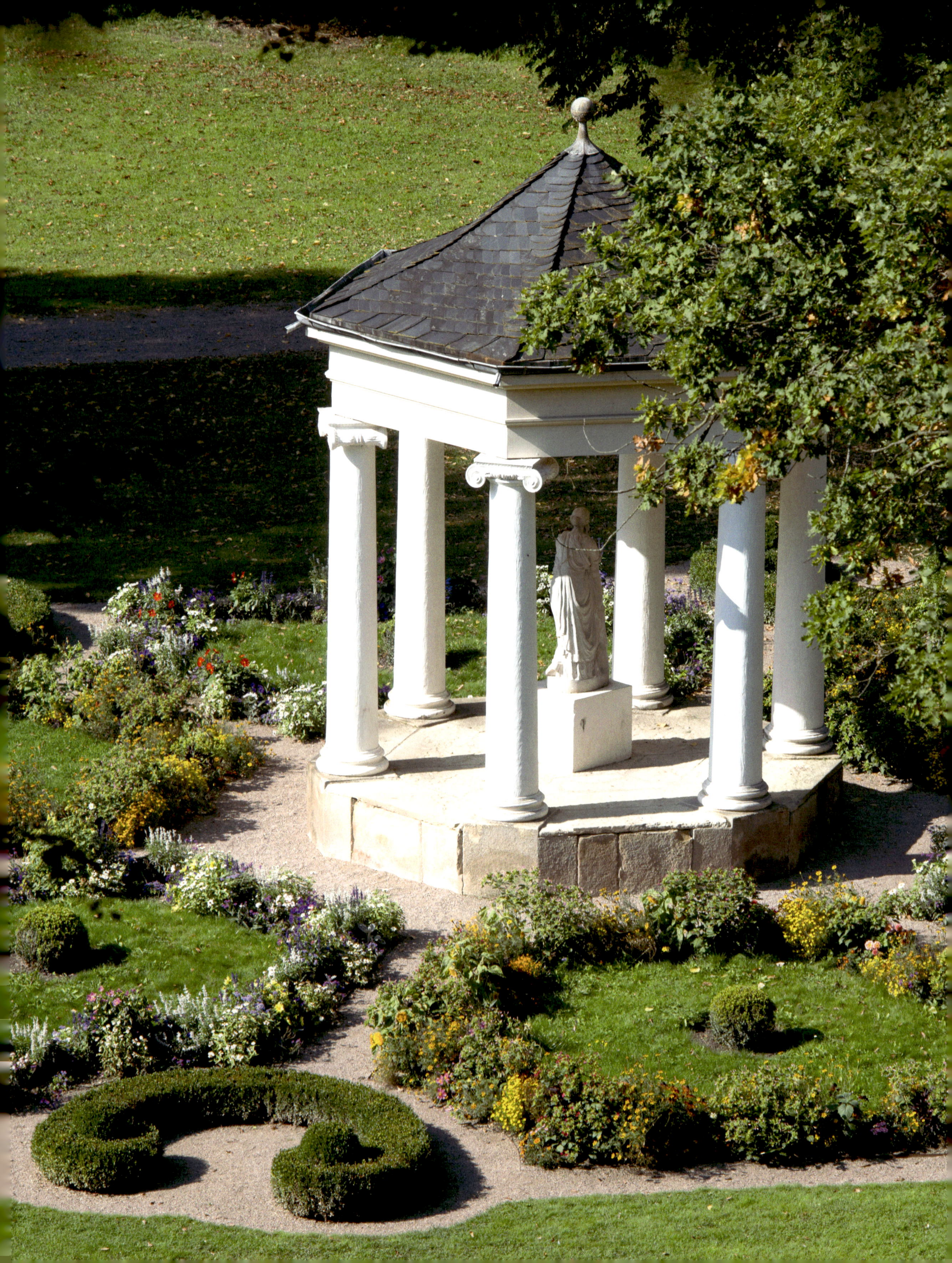

Copenhagen, Fürstenberg and Vienna, are among the high-points of the collection. From the courtyard one can catch a glimpse of the buffet kitchen with its many utensils and an array of deceptively realistic historical dishes moulded from porcelain, wax and papier mâché.

With the plundering of the mansion by French troops in 1806 and the death of Anna Amalia in 1807, Tiefurt fell silent. In connection with the regeneration of woodland, the court gardener, Eduard Petzold, reshaped the park for Grand Duke Carl Friedrich between 1846 and 1850. As Petzold held the monuments left by Anna Amalia, with their motifs of recollection and sentimental edification, in great respect, and no later additions changed the park, these elements still define the character of Tiefurt's garden landscape. Many stands of trees also date from this time.

Tiefurt Park, Temple of the Muses

Tiefurt Park, Salon

Tiefurt Mansion, Goethe Room

Trier

Roman city

Trier plays an outstanding role in the world's cultural heritage. Together with the city's cathedral and Liebfrauenkirche (Church of Our Lady), seven of its Roman monuments were adopted in 1986 onto the UNESCO list of World Cultural Heritage sites, justifying the city's designation as a "Centre of Antiquity". These are: the *Roman Bridge*, a nodal point in the Roman network of long-distance roads and waterways; *Porta Nigra*, the best-preserved Roman city gate north of the Alps; *Amphitheatre*, whose arena, tiers and vaults are still open to the public; *Barbara Baths*, a wellness oasis with cultural centre, library, restaurants, shops and beauty salons; *Imperial Baths*, originally a present from the Roman emperor to the people of Trier; *Basilica of Constantine*, the largest extant pillarless hall of classical antiquity, built as the audience hall of the imperial Palace; and the *Igel Column*, an impressive, 23 metre-tall Roman burial monument in the nearby municipality of Igel.

Founded in 17 BCE, Trier is Germany's oldest city. It was soon the biggest Roman city north of the Alps and possessed outstanding political and strategic importance. In Late Antiquity, after the reorganization of the Roman Empire into various large segments, Trier became the capital of the western empire. Roman emperors – the best known of whom is Constantine the Great – resided here, and the city was the administrative centre of an area that stretched from Gaul and the Germanic provinces to Britain, Portugal and North Africa. No other central European city can rival Trier in either Roman monuments or ancient history.

As well as the UNESCO sites mentioned above, the Cattle Market Baths (Thermen am Viehmarkt) – an excavation site today contained within a pro-

Porta Nigra from the north-east

Igel Column

DASWASSERISTEINKOSTBARGUT
DERMENSCHHAT'S
INDERHAND-
RUMMITIHM
UNFUGTUT
VERDIRBT DAS
VIEH
UNDLAND

tective glass building – offers visitors a glimpse of Trier's history from antiquity to the modern age. Finally, the city's Rhineland Museum (Rheinisches Landesmuseum Trier), established in 1877, is also important for an understanding of Trier's Roman history. As a branch of the State of Rhineland-Palatinate Archaeological Bureau, it holds findings from all local archaeological activities. These include the most comprehensive collection of ancient mosaics north of the Alps, and burial monuments with vivid scenes of everyday Roman life. A special highlight is the 18.5 kilogramme Roman imperial gold treasure – the biggest ever found. The city outskirts also possess some outstanding monuments witnessing to the importance of Trier in Roman times.

Amphitheatre from the north-east

Imperial Baths, interior view from the north-west

Trifels Imperial Castle
Mighty fortress of kings and safe stronghold

The first road-signs for Trifels already appear at the eastern edge of the Palatine Forest, and a short time later the castle itself rises into view atop the long rocky spur of the Sonnenberg near the small town of Annweiler. Trifels is one of the Palatinate's best-known castles and a popular tourist destination. Between 1088 and 1330 it stood at the centre of major political events.

The castle's origins date from the Salian period (10th–12th centuries). First mentioned in records in 1081, it reached the zenith of its importance under the Hohenstaufens (1138–1250), who had secured mastery of large parts of Swabia, Alsace and, above all, the Palatinate. Parts of the Trifels complex – including the first three storeys of the central tower, with the chapel on the second floor – date from this time. A second point of especial interest is the Well Tower, some 20 metres high. This is finished in the typical rough-hewn ashlars (stone blocks) of the Hohenstaufen age found throughout the castle.

The present appearance of Trifels is largely due to reconstruction work launched by the National Socialists in 1938. Then in ruins, the castle was to be resurrected as a national site sacred to the ideology of the regime. After the Second World War, Rudolf Esterer, who had planned this work, became president of the Bavarian Castles Administration. The construction of the Great Hall with the Kaisersaal (Imperial Hall) and the raising of the tower by another (fourth) storey are the most notable results of Esterer's work, which was continued well into the post-war period.

These measures, too, reflected the political importance of Trifels during the Hohenstaufen period, when it was

Trifels Castle from the south-east

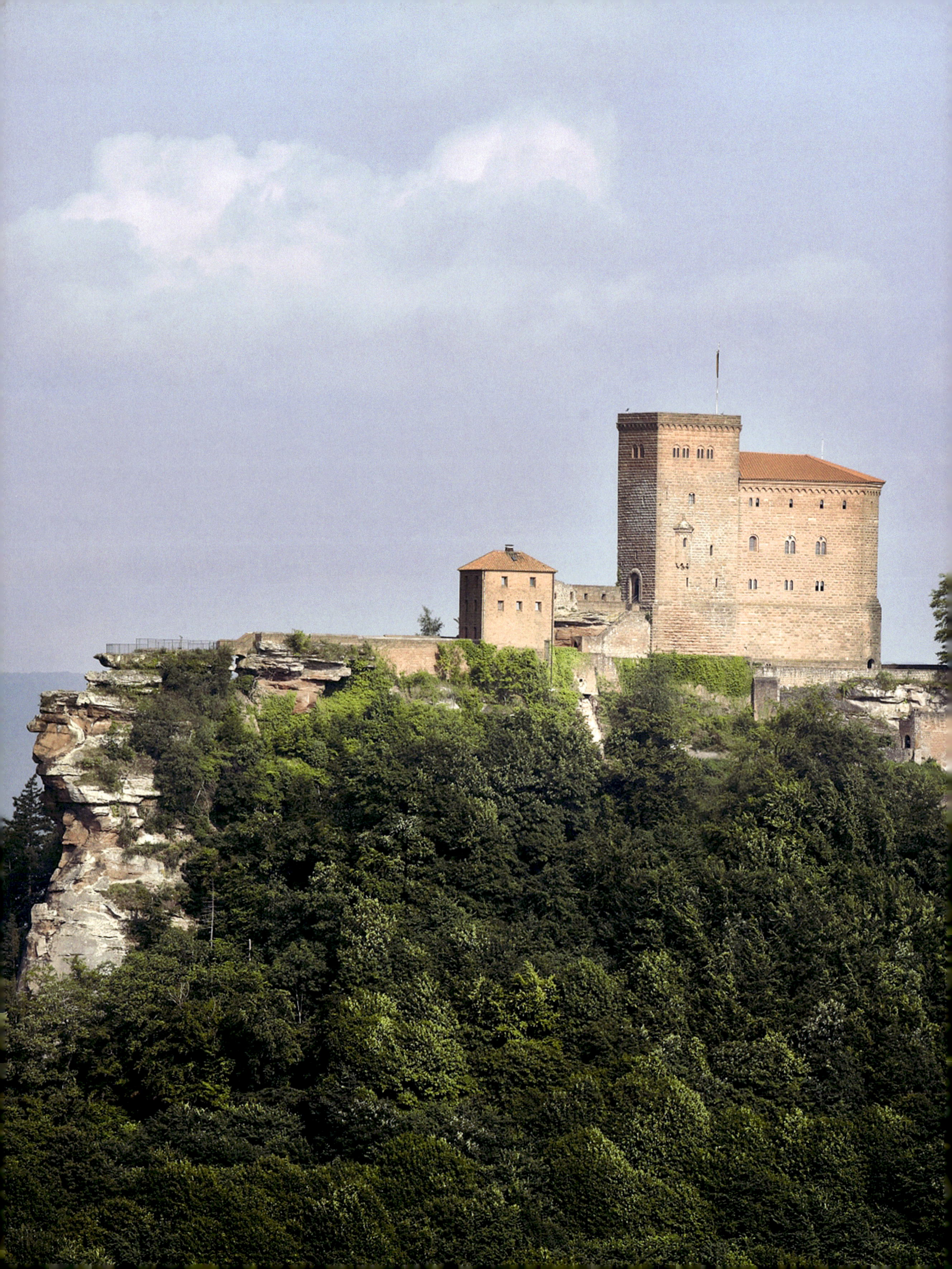

repeatedly at the focus of major historical developments. Legendary in the true sense of the word is the imprisonment of the English king, Richard the Lionheart, in "the emperor's safest castle". Heinrich VI intercepted him while he was on his way back from the Third Crusade and held him there briefly in 1193 against the gigantic ransom of 23 tons of silver – plus some political concessions. Only after fulfilling the Emperor's conditions was Richard allowed to return to England. The castle also served as a famously secure treasury for the imperial crown jewels, priceless symbols of regal power, which were kept there on several occasions under the Hohenstaufens. Today, valuable replicas of the crown, orb and sceptre, sword and cross of the Holy Roman Empire, as well as the so-called Holy Lance, are exhibited in Trifels Castle.

Trifels Castle from
the east

Kaisersaal (Imperial Hall)

Treasury with replicas of the imperial
Crown Jewels

207

Ulrichshusen Castle Estate

Cultural centre and jewel of Mecklenburg's lakeland

Entering Ulrichshusen, one is captivated by the magic of the place. A low dry-stone wall encircles a park landscaped in the English style with centuries-old oaks and chestnuts. Past reed-lined ponds one arrives at the schloss, which, standing serenely on its low hill, immediately absorbs all one's attention.

Ulrich von Maltzan built the Renaissance stronghold in 1562. To this day it remains embedded in the untouched landscape of Mecklenburg's lakeland, surrounded by golden fields, dense woods and tranquil waters. The commotion of an eventful history has died down – a history of destruction from the Thirty Years' War to the great fire of 1987. At the time of German reunification in 1990, when Helmuth, Baron Maltzahn, resolved to rebuild his family's ancestral seat, the Renaissance building was a ruin.

Out of that ruin has arisen a cultural-historical jewel, an arts centre filled with music not only in summer, but also at Christmas-time and in early January, when the New Year's concerts of the Mecklenburg-Western Pomeranian Festival take place. Ulrichshusen has long since established itself as one of the country's major festival venues. Every year the Great Barn, one of northern Germany's biggest concert halls, hosts the Mecklenburg-Western Pomeranian Festival, which attracts musicians from across the globe. When the great violinist and conductor Lord Yehudi Menuhin inaugurated the hall in 1994, he fell so in love with Ulrichshusen that he returned every year until

Schloss Ulrichshusen at dusk

Embedded between lake and meadows, fields and woods

A winter idyll

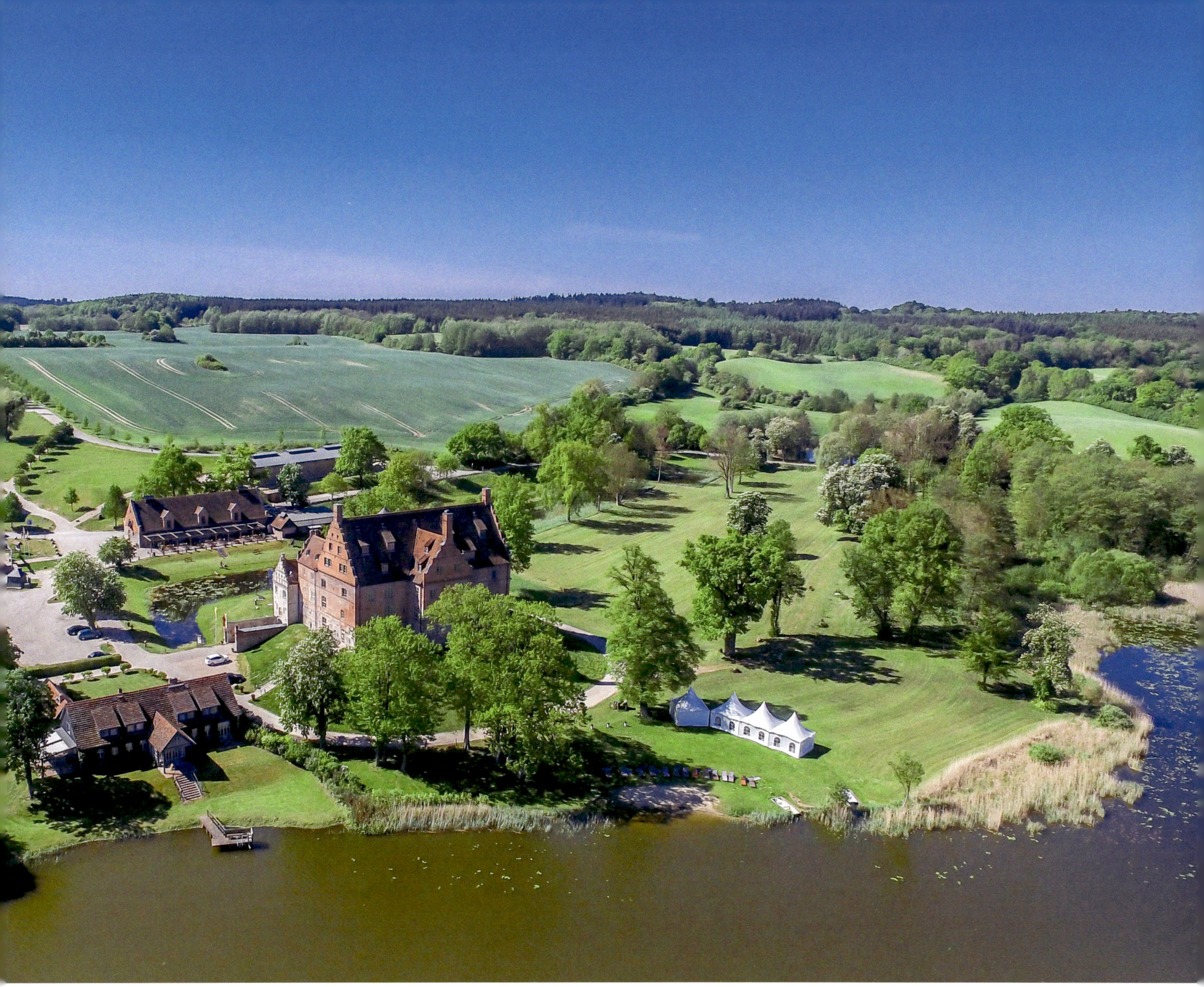

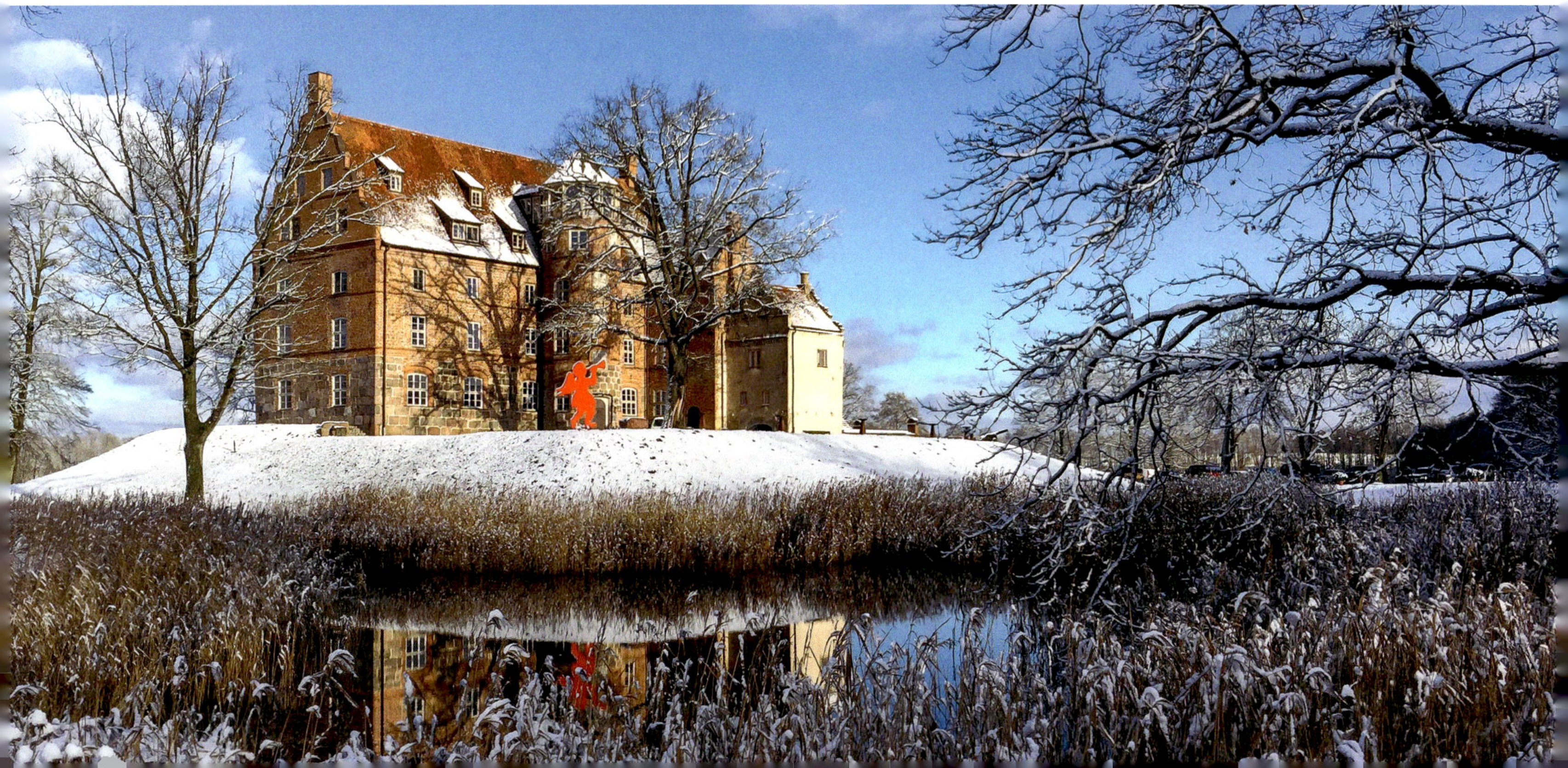

his death. And every year star musicians like Anne-Sophie Mutter, Daniel Hope, or Julia Fischer draw more than 80,000 classical music lovers to this village of 35 souls.

Like the music lovers, lovers of nature have every reason to visit Ulrichshusen. The castle park, meadowlands and lake unite with the castle itself to create a rural estate in line with its founder's ideas, where careful husbandry has given new life to an ancient cultural landscape. A comfortable restaurant in the old stables welcomes its guests with the elegance of simplicity: a country kitchen, home-baked bread and regional fare, with fish and crabs from the lakes and streams, game shot on the estate, and fruit and cereals from local farms – all of it prepared and served for the discriminating palate. Accommodation is available in the guestrooms and apartments of the castle and its ancillary buildings, as well as at nearby Ulrichshusen Farm. The historical ensemble provides space in abundance for individual vacations, weddings, conferences and major events of every kind, and its facilities include a generously equipped wellness centre. Set at the heart of Mecklenburg's beautiful lakeland, with its unique recreational potential, Ulrichshusen is one of the most popular and ecologically best sustained tourist destinations in Mecklenburg-Western Pomerania.

Restaurant by the moat

Great Hall

Wartburg World Heritage Site

Living history in ancient walls

For almost a thousand years Wartburg Castle has watched from its mountain fastness over the city of Eisenach in Thuringia. Its appearance has changed over the centuries, as have the perceptions of its visitors and inhabitants. The awed wonder that may have filled our forefathers in the presence of such might and authority has long since given way to an admiration of medieval architectural skill and a fascination with the magnificent view. Wartburg is the only German castle to have been adopted (in 1999) onto the UNESCO World Heritage list.

Entering the castle is like opening a thousand year-old history book: The 12th century Great Hall, a jewel of late Romanesque architecture, still testifies today to the Wartburg's former glory. Founded according to legend in 1067 as the seat of a landgrave, the castle became a home to the arts, famous above all for the songs of Walther von der Vogelweide and the epic verse of Wolfram von Eschenbach. The legendary "minstrels' contest", eternalized in Wagner's opera *Tannhäuser*, must be seen against this background. But the Wartburg was also where Elizabeth of Thuringia and Hungary – still venerated as a saint today – lived and ministered to the poor. And it provided the exiled Martin Luther with protection: it was here that he translated the New Testament into German. Finally, the Wartburg Fest of 1817 was one of the earliest occasions on which the student organizations of the time publicly embraced the vision of a free and democratic German nation.

Wartburg Castle provided the setting for all these great moments of German culture. It has been in turn a defensive stronghold, a noble residence, and a shelter and place of refuge for its inhabitants of long-gone centuries. At times derelict, but never forgotten, it underwent a resurrection in the 19th century. Medieval structures were restored and supplemented with Romantic historicist additions, the prime example being the ballroom in the Great Hall, today a backdrop for many events, including the well-known Wartburg summer concerts.

The castle's art collection, with treasures from eight centuries, owes its origin to a personal recommendation of Goethe's now almost 200 years ago. It has become a notable European collection with holdings totalling some 9000 works, among its highlights numerous paintings by Lucas Cranach the Elder.

And the Wartburg has maintained its tradition of hospitality, welcoming both the quickly passing visitor and those with more time, who can enjoy a meal in its tastefully appointed restau-

View of the first courtyard

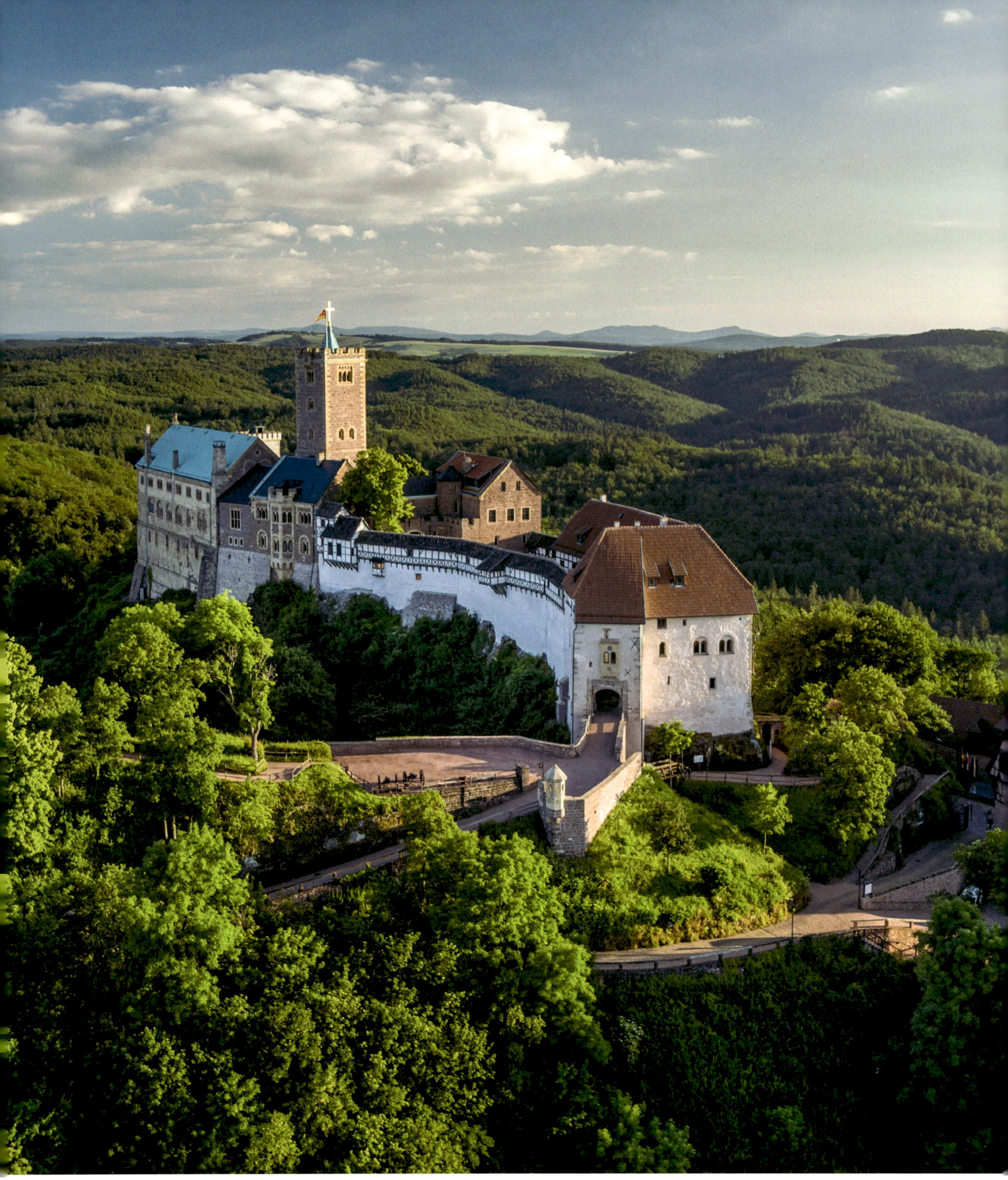

rants or stay a while in one of the 38 individually styled rooms of the "Hotel auf der Wartburg". Advent weekends are a special feast for lovers of romantic Christmas markets – they will certainly return for more.

Aerial view of Wartburg Castle

Great Hall

Luther's study – birthplace of the modern German language

Weilburg on the Lahn – Castle and Gardens

From medieval castle to Renaissance residence and Baroque palace

Prominently situated on a hilly spur above the Lahn, Weilburg Castle is one of the State of Hesse's foremost cultural monuments and a typical example of the residence of a minor German nobleman. Almost 400 metres of the eastern half of the ridge were raised and flattened to create space for the erection of a complex that fills almost half the old town centre of Weilburg.

The story begins in the 10th century with the Conradine line of German kings, who built an early defensive castle in Weilburg. After several further phases of construction this was transformed by Count Philipp III, starting in 1533, into a four-wing Renaissance palace – a measure made necessary by the various divisions and reunions of the house of Nassau-Weilburg, and one that promoted Weilburg to the rank of "residential city". The so-called High Castle remains almost unchanged to this day. A final stage of construction took place in the early 18th century under Count Johann Ernst, who commissioned the famous master builder Julius Ludwig Rothweil to extend the residence into a handsome Baroque ensemble. Careful matching of the façades ensured the architectural unity of the complex, and it is very largely Rothweil's work – with the addition of some ancillary buildings and the completion of the garden layout – that the visitor sees today.

A tour of Schloss Weilburg's interior takes one through every epoch: The elector's bedchamber and the "Chinese cabinet" are decorated in the ornate Baroque style, while the residential apartments were modernized in the early 19th century in the formally more severe Empire style exemplified in their imaged wall-coverings.

The two orangeries served different purposes: While the Lower Orangery was used principally as a conservatory

With its striking interior design, the Upper Orangery was not only used as a winter conservatory.

Weilburg Castle and its gardens – enthroned high above the Lahn

214

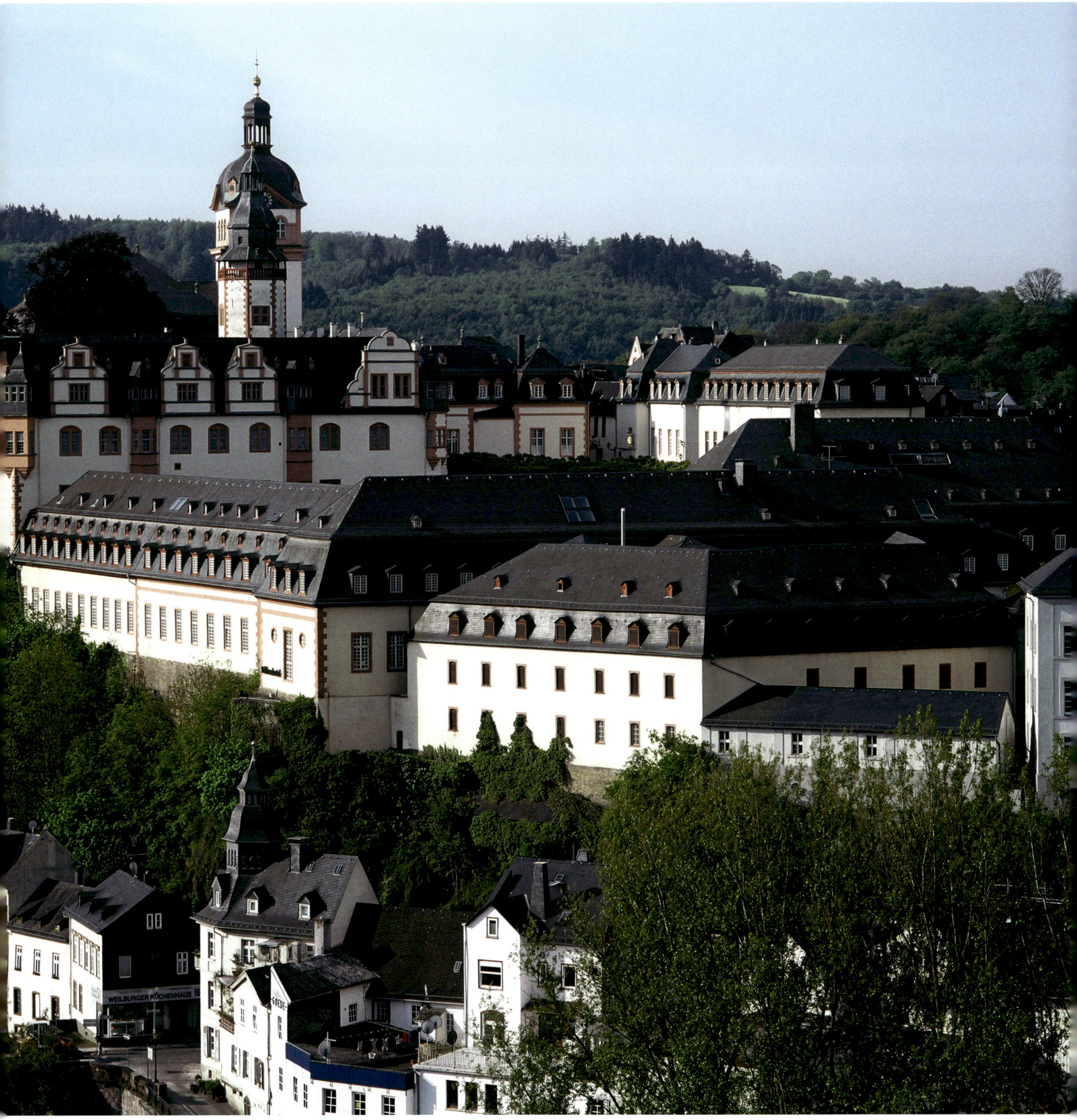
WEILBURGER KÜCHENHAUS

for plants in winter, the more richly decorated Upper Orangery with its French windows provided not only a corridor connecting the palace and church but also a fitting place for courtly entertainment and festivities.

Outside the Castle, the splendour and influence of the court is evident in the town and gardens of Weilburg. These latter cover a number of terraces, each notable for their typically Baroque symmetry – only the grid patterned "Lime-Tree Hall" and the steeply wooded slope down to the River Lahn form a marked contrast to this order. Eye-catching aspects here, as well as the richly variegated flower beds and lawns, are a number of small architectural features like the Hercules Fountain in the Upper Garden, which depicts a scene from classical mythology, or the fountain in front of the Lower Orangery, which is flanked by two life-size gilded lead figures.

Gilded figure of a discus thrower in front of the Lower Orangery

Upper Garden with "Lime-Tree Hall"

Weimar City Castle and Park on the Ilm

An ensemble of castle, park and artworks

Weimar's City Castle on the banks of the Ilm was from the mid-16th century the permanent residence of the Dukes of Saxe-Weimar and Eisenach. First mentioned in 10th century records as a moated castle, the ensemble grew under the auspices of the later dukes into a three-winged Baroque castle open to the south which, however, largely burned down in 1774. Its rebuilding – in which Johann Wolfgang Goethe played a significant role – bore fruit in the Neoclassical interior that has come down to us today, its high-point being the staircase and ballroom by Heinrich Gentz. A tour of the castle takes in these architectonic masterworks, as it does the Poets' Room, which the Grand Duchess and Tsar's daughter Maria Pawlowna created in the 19th century in honour of Christoph Martin Wieland, Johann Gottfried Herder, Friedrich Schiller and Johann Wolfgang Goethe.

The former Grand Ducal art collection is today housed in these historic rooms, whose fixed elements are for the most part original. The collection includes masterpieces from the Middle Ages to the Modern period around 1900, with the Cranach gallery on the ground floor, as well as works by Caspar David Friedrich, Johann Heinrich Wilhelm Tischbein, Auguste Rodin and Max Beckmann. The *bel étage* contains sculptures and applied art from the early years of the 19th century, including some items from Maria Pawlowna's dowry. Works of the Weimar School, and of German and French Modernism, can be seen on the second floor. Added in 1914 to close off the inner courtyard from the park along the Ilm, the south wing houses the administrative headquarters of Classical Foundation Weimar.

Adjoining the castle is a 50 hectare (c. 125 acre) park on either side of the Ilm. The first architectonic and scenic elements were installed here in 1778 at the rocky western escarpment. The landscaped garden was then extended across the water-meadows of the Ilm and above the escarpment – the older Star and Southern Gardens were adapted and integrated into the overall concept. The Neoclassical Roman House that marks the formal climax of the southern park was installed by Duke Carl August between 1791 and

NOTE: Weimar City Castle as a whole will remain closed for general refurbishment until (on present estimates) 2028. It is, however, planned to admit museum visitors from 2023

Weimar City Castle, east wing

1797. Another characteristic feature of the park is the sightlines that heighten the impact not only of elements like Goethe's Garden House, the Roman House, and Bark Cottage, but also – outside the park – the tower of the city's Oberweimar church. Landscaping work in the park essentially ended with the death of Duke Carl August, its leading spirit, in 1828.

Roman House in the Park on the Ilm

Weimar City Castle, Goethe Gallery

Weimar City Castle, staircase by Heinrich Gentz, looking south-west

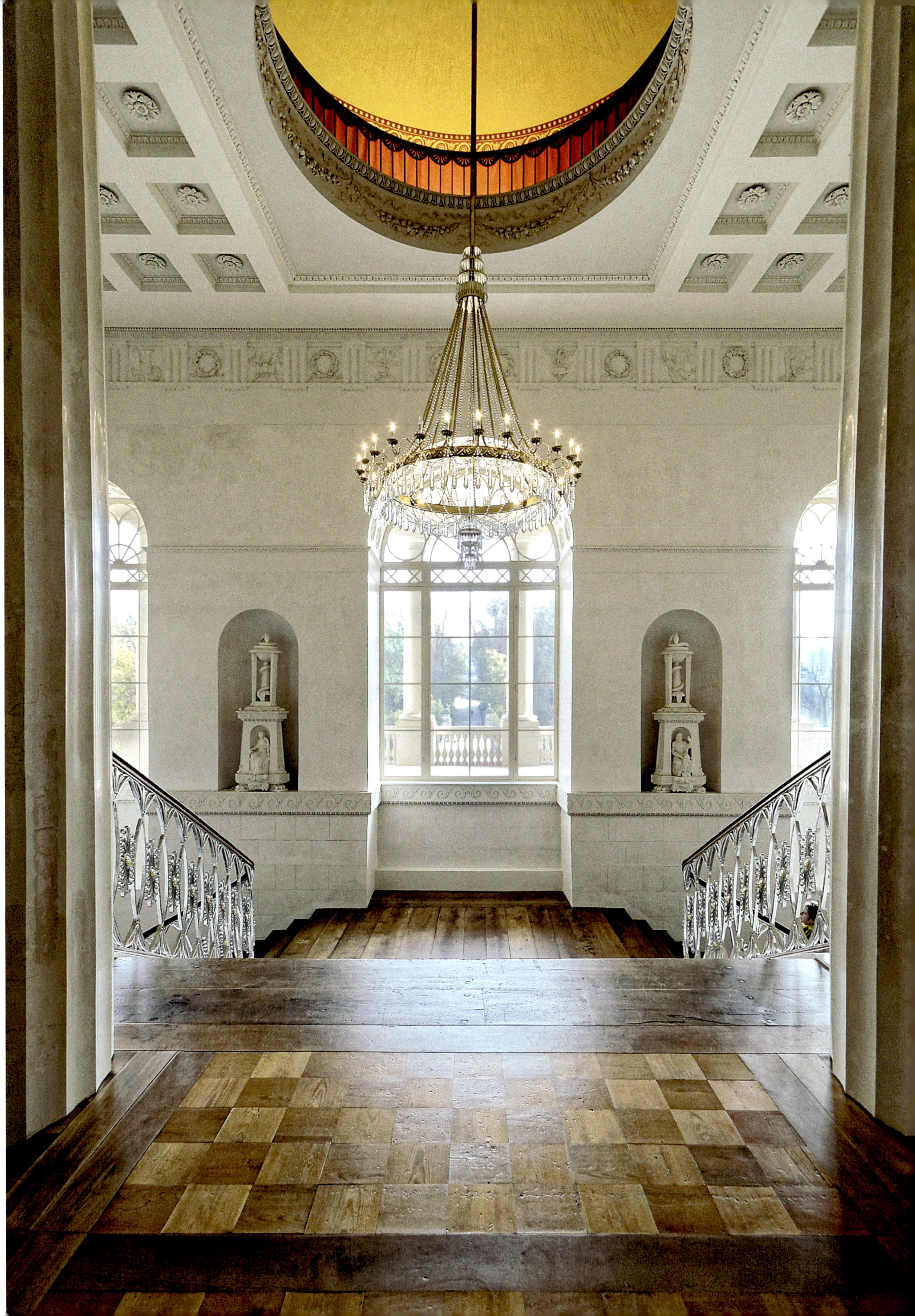

Weissenstein Palace

Baroque splendour in the Steigerwald

Weissenstein Palace near Bamberg was built between 1711 and 1718 as the private summer residence of Bishop-Elector Lothar Franz von Schönborn. It has remained to the present day in the ownership of the Counts of Schönborn, who still enjoy spending the summer months in Pommersfelden. With its rural position on the edge of the Steigerwald, the Baroque palace remained largely undisturbed by war and pestilence, and ranks today as one of Europe's best preserved cultural monuments.

The master builders Johann Dientzenhofer and – in a more consultative capacity – Johann Lukas von Hildebrandt were responsible for drawing up the plans for the palace. But the bishop himself played a major role in their realization, evident above all in the great staircase, which he spoke of as his "masterpiece". The imposing flight of steps served the extravagant purposes of Baroque court ceremonial – for example in the greeting of guests – as much as it did simply to gain access to the upper floors. Crowning the 8000 cubic metres of light-flooded space around it in the entrance hall is a magnificent ceiling fresco by Rudolf Byss and Giovanni Francesco Marchini.

Completely covered with shells, minerals, and stones, the Sala Terrena is a grotto-like room whose thick walls served to keep it cool in summer. Sculptures of the four elements and four seasons underline the proximity of nature, and form a link with the garden, whose original Baroque layout was modernized in the 19th century to a park landscaped in the English fashion.

The Marble Hall in the *piano nobile* serves today as a concert room. Decorated with marble and marbled stucco, as well as with stucco work by Daniel Schenk, it displays on its walls a genealogical portrait gallery of the Counts of Schönborn. The ceiling fresco by the Austrian artist Johann Michael Rottmayer is a symbolic depiction of virtue.

As well as an obsessive builder, Lothar Franz von Schönborn was a collector of paintings, books, silver, porcelain and other curiosities, many of which are today on view for visitors. His several hundred paintings still hang, in typical Baroque order, in the special gallery he had installed for that purpose. Further paintings, as well as elaborate stucco work, adorn the Flower Room and other spaces, including the Bishop-Elector's study and his personal suite of domestic and guest rooms.

For the exceptionally fine marquetry in the Mirror Room the cabinet maker Ferdinand Plitzner used wood from var-

Weissenstein Palace in Pommersfelden, with princely stables and outbuildings

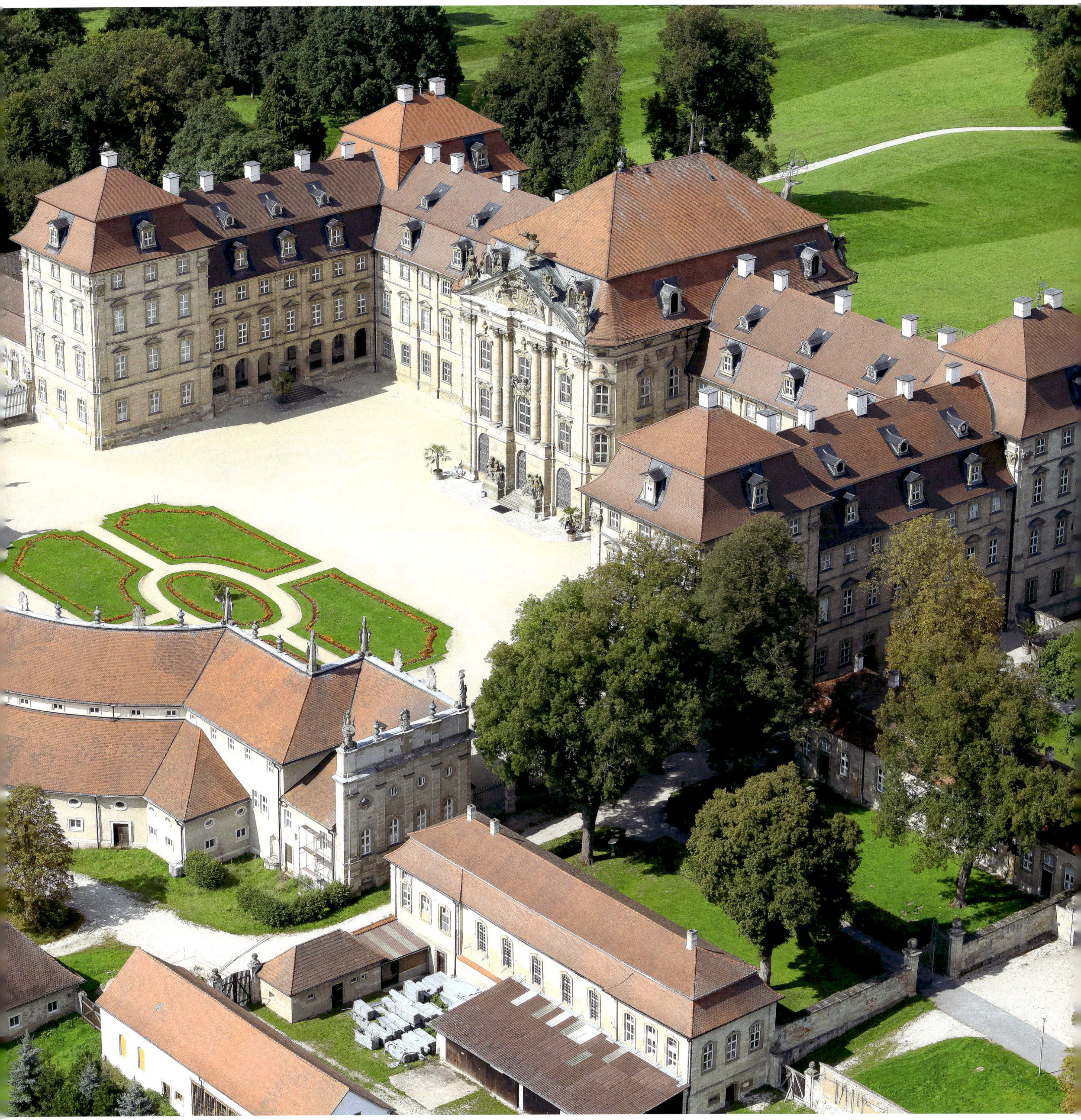

Weissenstein Palace

ious fruit trees and conifers. Based on French models, the mirrors themselves capture and multiply not only the extravagant room furnishings but also the valuable collection of Far Eastern porcelain displayed there.

Mirror Room by Ferdinand Plitzner

Marble Hall

Wernigerode Castle®

Centre for the History of 19th Century Art and Culture

Wernigerode Castle is one of Germany's great historicist edifices – a fairytale castle with an aura calculated to impress. Its history began in 1121, with the first documentary mention of a *comes de wernigerothe* and of the castle and wooded settlement of Wernigerode ("Werniger clearing"). The buildings were altered at various times in the Middle Ages; a stone coat of arms in the inner courtyard dates the final Late Gothic additions to 1494.

After 1429 the castle passed from the House of Wernigerode to the related House of Stolberg, whose counts thereupon took the name of Stolberg-Wernigerode. In the early 16th century, Botho III of that line strengthened the fortifications. The castle suffered greatly in the Thirty Years' War, but considerable portions of the medieval and Renaissance buildings have nevertheless been preserved intact. From 1710 the castle increasingly took on the aspect of a Baroque ensemble.

A comprehensive transformation under the influence of historicism took place between 1862 and 1885 under Count Otto zu Stolberg-Wernigerode, whose meteoric rise to political power had brought with it a need for suitably imposing, as well as comfortable, accommodation. The task was entrusted to the Blankenburg architect and master builder Carl Frühling who, with the Vienna cathedral architect Friedrich von Schmidt – who also built the neo-Gothic Vienna Town Hall – was responsible for the castle church of Sts. Pantaleon and Anna.

In its present-day – still largely authentic – form, Wernigerode Castle is an artistic synthesis on historicist lines. Three architectural ideas guided Frühling's work: first, the castle ensemble should express a single organic principle; then, every 45° around the castle should provide a different perspective; and, finally, there should be no repetition of either architectonic form or interior design. Recourse to the architectonic idiom of former ages should evoke a specific mood or cite a historical motif.

After 1929 the Stolberg-Wernigerode family no longer lived in the castle, and from 1930 it functioned as a museum. In 1949 this became Wernigerode Castle Feudal Museum, which in the 1950s was considered "the biggest socio-historical museum of the German

Wernigerode Castle from the Agnesberg

Democratic Republic". Restoration of the valuable historicist interior architecture began in the 1980s, and in 1998 Wernigerode Castle became the country's first Centre for the History of 19th Century Art and Culture. The castle ensemble includes three major gardens: the *Jardin de Plaisance* with the Orangery, the *Tiergarten* (a landscaped park), and the Castle Terrace Gardens.

Banqueting Hall

Historic Hall

Wernigerode Castle at sunset from the south-east

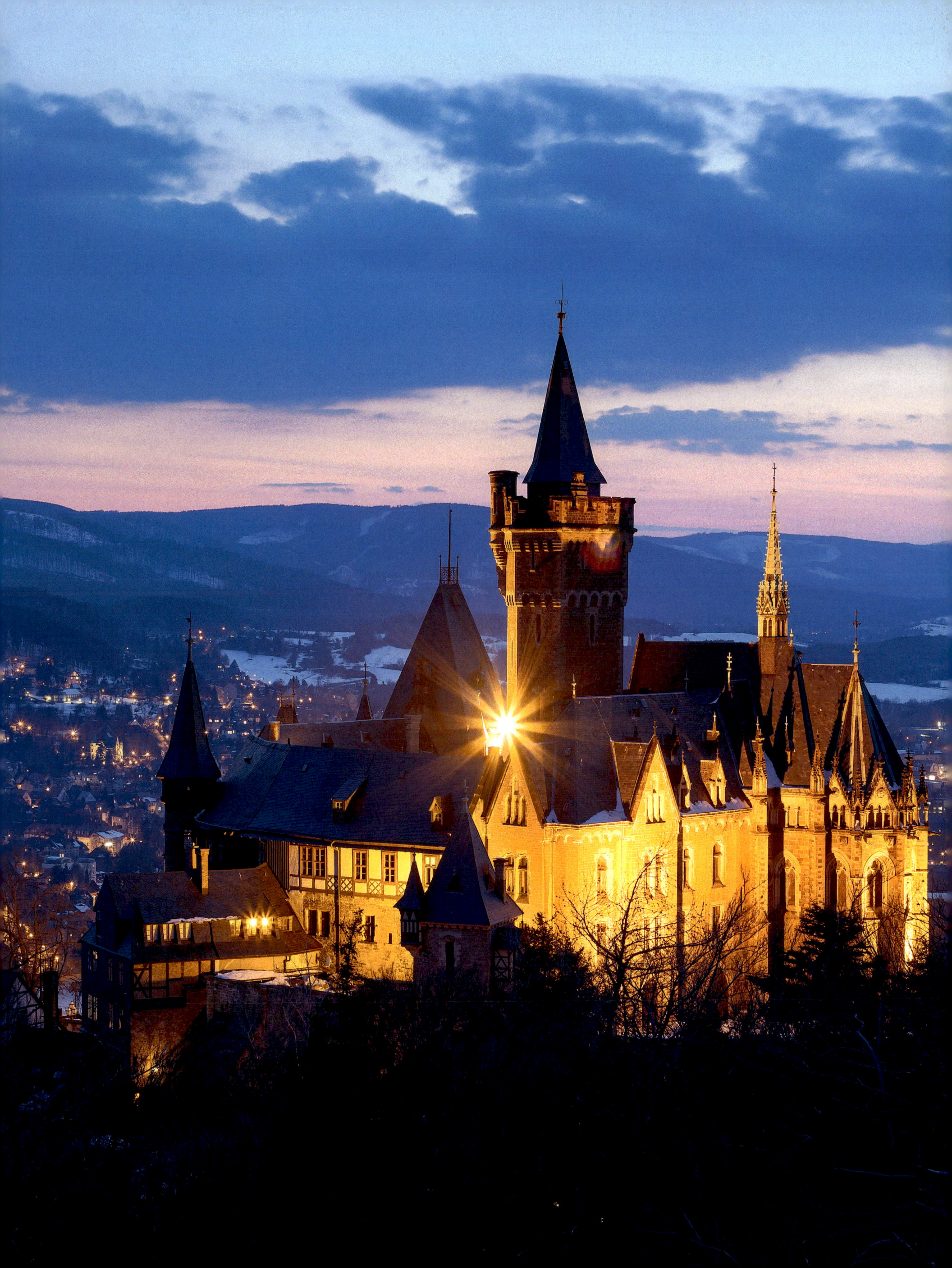

Wilhelmsburg Castle in Schmalkalden

A Hessian castle in Thüringia

Set on a gentle slope of the Thuringian Forest foothills above the timber-framed town of Schmalkalden, Wilhelmsburg Castle began its life in 1585 as a secondary residence of the Landgraves of Hesse-Kassel. With its excellent overall state of conservation and exceptional interior decor, it is considered one of Germany's most important Renaissance mansions.

A lover of the arts, with wide experience of building projects, Landgrave Wilhelm IV of Hesse-Kassel (1532–1592) took a personal interest in the design and completion of his Castle, as well as in its equipment and furnishing. The terraced garden and outbuildings, which today ear unusual witness to the horticultural practices of the period, date from the early 17th century. A permanent exhibition in Wilhelmsburg Castle Museum presents the history of the mansion, set in the context of the aristocratic residential culture of the Renaissance and the history of the Reformation.

As a regularly proportioned four-wing ensemble, with staircase towers in each corner of its inner courtyard, Wilhelmsburg Castle embodies the Renaissance ideal of the *castello*. In the arrangement of its rooms it foreshadowed later developments in Early Modern noble houses, with master apartments of three or four rooms interconnected by salons. The private apartments and formal reception rooms, as well as the great ground floor kitchen, separate administrative and service buildings and many-faceted grounds, present an impressive picture of courtly culture at the turn of the 17th century. Particularly striking are the illusionistic wall decorations, which weave human, vegetable and abstract motifs playfully together.

The chapel in the south wing is a galleried hall church in the tradition of the chapel in Torgau Castle inaugurated by Martin Luther in 1544. Its ordering of altar, baptismal font, pulpit and organ along a central axis pioneered the pulpit-altar alignment of many future Lutheran churches. The organ, completed in 1589, is of particular interest for its ranks of wooden pipes; it is one of the oldest still playable instruments in Germany.

In 1602 Landgrave Moritz laid down a terraced garden to the south of the schloss. In the spirit of the Renaissance garden, this combined crop and decorative plants in geometrically ordered beds, flowers alternating with medicinal herbs, vegetables and vines for the use of the court. A high point of horticultural art was the water supply, which took different forms over the course of time. After the 18th century, the garden fell into neglect and at

Great Hall

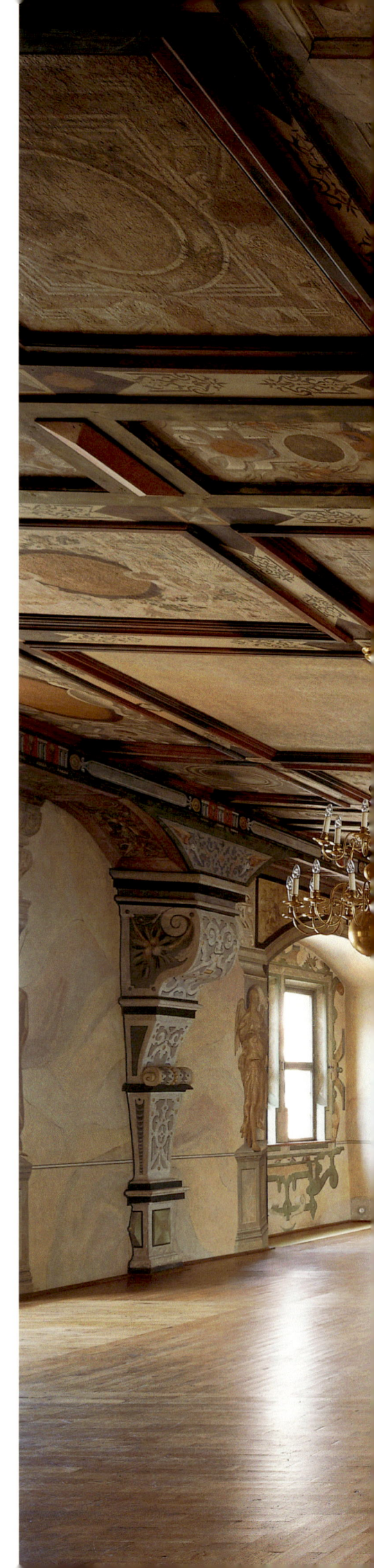

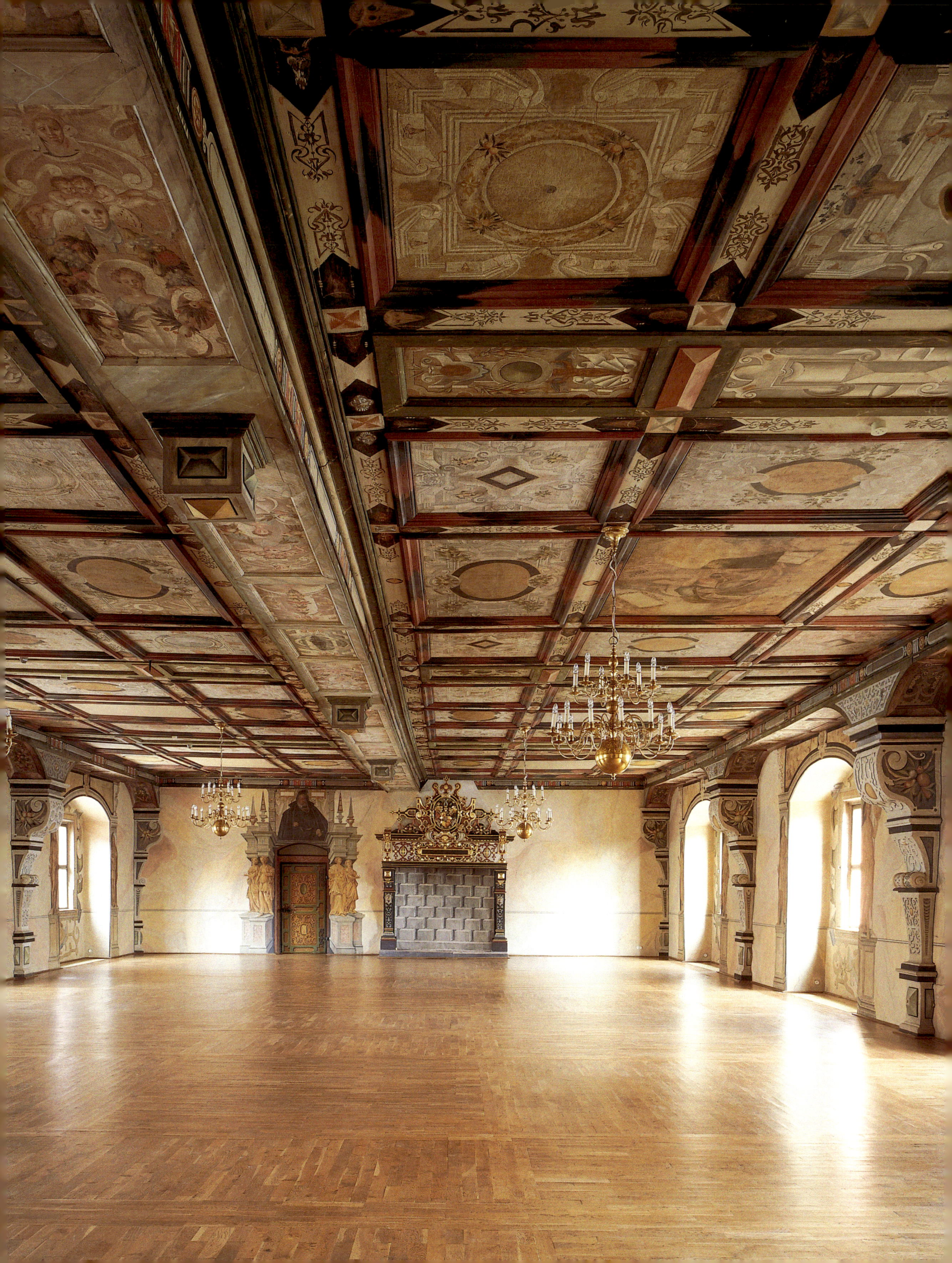

times underwent severe simplification. More recently, from 2013 to 2015, work has been undertaken to restore it to its basic original form.

Wilhelmsburg Castle with terraced garden and view of the town

Wilhelmsgemach (Landgrave Wilhelm's apartment) – reception room with wall decoration

Schloss Wilhelmshöhe
Palace with international flair

The foundation stone for Wilhelmshöhe Palace was laid in 1786 on a plateau above the central German city of Kassel. Today, as part of the artistic synthesis of Bergpark Wilhelmshöhe – a UNESCO World Heritage site – Wilhelmshöhe Palace houses the Old Masters Gallery, the Collection of Antiquities, the Collection of Prints and Drawings, and the Palace Museum in the Weissenstein Wing.

As one of the most important collections of its kind, the Old Masters Gallery enjoys worldwide renown. Some 500 paintings on three floors represent European art from the Late Gothic to the Neoclassical period. A special focus is put on Dutch and Flemish paintings of the 17th century, with numerous masterpieces by Rubens, Frans Hals, Van Dyck and Jordaens. The gallery's holdings of Rembrandt, with famous paintings like *Jacob Blessing the Sons of Joseph* or the *Portrait of Saskia van Uylenburgh*, is one of the biggest worldwide. The schools of Old German, Italian, French and Spanish painting are represented by Dürer, Tizian, Poussin and Murillo, among others.

The Collection of Antiquities on the ground floor and basement provides a fascinating overview of bygone cultures of the Mediterranean countries. Its extensive holdings, counting some 800 exhibits – among them around 60 sculptures – illustrate the development of different cultures with artefacts from the Bronze Age to the Golden Age of Greece and the Roman Empire.

The Collection of Prints and Drawings of Hesse-Kassel comprises more than 60,000 works on paper, among them water-colours, pencil and charcoal sketches, gouaches, copperplate engravings, woodcuts, posters, and illustrated books, as well as many other prints from the Late Middle Ages to the present – from Albrecht Dürer to Georg Baselitz. By prior (telephonic) arrangement, items from this collection may be examined close-up in the study room of the Collection of Prints and Drawings in the Kirchflügel, part of Wilhelmshöhe Palace.

The south wing of Wilhelmshöhe Palace (Weissenstein Wing) originally contained the reception and state rooms, as well as the private apartments of the landgravial family and

Wilhelmshöhe Palace – Bergpark
Wilhelmshöhe UNESCO World Heritage site

their high-ranking guests. The Weissenstein Wing is unique among Kassel's stately homes in having survived the Second World War largely undamaged, with its historical furnishings intact. As such, it offers interesting insights into the courtly domestic culture of the period around 1800. In particular, the dining room, portrait gallery, and Empire-style apartments of the Elector, with their splendid marble bathroom, are worth closer examination.

Elector's room in the Weissenstein Wing

Detail of a Rembrandt painting with viewer's profile, Old Masters Gallery

Rembrandt room in the Old Masters Gallery

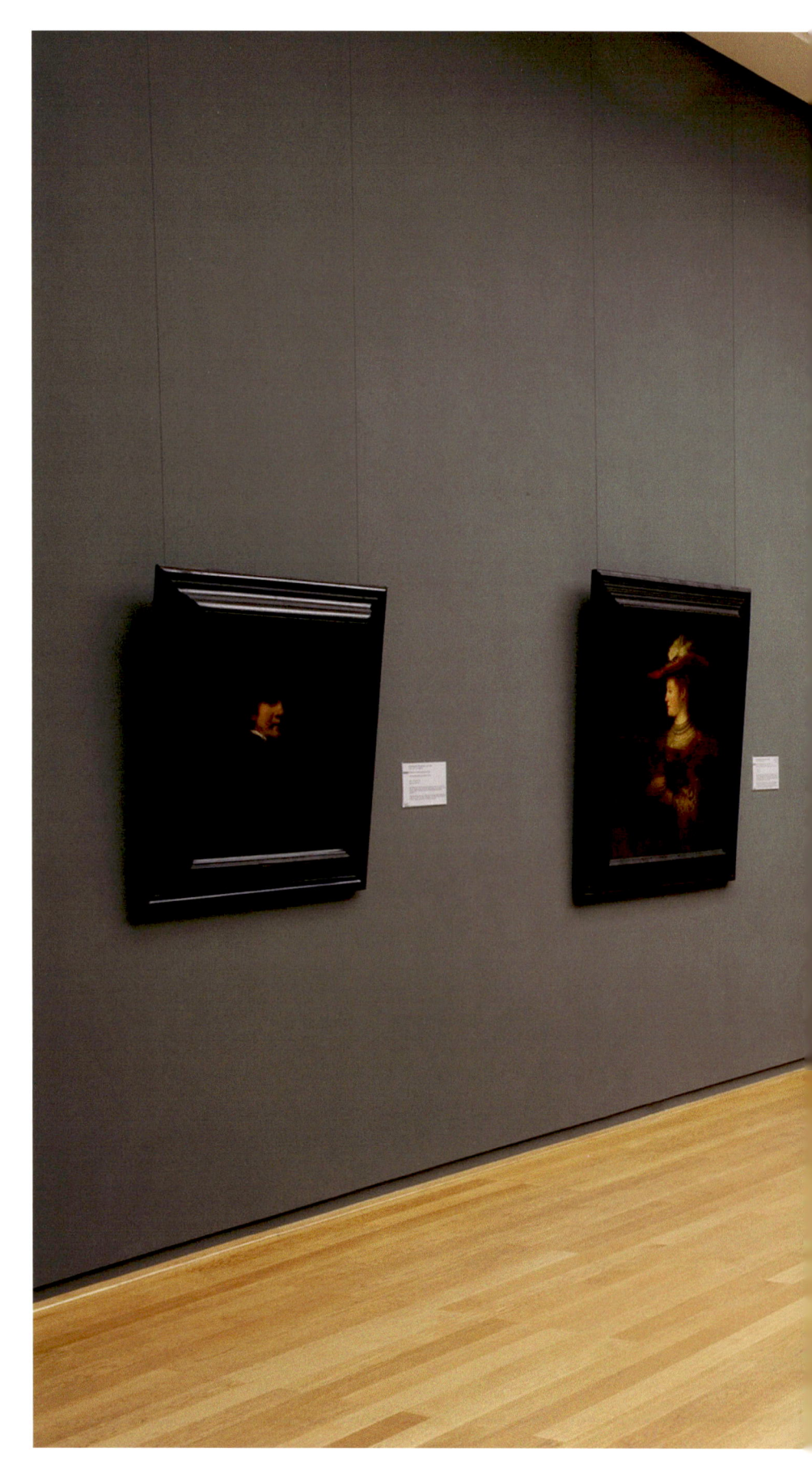

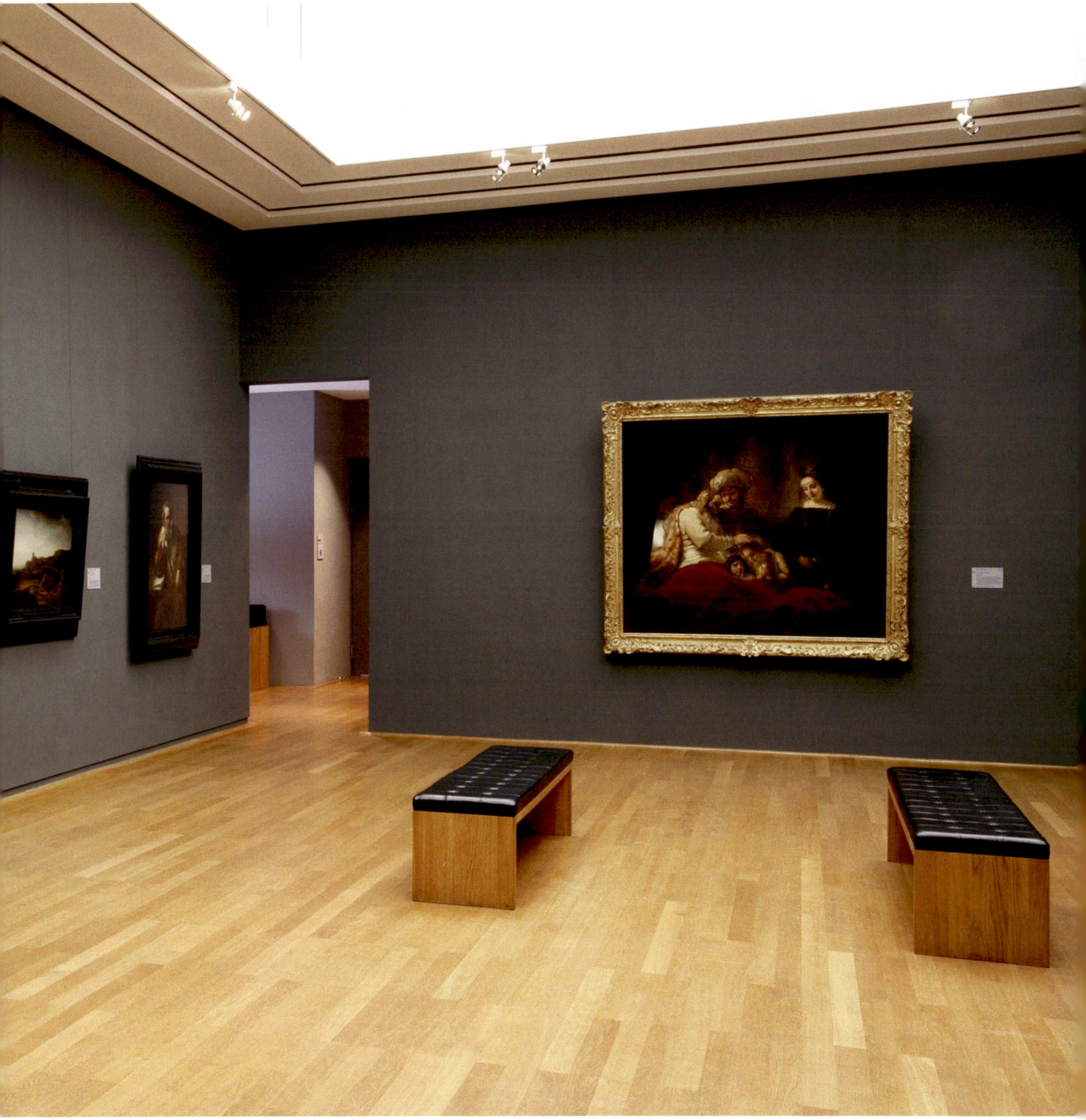

Schloss Wilhelmsthal

A Rococo pearl

One of Germany's finest Rococo palaces is situated in the picturesque garden of Wilhelmsthal Palace near Calden (north of Kassel). The three-wing ensemble was built between 1747 and 1761 as a *maison de plaisance* by Landgrave Wilhelm VIII of Hessen-Kassel (in office 1751–1760). With the virtually unchanged disposition of its rooms, it provides an insight into the life of the aristocracy and their household in the Late Absolutist period.

Among the many items of outstanding quality in this impressive setting are some excellent pieces of European and Far Eastern porcelain. Other objects of special interest include lacquered French furniture, a writing desk by Abraham Roentgen (1711–1793), and a peacock-feather dresser (c. 1755) notable for its appliqué technique. The important painter Johann Heinrich Tischbein (1722–1789) contributed widely to the collection of paintings, which include a Telemachus cycle, as well as a series of ancestral portraits (still kept in the gallery dedicated to that purpose), and a Gallery of Beauties – a series of portraits of beautiful women of Landgrave Wilhelm VIII's acquaintance.

The singular charm of Wilhelmsthal Palace lies in the almost intact historical sequence of its rooms, which allows the visitor to reconstruct life both above and below stairs. The main kitchen, for example, is a particularly popular attraction, with its still functioning roast-turning machine. The interior of the house can be visited on a guided tour.

Embedded in a natural hollow, the gardens at Calden complete the historical triad of the Hessian Landgrave's parks in and around Kassel. Like those at Wilhelmshöhe and, in the city of Kas-

Wilhelmsthal Palace: Gallery of Beauties

View of Wilhelmsthal Palace from the garden

An example of outstanding art and craftsmanship: the peacock-feather casket

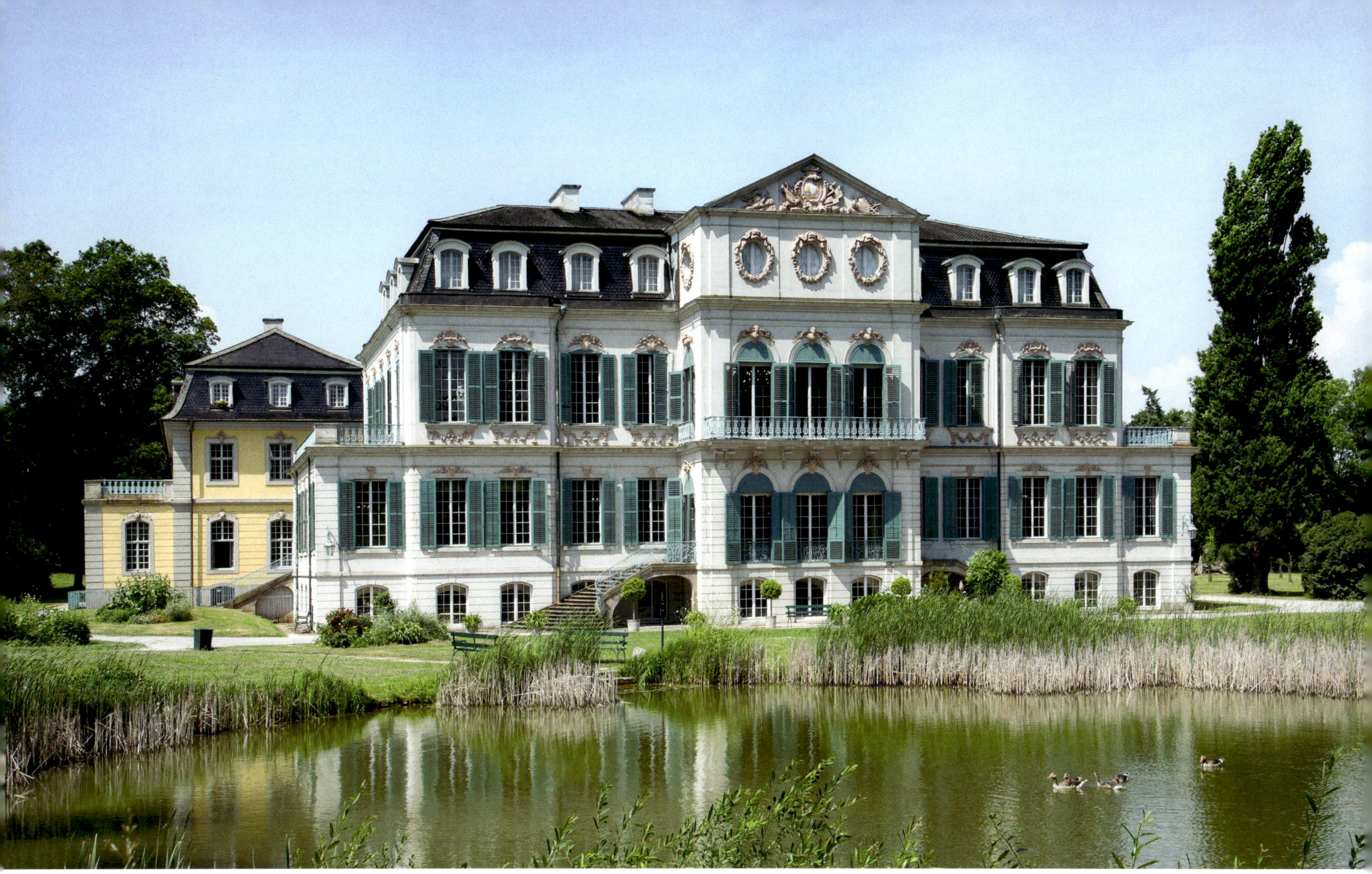

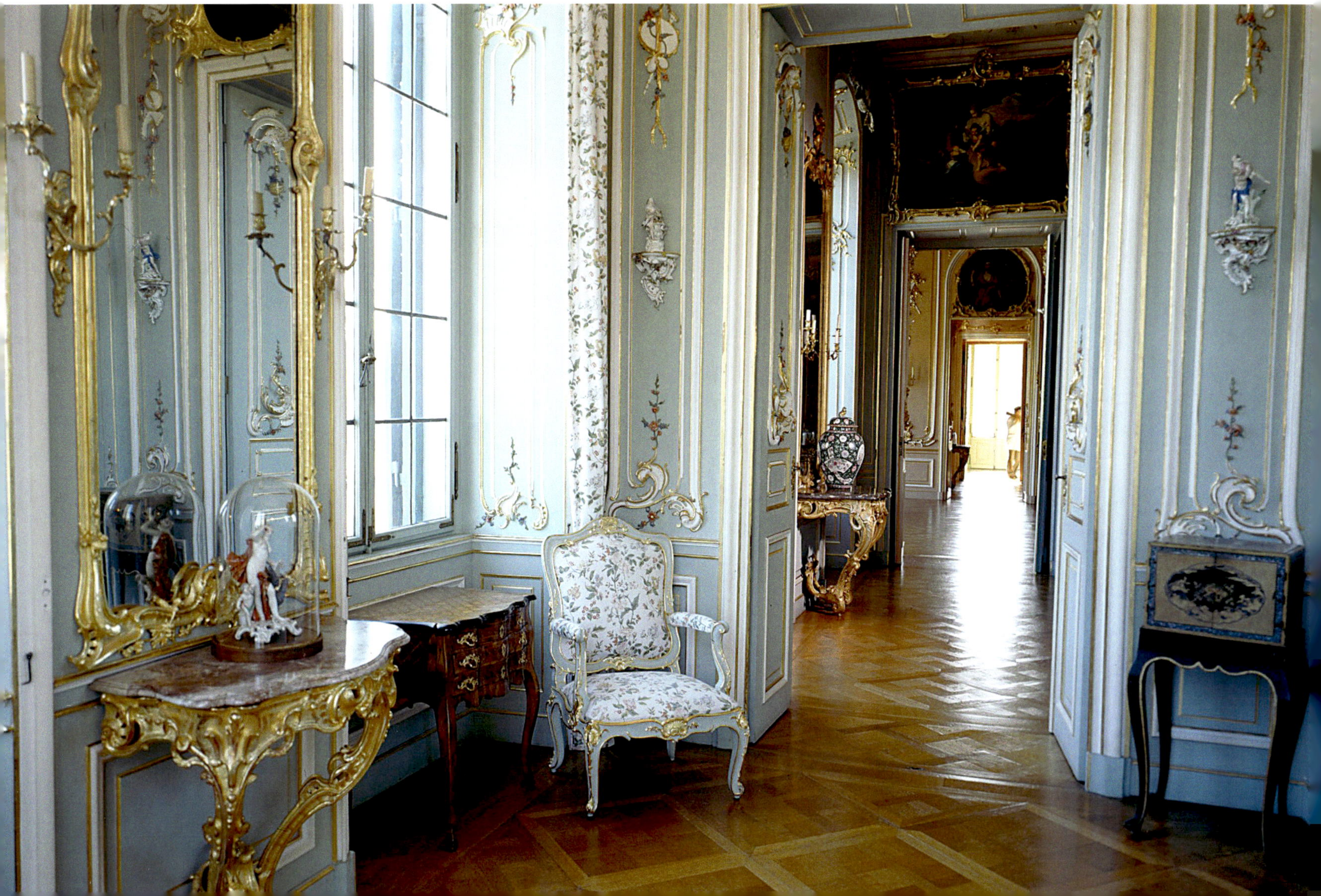

sel, Karlsaue, the c. 30 hectare (c. 74 acre) estate was originally planned in the Rococo style and only later transformed into a landscaped garden with elements of woodland, a neo-Gothic tower created as an artificial ruin by the Kassel architect Simon Louis Du Ry, and – from the early Rococo period – a water grotto. For both art and nature lovers, the garden of Wilhelmsthal Palace provides a delightful setting for a walk at every season, or simply an opportunity to spend some time, with new perspectives opening literally at every turn.

Wilhelmsthal Palace: Hall of the Muses

Wittumspalais in Weimar
Dowager seat of Duchess Anna Amalia

The Wittumspalais (Wittum House), dowager seat of Duchess Anna Amalia (1739–1807), fronts onto Weimar's present-day Schillerstrasse. A stately Baroque town house, it stands on land that belonged in the Late Middle Ages to a Franciscan friary. The Weimar state minister, Baron Jakob Friedrich von Fritsch, bought the land in 1767 and built the Wittumspalais on it. However, when the 1774 fire at Weimar City Castle destroyed the ducal apartments, he sold the house to Duchess Anna Amalia; she, over the years, adapted it to her own requirements. The rooms were refashioned to plans by Adam Friedrich Oeser, director of the Leipzig Academy of Drawing, who was also responsible for the ceiling frescoes in the second floor state room and in the private apartments on the first floor.

Anna Amalia lived in the Wittumspalais for more than thirty years. Here she received her "round table", where members of the ducal family and court interested in art, literature and science met with writers, artists and scholars from the educated bourgeoisie. Here music was composed and played, readings were given, plays performed and drawings made – a lively, not to say exuberant, gathering of cultivated society that included such figures as Johann Wolfgang von Goethe, Christoph Martin Wieland and Johann Gottfried Herder, as well as Carl Ludwig von Knebel, the painter Georg Melchior Kraus, the Weimar entrepreneur Friedrich Justin Bertuch, and the writer and translator Johann Joachim Bode. After the death of the duchess the house was no longer permanently inhabited. The large garden to the north, with its attractive pavilion, fell victim to the city expansion of the early 19th century. Today only a staircase in the courtyard remains as a silent witness.

In the 1870s Anna Amalia's great-grandson, Grand Duke Carl Alexander (1818–1901), had the Wittumspalais – by then derelict – restored to the condition it had enjoyed around 1800, and opened it to the public as a museum. As such it still reflects to the letter the refined domestic culture of that age, and is one of Weimar's most attractive museums. Visitors can see Anna Amalia's apartments and the rooms in which classical Weimar met, socialized

Wittumspalais from the courtyard

235

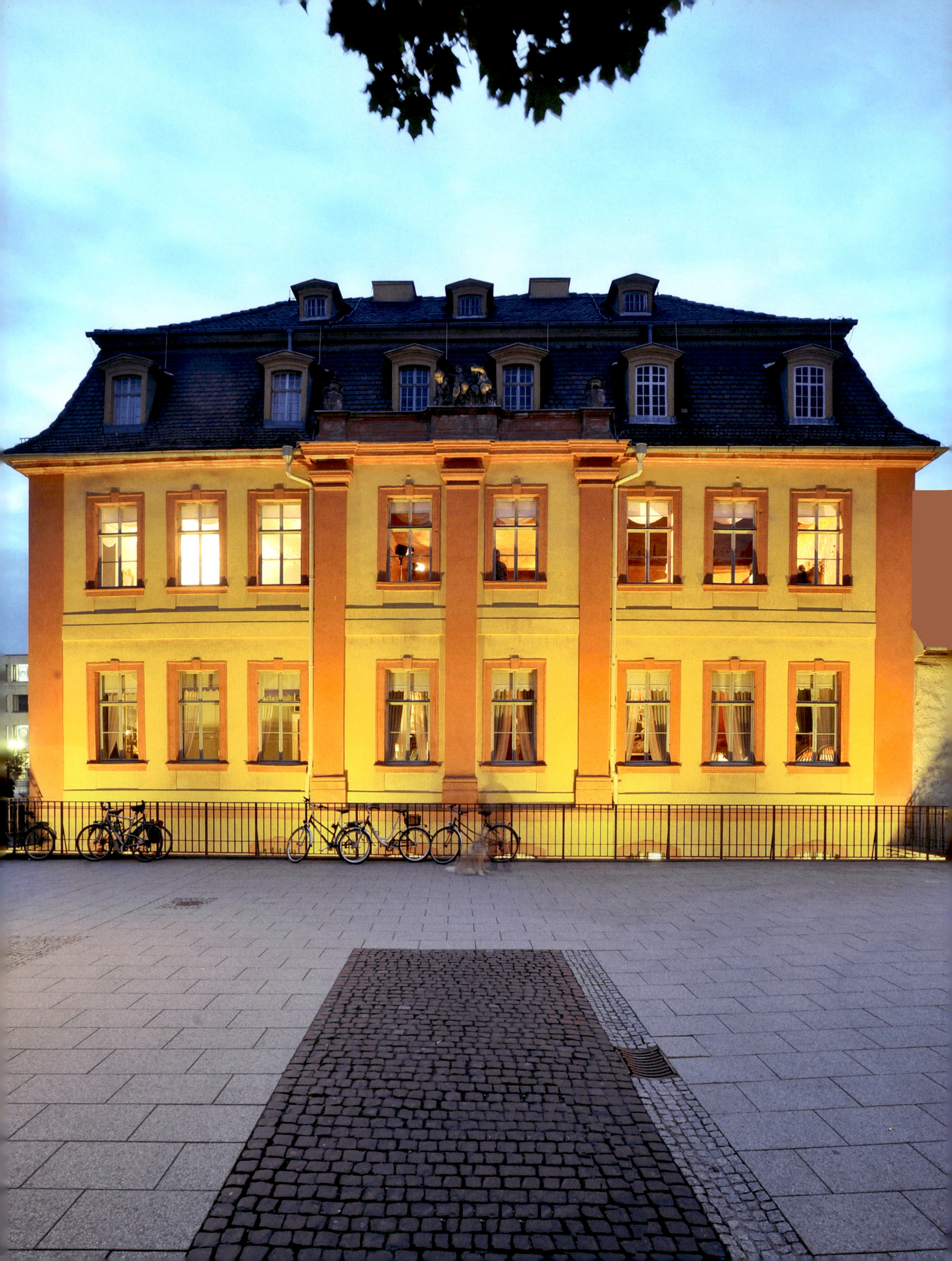

and exchanged ideas. The furnishings there demonstrate the seamless transition from Rococo to Empire styles, and although by no means all the items on view belonged to the duchess's household, and many of her own possessions are absent, the rooms still breathe something of the atmosphere that would have informed them in Anna Amalia's day.

Wittumspalais at night

Wittumspalais – "round table" room

Wittumspalais – main staircase

Schloss and Park Wörlitz

Iconic classicism

The foundation stone for Schloss Wörlitz, the prototype of German Neoclassicism, was laid in 1769. Friedrich Wilhelm von Erdmannsdorff (1736–1800) designed the building on the model of an English stately home, and it was inaugurated in March 1773 as the summer residence of Prince Leopold Friedrich Franz of Anhalt-Dessau (1740–1817).

The balanced façade, plain wall surfaces free of any decorative extravagance, and elegant four-columned portico give the building a dignity and charm suggestive of antiquity. Erdmannsdorff's "country house" was an innovation in German architectural history: it is a building whose external form documents its functionality in a strikingly modern way.

For the architect, the design and decoration of the interior was an integral aspect of this artistic synthesis. Wall and ceiling paintings, for instance, marked the earliest and most important artistic reaction north of the Alps to the excavation of the ancient cities of Pompeii and Herculaneum. Overall, the rich décor – with ancient sculptures, Italian

Wörlitz Castle and St. Peter's Church

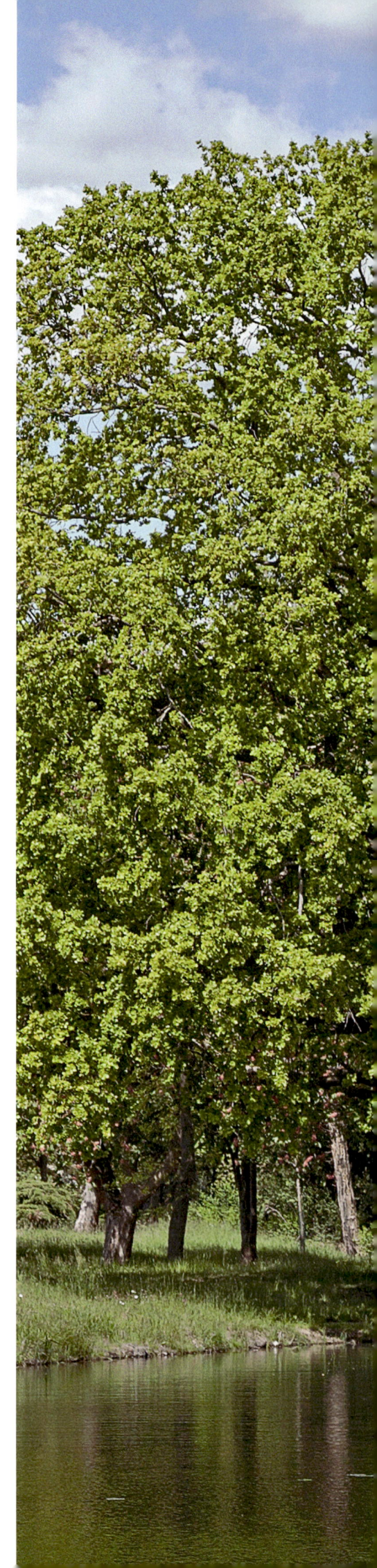

View of the Hohe Brücke (High Bridge)

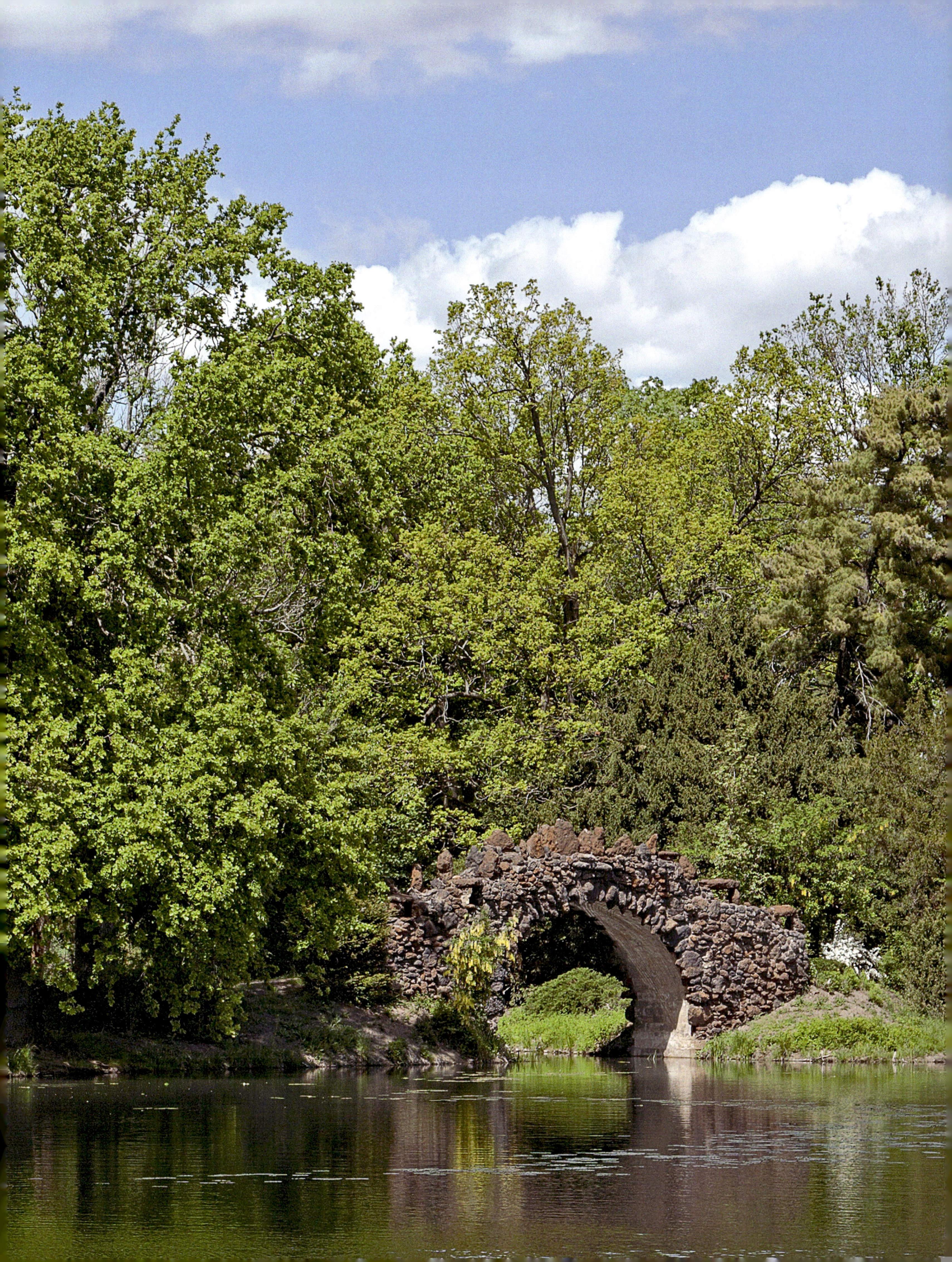

and Dutch paintings, and English Wedgwood china (almost all of which is preserved) – reflected the spirit and interests of the Prince's travels. Restoration work over the past 20 years has included the façade, roof, noble first floor apartments, mezzanine, Belvedere, and Palm Hall with its wall decoration featuring a painted pomegranate hedge.

Schloss Wörlitz is set in the first significant garden on the European mainland landscaped in the English manner: the fruit of a unique programme initiated by the prince for the enhancement of landscape and lifestyle, according to the principle of "combining the useful with the pleasant". The five gardens contained orchards, arable crops and pastures. At the same time they were linked with a carefully planned system of paths, canals and sightlines far and near, often beginning and ending with buildings, statues or stands of trees.

1773 also saw the laying of the foundations of the Gothic House in the garden of Schloss Wörlitz, one of the earliest and best preserved neo-Gothic buildings on the European mainland. Its interior is notable for its neo-Gothic décor and furnishings, as well as for a fine collection of early German and Dutch paintings.

Since 2000, Schloss Wörlitz and its gardens have formed part of the cultural heritage and tourist network "Garden Dreams – Historic Parks in Saxony-Anhalt".

The garden façade of the Gothic House quotes stylistic elements of English Tudor Gothic.

Moulded replicas of classical statues in the entrance hall introduce the mood and style of the castle.

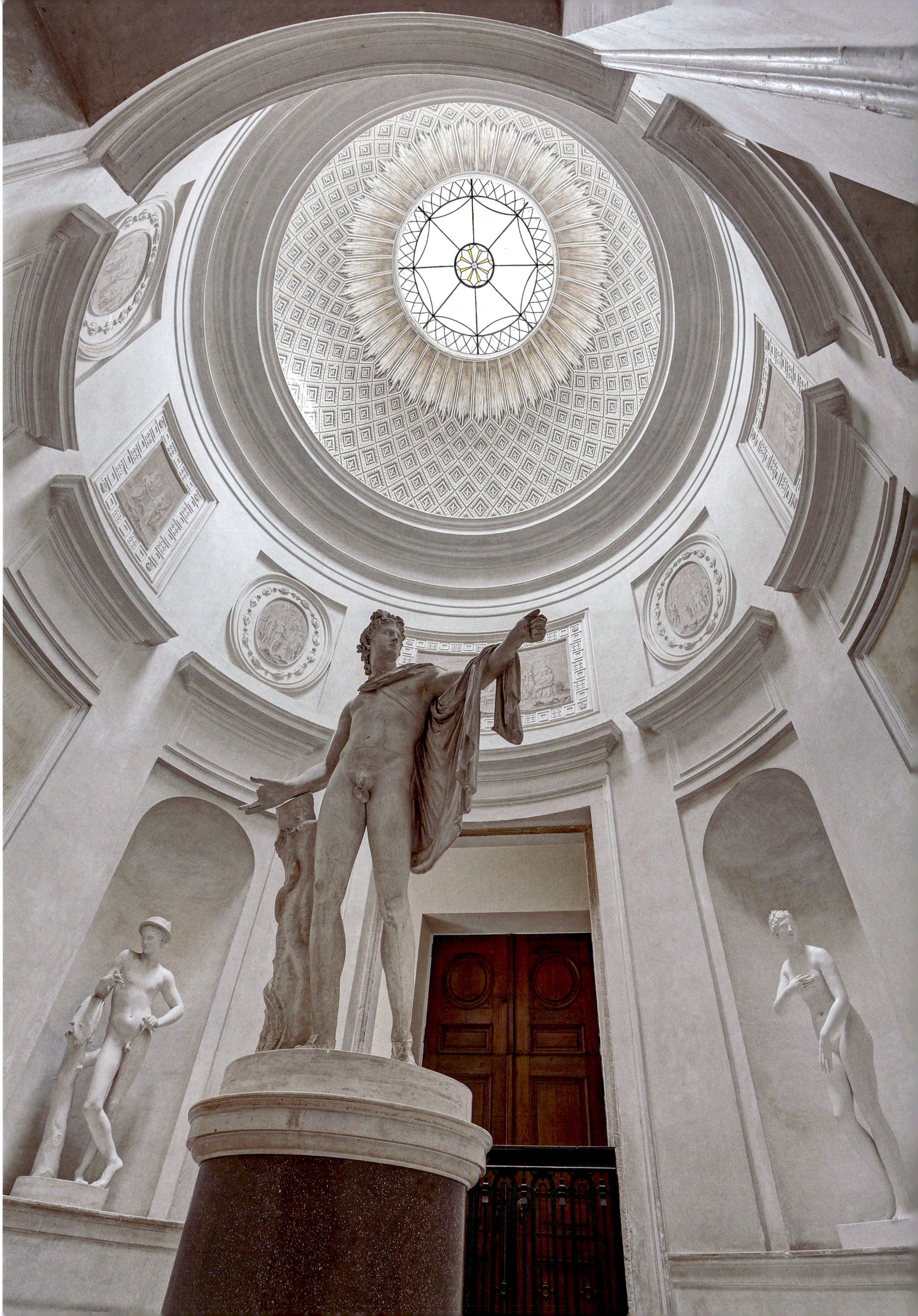

Index

Places

Altenmünster 126
Annweiler 205–207
Assmannshausen 64
Augustusburg 189–192
Bad Arolsen 17–19
Bad Bentheim 29–31
Bad Homburg vor der Höhe 20–22
Bad Liebenstein 11–13
Bad Muskau 47
Bad Pyrmont 96
Bamberg 220
Bendorf-Sayn 177–182
Bensheim-Auerbach 81–83
Berlin 40, 75, 93, 183
Binz 87–89
Braubach 144–146
Bückeburg 38–40
Hohenzollern Castle 114–116
Calden 232–234
Celle 41–43
Chemnitz 189
Cochem 44–46
Copenhagen 75, 201
Cottbus 35–37
Darmstadt 81
Detmold 50–52
Dornburg-Camburg 53–55
Drehbach-Scharfenstein 189–192
Dresden 56–59, 103, 156, 165–167
Düsseldorf 26–28
Edenkoben 132–134
Eichenzell 75–77
Eisenach 211–213
Eltville 63–65
Emmerthal 96–98

Frankfurt am Main 72, 93
Fulda 75–77
Fürstenberg 201
Glücksburg 84–86
Gotha 78–80
Granitz, Binz 87–89
Greifswald 88
Greiz 90–92
Gunzenhausen 47
Haldensleben 117–119
Halle 118
Hameln 96
Hanau 99–101
Hanover 111–113, 118, 141, 165
Harbke 118
Hechingen 114–116
Heidelberg 93, 108–110
Herculaneum 239
Hildesheim 141
Honau (Lichtenstein) 123–125
Hundisburg 117–119
Igel 202
Isselburg-Anholt 14–16
Jena 53
Jüchen 60–62
Kassel 99, 100, 118, 229–232, 234
Klütz 32–34
Koblenz 66–68, 144, 196–198
Kołobrzeg (Kolberg) 88
Langenburg 120–122
Leipzig 103
London 32, 165
Lorsch 126–128
Ludwigsburg 129–131
Ludwigslust 135–137, 183
Mainau Island 138–140
Mannheim 108, 186

Maulbronn 147–149
Meissen 8–10, 75, 201
Mirow 153–155
Moltzow-Ulrichshusen 208–210
Moritzburg 156–158
Mühlberg 103
Munich 188
Neustadt an der Weinstrasse 93–95
Niederwiesa-Lichtenwalde 189–192
Oettingen 159–161
Oranienbaum-Wörlitz 99, 238–240
Pappenheim 162–164
Pattensen 141–143
Pommersfelden 220–222
Pompeii 238
Prague 108
Putbus 87, 88
Regensburg 72–74
Rochlitz 168–170
Rüdesheim am Rhein 144
Rudolstadt 105–107
Salem 171–173
Sangerhausen 174–176
Schmalkalden 226–228
Schwerin 135, 183–185
Schwetzingen 186–188
Sèvres 75
Sigmaringen 193–195
Speyer 93
St. Petersburg 180
Stadthagen 38
Stralsund 88
Stuttgart 114, 130
Torgau 102–104, 226
Trier 202–204
Ulrichshusen 208–210
Unterschwaningen 47–49

243

Vienna   14, 75, 108, 165, 201
Weilburg/Lahn   214–216
Weimar   23–25, 199–201, 217–219, 235–237
Wernigerode   223–225
Wierschem   69–71
Wittenberg   103
Worms   93

Castles

Albrechtsburg Castle Meissen   8–10, 168
Altenstein Palace and Park, Bad Liebenstein   11–13
Althaldensleben Landscape Park, Hundisburg   117–119
Anholt (Wasserburg), Isselburg   14–16
Arolsen Palace   17–19
Augustusburg Castle   189–192
Bad Homburg Castle and Park   20–22
Belvedere Castle and Park, Weimar   23–25
Benrath Palace, Düsseldorf   26–28
Bentheim Castle   29–31
Bothmer House, Klütz   32–34
Branitz Palace and Park, Cottbus   35–37
Bückeburg Palace   38–40
Celle Castle   41–43
Cochem Imperial Castle   44–46
Dennenlohe Castle, Unterschwaningen   47–49
Detmold Castle   50–52
Dornburg Castles   53–55
Dresden Zwinger   56–59
Dyck Castle, Jüchen   60–62
Eberbach Monastery, Eltville   63–65
Ehrenbreitstein Fortress, Koblenz   66–68
Eltz Castle, Wierschem   69–71
Fasanerie – The Pheasantry, Eichenzell   75–77

Friedenstein Castle, Gotha   78–80
"Fürstenlager" State Park, Bensheim-Auerbach   81–83
Glücksburg Castle   84–86
Granitz Hunting Lodge, Binz   87–89
Greiz – Summer Palace and Princely Park   90–92
Hambach Castle, Neustadt an der Weinstrasse   93–95
Hämelschenburg Castle, Emmerthal   96–98
Hanau-Wilhelmsbad – State Park   99–101
Hartenfels Castle, Torgau   102–104
Heidecksburg Palace, Rudolstadt   105–107
Heidelberg Castle   108–110
Royal Gardens of Herrenhausen, Hanover   111–113
Hohenzollern Castle, Hechingen   114–116
Hundisburg Palace and Baroque Garden   117–119
Langenburg Castle   120–122
Lichtenstein Castle   123–125
Lichtenwalde Castle & Park, Niederwiesa   189–192
Lorsch Abbey   126–128
Ludwigsburg Palace   129–131
Ludwigshöhe Castle, Edenkoben   132–134
Ludwigslust Palace   135–137, 183
Mainau Island   138–140
Manorial Estates and Houses – Cultural Landscape, Mecklenburg-Western Pomerania   150–152
Marienburg Castle, Pattensen   141–143
Marksburg   144–146
Maulbronn Monastery   147–149
Mirow Palace   153–155
Moritzburg Castle   156–158
Oettingen Castle   159–161

Pappenheim Castle   162–164
Pillnitz Palace & Park, Dresden   165–167
Rochlitz Castle   168–170
Salem Monastery and Palace   171–173
Sangerhausen, Europa-Rosarium   174–176
Sayn – Castle and Palace, Bendorf   177–179
Sayn Palace Gardens, Bendorf   180–182
Schloss Wilhelmshöhe, Kassel   229–231
Schloss Wilhelmsthal, Calden   232–234
Schwerin Palace   183–185
Schwetzingen Palace and Gardens   186–188
Sigmaringen Palace   193–195
St. Emmeram's Palace, Regensburg   72–74
Stolzenfels Castle   196–198
Three Saxon Highlights   189–192
Tiefurt Mansion and Park 199–201
Trier – Roman city   202–204
Trifels Imperial Castle, Annweiler   205–207
Ulrichshusen Castle Estate   208–210
Wartburg World Heritage Site   211–213
Weilburg on the Lahn – Castle and Gardens   214–216
Weimar City Castle and Park on the Ilm   217–219
Weissenstein Palace, Pommersfelden   220–222
Wernigerode Castle®   223–225
Wilhelmsburg Castle, Schmalkalden   226–228
Wittumspalais, Weimar   235–237
Wörlitz – Schloss and Park, Oranienbaum-Wörlitz   99, 238–240

Winter paradise at Lichtenstein Castle

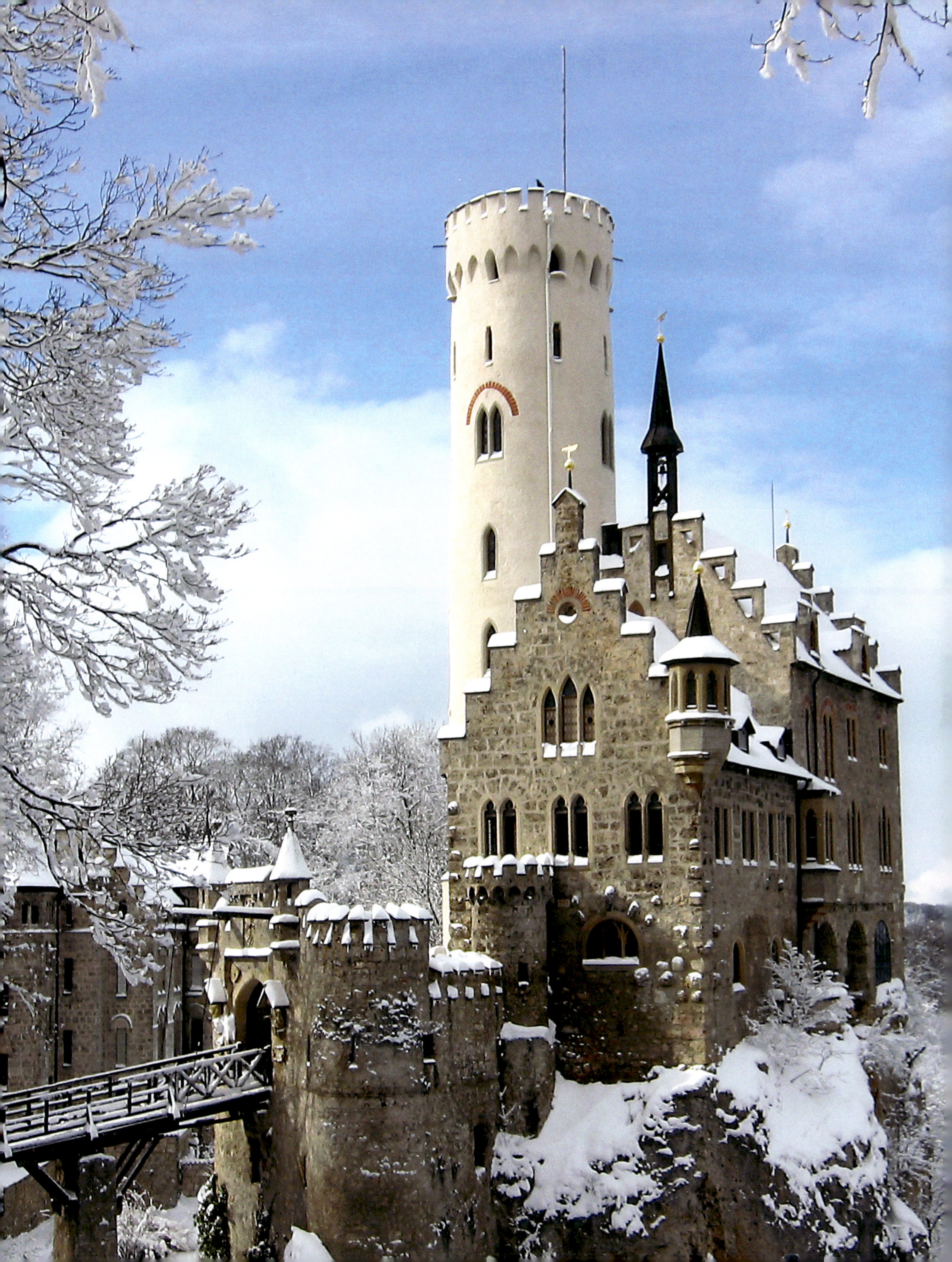

Addresses

Baden-Württemberg

Heidelberg Castle
Schlosshof 1
69117 Heidelberg
www.schloss-heidelberg.de

Hohenzollern Castle
72379 Burg Hohenzollern
www.burg-hohenzollern.com

Mainau Island
78465 Insel Mainau
www.mainau.de

Langenburg Castle
Schloss 1
74595 Langenburg
www.schloss-langenburg.de

Lichtenstein Castle
72805 Lichtenstein
www.schloss-lichtenstein.de

Ludwigsburg Palace
Schlossstrasse 30
71634 Ludwigsburg
www.schloss-ludwigsburg.de

Maulbronn Monastery
Klosterhof 5
75433 Maulbronn
www.kloster-maulbronn.de

Salem Monastery and Palace
88682 Salem
www.salem.de

Schwetzingen Palace and Gardens
Schloss Mittelbau
68723 Schwetzingen
www.schloss-schwetzingen.de

Sigmaringen Palace
Karl-Anton-Platz 8
72488 Sigmaringen
www.hohenzollern-schloss.de

Bayern

Dennenlohe Castle – House and Park
Dennenlohe 1
91743 Unterschwaningen
www.dennenlohe.de

St. Emmeram's Palace, Regensburg
Emmeramsplatz 5
93047 Regensburg
www.thurnundtaxis.de

Oettingen Castle
Schlossstrasse 1
86732 Oettingen
www.oettingen-spielberg.de

Pappenheim Castle
Marktplatz 5
91788 Pappenheim
www.grafschaft-pappenheim.de

Weissenstein Palace
96178 Pommersfelden
www.schloss-weissenstein.de

Brandenburg

Branitz Palace and Park
Robinienweg 5
03042 Cottbus
www.pueckler-museum.de

Hesse

Arolsen Palace
Schlossstrasse 27
34454 Bad Arolsen
www.schloss-arolsen.de

Bad Homburg Castle and Park
61348 Bad Homburg vor der Höhe
www.schloesser-hessen.de

Eberbach Monastery
65346 Eltville im Rheingau
www.kloster-eberbach.de

Schloss Fasanerie (The Pheasantry)
36124 Eichenzell
www.schloss-fasanerie.de

"Fürstenlager" State Park, Bensheim-Auerbach
64625 Bensheim-Auerbach
www.schloesser-hessen.de

State Park Hanau-Wilhelmsbad
Parkpromenade 7
63454 Hanau
www.schloesser-hessen.de

Lorsch Abbey
Nibelungenstrasse 35
64653 Lorsch
www.schloesser-hessen.de;
www.kloster-lorsch.de

Weilburg on the Lahn – Castle and Gardens
Schlossplatz 3
35781 Weilburg
/Lahn
www.schloesser-hessen.de

Schloss Wilhelmshöhe
Schlosspark 1
34131 Kassel
www.museum-kassel.de

Schloss Wilhelmsthal
34379 Calden
www.museum-kassel.de

Mecklenburg-Western Pomerania

Bothmer House
Am Park
23948 Klütz
www.mv-schloesser.de

Granitz Hunting Lodge
Postfach 1101
18609 Ostseebad Binz
www.mv-schloesser.de

A Cultural Landscape of Manorial Estates and Houses
Verein der Schlösser, Guts- und Herrenhäuser Mecklenburg-Vorpommern V e.V.
Rondell 7-8, 17207 Südmüritz OT Ludorf
www.mein-urlaub-im-schloss.de

Ludwigslust Palace
Schlossfreiheit
19288 Ludwigslust
www.mv-schloesser.de

Mirow Palace
Schlossinsel
17252 Mirow
www.mv-schloesser.de

Schwerin Palace
Lennéstr. 1
19053 Schwerin
www.mv-schloesser.de

Ulrichshusen Castle Estate
Seestrasse 14
17194 Ulrichshusen
www.ulrichshusen.de

Lower Saxony

Bentheim Castle
Schloss
48455 Bad Bentheim
www.burg-bentheim.de

Bückeburg Palace
Schlossplatz 1
31675 Bückeburg
www.schloss-bueckeburg.de

Celle Castle
Schlossplatz 1
29221 Celle
www.residenzmuseum.de;
www.celle-tourismus.de

Hämelschenburg Castle
Schlossstrasse 1
D-31860 Emmerthal
www.schloss-haemelschenburg.de

Royal Gardens of Herrenhausen, Hanover
Herrenhäuser Strasse 3c
(Besucherparkplatz)
30419 Hannover
www.hannover.de/herrenhausen

Marienburg Castle
Marienberg 1
30982 Pattensen
www.schloss-marienburg.de

North Rhine-Westphalia

Wasserburg Anholt
Schloss 1
46419 Isselburg-Anholt
www.wasserburg-anholt.de

Benrath Palace
Benrather Schlossallee 100–108
40597 Düsseldorf
www.schloss-benrath.de

Detmold Castle
Schlossplatz 1
32756 Detmold
www.schloss-detmold.de

Dyck Castle
Zentrum für Gartenkunst und Landschaftskultur
Schloss Dyck
41363 Jüchen
www.stiftung-schloss-dyck.de

Rhineland-Palatinate

Cochem Imperial Castle
Reichsburg Cochem GmbH
Schlossstrasse 36
56812 Cochem
www.reichsburg-cochem.de

Ehrenbreitstein Fortress
Greiffenklaustrasse
56077 Koblenz
www.tor-zum-welterbe.de

Eltz Castle
Burg Eltz 1
56294 Wierschem
www.eltz.de

Hambach Castle
67434 Neustadt an der Weinstrasse
www.hambacher-schloss.de

Ludwigshöhe Castle
Villastrasse 64
67480 Edenkoben
www.schloss-villa-ludwigshoehe.de

Marksburg
56338 Braubach
www.marksburg.de

Sayn – Castle and Schloss /Sayn Palace Gardens
Schloss-Str. 100
56170 Bendorf-Sayn
www.sayn.de

Stolzenfels Castle
56075 Koblenz
www.schloss-stolzenfels.de

Trier – The Centre of Antiquity
Porta Nigra
Simeonstrasse 60
54290 Trier
www.zentrum-der-antike.de

Trier – The Centre of Antiquity
Imperial Baths
Weberbach 41
54290 Trier
www.zentrum-der-antike.de

Trier – The Centre of Antiquity
Amphitheatre
Olewiger Strasse
54295 Trier
www.zentrum-der-antike.de

Trier – The Centre of Antiquity
Barbara Baths
Viehmarktplatz
54290 Trier
www.zentrum-der-antike.de

Trier – The Centre of Antiquity
Igel Column
54298 Igel
www.zentrum-der-antike.de

Trifels Imperial Castle
76855 Annweiler
www.reichsburg-trifels.de

Saxony

Albrechtsburg Castle, Meissen
Domplatz 1
01662 Meissen
www.albrechtsburg-meissen.de

Dresden Zwinger
Theaterplatz
01067 Dresden
www.der-dresdner-zwinger.de

Hartenfels Castle, Torgau
Schlossstrasse 27
04860 Torgau
www.schloss-hartenfels.de

Moritzburg Castle
Schloßallee
01468 Moritzburg
www.schloss-moritzburg.de

Pillnitz Palace & Park
August-Böckstiegel-Str. 2
01326 Dresden
www.schlosspillnitz.de

Rochlitz Castle
Sörnziger Weg 1
09306 Rochlitz
www.schloss-rochlitz.de

Three Saxon Highlights:

Augustusburg Castle
Schloss 1
09573 Augustusburg

Lichtenwalde Castle & Park
Schlossallee 1
09577 Niederwiesa
/OT Lichtenwalde

Scharfenstein Castle
Schlossberg 1
09430 Drebach/OT Scharfenstein
www.die-sehenswerten-drei.de

Saxony-Anhalt

Hundisburg Palace and Baroque Garden, Althaldensleben Landscape Park
Schloss 1
39343 Hundisburg
www.schloss-hundisburg.de

Europa-Rosarium Sangerhausen
Am Rosengarten 2a
06526 Sangerhausen
www.europa-rosarium.de

Wernigerode Castle®
Am Schloss 1
D-38855 Wernigerode
www.schloss-wernigerode.de

Schloss and Park Wörlitz
Kirchgasse
06785 Oranienbaum-Wörlitz –
OT Wörlitz
www.gartenreich.com

Schleswig-Holstein

Glücksburg Castle
Schloss
24960 Glücksburg
www.schloss-gluecksburg.de

Thuringia

Altenstein Palace and Park
36448 Bad Liebenstein
www.thueringerschloesser.de

Belvedere Castle and Park
Weimar-Belvedere
99425 Weimar
www.klassik-stiftung.de/einrichtungen

Dornburg Castles – a Triad of Stately Homes
Max-Krehan-Strasse 2
07774 Dornburg-Camburg
www.thueringerschloesser.de

Friedenstein Castle
Schlossplatz 1
99867 Gotha
www.stiftung-friedenstein.de

Greiz – Summer Palace and Princely Park
Greizer Park 1
07973 Greiz
www.thueringerschloesser.de

Heidecksburg Palace, Rudolstadt
Schlossbezirk 1
07407 Rudolstadt
www.thueringerschloesser.de

Tiefurt Mansion and Park
Hauptstrasse 14
99425 Weimar-Tiefurt
www.klassik-stiftung.de/einrichtungen

Wartburg World Heritage Site
Auf der Wartburg 1
D-99817 Eisenach
www.wartburg.de

Weimar City Castle and Park on the Ilm
Burgplatz 4
99423 Weimar
www.klassik-stiftung.de/einrichtungen

Wilhelmsburg Castle in Schmalkalden
Schlossberg 9
98574 Schmalkalden
www.thueringerschloesser.de

Wittumspalais in Weimar
Am Palais 3
99423 Weimar
www.klassik-stiftung.de/einrichtungen

Chimney corner in St Elizabeth's Bower, Wartburg World Heritage Site

Photo copyright and credits

Note: The following list names the copyright owner of each group of images and (indented) the photographer of each image. Images are denoted by page and position on page. Where no photographer is named, the page reference directly follows the name of the copyright owner.

Archiv Schloss Langenburg:
Katrin Artmann: 122 (bottom)
/ David König: 121
/ Achim Mende: 120, 122 (top)

Archiv Schloss Sayn: 177, 178 (left), 178/179, 180, 181, 182 (top)
/ Blaese: 182 (bottom left)
/ Naethe: 182 (bottom right)

ASL Schlossbetriebe gGmbH:
/ Sylvio Dittrich: 189, 191 (top), 192 (top, bottom left)
/ Rainer Weißflog: 190 (top)
/ Lutz Zimmermann: 190 (bottom right), 191 (bottom), 192 (bottom right),

Roland Beck, Burg Hohenzollern: 114, 116

Burg Bentheim GmbH: 29, 30 (bottom), 31 (bottom)
/ S.Trocoli Castro: 30 (top), 31 (top)

Deutsche Burgenvereinigung e.V.: 144–146

Düsseldorf Marketing & Tourismus GmbH: 26/27

St. Emmeram, Fürst Thurn und Taxis Zentralarchiv:
/ Clemens Mayer: 72–74

Fürst zu Oettingen-Spielberg'sche Verwaltung: 159–161

Fürst zu Salm-Salm, Anholt:
/ Andreas Lechtape, Münster: 14–16

Gartenträume – Historische Parks in Sachsen-Anhalt e. V.
/ Felicitas Remmert: 118, 175 (top)

Gemeinnützige Stiftung Schloss Weissenstein in Pommersfelden: 220/221
/ Michael Aust: 222

Generaldirektion Kulturelles Erbe Rheinland-Pfalz:
/ Lufthelden: 68
/ Fitting: 203
/ Pfeuffer 66, 67, 132 134, 196–198, 202, 204–207

Gräflich Pappenheim'sche Verwaltung: 162–164

Herrenhäuser Gärten:
/ Coptograph: 112/113
/ Hassan Mahramzadeh: 111

Insel Mainau:
/ Peter Allgaier: 138–140

M. Jermann, Zeitz Verlag, Königsee: 69, 70

Klassik Stiftung Weimar: 23 25, 199–201, 218, 235–237
/ Johann Philipp Jung: 219
/ Jens Hauspurg: 217

KULTUR-Landschaft Haldensleben-Hundisburg e.V.: 119
/ Dr. Harald Blanke: 117

Kulturstiftung Dessau-Wörlitz, Bildarchiv:
/ Heinz Frässdorf: 238 (left), 238/239, 240, 241

Kulturstiftung des Hauses Hessen:
/ Andreas von Einsiedel: 75, 76 (bottom right)
/ Klaus Lorke: 76 (top right)
/ Christian Tech: 76/77

Landesamt für Kultur und Denkmalpflege:
/ Achim Bötefür: 155 (top)

Landratsamt Nordsachsen:
/ Andreas Franke: 103
/ Jens Klöppel: 102
/ Wolfgang Sens: 104

Thomas Monhof: 145

Museumslandschaft Hessen Kassel:
/ Ute Brunzel: 233 (bottom)
/ Arno Hensmanns: 229, 230 (top left), 230/231
/ Mirja Loewe: 232, 234
/ Volker Straub: 233 (top)
/ Uwe Zucchi: 230 (bottom left)

Reichsburg Cochem GmbH: 44
/ Foto Gossler: 45 (bottom), 46
/ Zeitz: 45 (top)

Residenzmuseum im Celler Schloss / Foto: Fotostudio Loeper, Celle: 41–43

Rosenstadt Sangerhausen GmbH: 174, 175 (bottom), 176

R. Rossner, Bad Godesberg: 71

SBG gGmbH (Schlösserland Sachsen):
/ Carlo Böttger: 158
/ Sylvio Dittrich: 166/167 (top), 167 (unten rechts), 169 (top)
/ Wolfgang Friebel: 167 (bottom left)
/ Andy Gosch: 170 (top)
/ Gabriele Hilsky: 156
/ Peter Hirth: 10 (bottom), 56, 57
/ Frank Höhler: 10 (top)
/ Peter Knierriem: 169 (bottom)
/ Marcel Quietzsch: 58/59
/ Holm Röhner: 157
/ René Schleichardt: 8
/ Lothar Sprenger: 168, 170 (bottom)
/ Anja Ligaya Weiss: 9
/ H.& D. Zielske: 165

Schatzkammer Thüringen:
/ Marcus Glahn: 11, 53, 54/55, 90, 91, 92

Schloss Bückeburg: 38 (left), 40
/ Müller Luftbild: 38/39

Schloss Dennenlohe: 47 (left), 48
/ Roland Mimberg: 49

Schloss Dyck:
/ Anja Spanjer:61
/ Jens Spanjer: 60, 62

Schloss Hämelschenburg:
/ C. v. Klencke: 96 f., 98 (bottom)
/ Achim Werner: 97, 98 (top)

Schloss Lichtenstein: 223–225, 245

Schloss Marienburg GmbH:
/ Diana Frohmöller Photography: 141, 142 (bottom)
/ Patrice Kunte: 142 (top), 143

Hohenzollernschloss Sigmaringen
/ Melanie Straub: 193–195

Schloss Ulrichshusen: 207/208, 253
/ DOMUSimages Alexander Rudolph: 208 (bottom), 210 (top)
/ Thorsten Scherz: 208 (left), 210 (bottom)

Schloss Wernigerode® GmbH: 223–225

Staatliche Schlösser und Gärten Baden-Württemberg: 131, 130 (bottom left), 172/173
/ Günther Bayerl: 108, 109 (top), 110 (top), 147–149
/ Julia Haseloff: 109 (bottom)
/ Achim Mende: 110 (bottom), 129, 130 (top), 171, 172 (middle left), 186/187, 188 (top)
/ Birgit Rückert: 172 (bottom left)
/ Arnim Weischer: 130 (bottom right)
/ Ursula Wetzel: 186 (left), 188 (bottom)

Staatliche Schlösser und Gärten Hessen:
/ Petrus Bodenstaff: 99
/ espelohra: 22, 101
/ Roman von Götz: 22
/ Olli Heimann: 81, 128
/ Robert Hill: 20/21
/ Michael Joest: 100 (bottom)
/ Gerd Kittel: 214/215
/ Boris Laicht: 100 (top)
/ Michael Leukel: 82, 83 (top), 216
/ Yasmine Schüssler: 214 (left)

Staatliche Schlösser, Gärten und Kunstsammlungen Mecklenburg-Vorpommern: 88
/ Timm Allrich: 34 (top), 87, 89, 137 (both), 153, 154, 155 (bottom), 183, 185 (bottom)
/ Thomas Grundner: 135, 184, 185 (top),
/ Bernd Lasdin: 33
/ Jörn Lehmann: 136
/ Stephan Rudolph-Kramer: 32
/ Helmut Strauß: 34 (bottom)

Stiftung des Fürstlichen Hauses Waldeck und Pyrmont: 17
/ Michaela Hundertmark, Michael Mehle: 18/19

Stiftung Fürst-Pückler-Museum Park und Schloss Branitz:
/ Hans Bach: 37 (bottom left, middle right)
/ Peter-Michael Bauers: 37 (bottom right)
/ Andreas Franke: 35, 36
/ Ben Peters: 37 (top)

Stiftung Hambacher Schloss:
/ Stefan Müller: 93, 94
/ Nikolai Benner: 94/95

Stiftung Kloster Eberbach: 63, 64, 65 (top)
/ Hermann Heibel: 65 (bottom)

Stiftung Residenzschloss Detmold gGmbH: 52 (bottom)
/ Fotoarchiv Marburg: 50–52 (top)

Stiftung Schloss Friedenstein Gotha:
/ Marcus Glahn: 78, 79, 80 (top)
/ Bernhard Hartmann: 80 (bottom)

Stiftung Schloss Glücksburg:
/ Foto Raake Flensburg: 84
/ Sven Geissler: 86 (left)
/ Olff Appold: 85, 86 (top right)

Stiftung Schloss und Park Benrath
/ Marcus Schwier: 26 (left), 28

Stiftung Thüringer Schlösser und Gärten:
/ Constantin Beyer: 12, 13, 55 (right), 78/79, 106, 107, 217, 226/227, 228 (bottom)
/ Franz Nagel: 105
/ Helmut Wiegel: 228 (top)

Verein der Schlösser, Guts- und Herrenhäuser Mecklenburg-Vorpommern e. V.:
/ Hans Blossey, Alamy Stock Photo: 151
/ DOMUSimages - Alexander Rudolph: 150, 151 (bottom right)
/ Christin Druehl: 152 (bottom)
/ gutshaus_stolpe: 151 (bottom left)
/ Holger Martens: 152 (top)
/ Stefan von Stengel: 152 (middle), 254

Wartburg-Stiftung: 211, 213, 250
/ Dominik Ketz: 212

Water Mill, Ulrichshusen Castle Estate

Kaarz Manor House viewed from the park, Mecklenburg-Western Pomerania

Im Programm des Verlags Schnell & Steiner ist außerdem lieferbar:

Große Residenzen, romantische Entdeckungen, versteckte Schönheiten

Ein Reiseführer zu Deutschlands schönsten Schlössern, Burgen und Gärten

Herausgegeben von
Schlösser und Gärten in Deutschland e. V.

ISBN 978-3-7954-3244-7

Front cover: Hohenzollern Castle in a sea of fog, © Roland Beck, Burg Hohenzollern
Back cover: Banqueting Hall at Friedenstein Castle, Gotha © Schatzkammer Thüringen, photo: Marcus Glahn

Coordination and compilation
Andrea Hahn | Text & Presse, Marbach am Neckar

Cover design: typegerecht berlin
Layout: typegerecht berlin
Print: Grafisches Centrum Cuno GmbH & Co. KG, Calbe, printed in Ultra HD Print
Translation: Joseph Swann

Bibliographic information published by the Deutsche Nationalbibliothek:
The Deutsche Nationalbibliothek lists this publication in the Deutsche Nationalbibliografie;
detailed bibliographic data are available in the Internet at http://dnb.dnb.de.

First edition 2020
© 2020 Verlag Schnell & Steiner GmbH, Leibnizstr. 13, D-93055 Regensburg
© 2020 Schlösser und Gärten in Deutschland e.V., Schlossraum 22a, 76646 Bruchsal

ISBN 978-3-7954-3539-4

All rights reserved. This book may not be reproduced in whole or in part by photo-
mechanical or electronic means without the express permission of the publisher.

Further information about the Verein »Schlösser und Gärten in Deutschland e. V.«
can be found under: www.schloesser-gaerten-deutschland.de

Further information about our publications can be found under:
www.schnell-und-steiner.de